CATO'S TEARS
AND THE MAKING
OF ANGLO-AMERICAN
EMOTION

Julie Ellison

Cato's Tears and the Making of Anglo-American Emotion

THE UNIVERSITY OF CHICAGO PRESS

CHICAGO & LONDON

Julie Ellison is professor of English at the University of Michigan, Ann Arbor and director of "Imagining America: Artists and Scholars in Public Life," a national initiative. She is the author of *Emerson's Romantic Style* and *Delicate Subjects: Romanticism, Gender, and the Ethics of Understanding.*

The University of Chicago Press, Chicago 60637
The University of Chicago Press, Ltd., London

© 1999 by The University of Chicago
All rights reserved. Published 1999
Printed in the United States of America

08 07 06 05 04 03 02 01 00 99   1 2 3 4 5
ISBN: 0-226-20595-9 (cloth)
ISBN: 0-226-20596-7 (paper)

Library of Congress Cataloging-in-Publication Data

Ellison, Julie K.
    Cato's tears and the making of Anglo-American emotion / Julie Ellison.
      p.   cm.
    Includes bibliographical references (p.   ) and index.
    ISBN 0-226-20595-9 (cloth : alk. paper). — ISBN 0-226-20596-7 (pbk.)
    1. English literature—18th century—History and criticism.   2. Emotions in literature.   3. Cato, Marcus Porcius, 234–149 B.C.—In literature.   4. Politics and literature—Great Britain—History.   5. American literature—History and criticism.   6. Addison, Joseph, 1672–1719—Influence.   7. Addison, Joseph, 1672–1719. Cato.   8. Sentimentalism in literature.   9. Masculinity in literature.   10. Sex role in literature.   11. Men in literature.   I. Title.
PR448.E46E45   1999
820.9'353—dc21   99-23105
                                                      CIP

For Peter

CONTENTS

ACKNOWLEDGMENTS

*T*hrough writing this book I learned how to be a colleague. The project originated in a memorable term of team teaching with my friend James Winn, who helped me to overcome my prejudices against the eighteenth century. Chris Blouch, Wendy Motooka, Anne Krook, and Shawn Maurer were part of this benevolent conspiracy, as well. Adela Pinch's arguments about intersubjective emotion were fundamental to my understanding of sensibility. Because she was so important at the beginning of the project, it is a joy to welcome her back to Ann Arbor at the end. June Howard is another key member of the Michigan school of sentimental studies. Her work on emotion has been profoundly clarifying, and so has her overall sanity. In Nanora Sweet, I have had, throughout the years of writing this book, a subtle feminist interlocutor deeply engaged in women's poetry. Carroll Smith-Rosenberg has lured me into a more active engagement with historians. I am particularly indebted to her response to my paper, "Cato Discourse, Algerine Captives, and Comparative Slavery in the Early Republic," which I presented at the First Annual Conference of the Institute of Early American History and Culture in June 1995. Liz Barnes and P. A. Skantze offered invaluable suggestions. Chris Flint, Donna Landry, Sarah Robbins, Marlon Ross, and Tobin Siebers shared their expertise and generously offered timely reactions to queries. I was unusually blessed by the remarkably generous and insightful suggestions provided by Terry Castle and Julia Stern. I am indebted, too, to the expert management of Alan Thomas and Randy Petilos, editor and assistant editor respectively, and the discerning work of senior manuscript editor Jennifer Moorhouse at the University of Chicago Press.

Cato's Tears has emerged from many conversations. My friend and colleague Joanne Leonard was my office mate for a year at the University of Michigan Institute for the Humanities, and a member of a writing group that also included Ruth Behar, Anne Ruggles Gere, and Patricia Yaeger. They provided excellent feedback, but that is the least of the ways in which they were supportive. Lemuel Johnson invited me to "go further" at the 1991 Berkeley Conference on Alienation: The Production of Strangers and the Boundaries of Culture. Kathleen Woodward and her wonderful colleagues at the Institute for Twentieth-Century Studies were illuminating partners in a conversation about liberal guilt, as were the members of the faculty seminar of the program in Comparative Studies in Social Transformation—especially Ann Stoler, whose question "But what about the state?" I am still trying to answer. The spring 1993 faculty seminar on emotion, supported by the dean of the College of Literature, Science, and the Arts at the University of Michigan, offered a challenging opportunity to test theoretical perspectives. A weekend in the company of Michael Warner, Cora Kaplan, Harryette Mullen, and the faculty and graduate students at the Miami University of Ohio helped catalyze the final phases of the book.

Writing this book would have been impossible without a long series of teaching experiments and without the inspiration of a cadre of present and former doctoral students whose work on gender, genre, and emotion has been an important part of my education. This group includes David Anthony, Linda Bachman, Lee Behlman, Eliza Richards, and Laura Stevens. The discerning research efforts of James Crane, Stephen Hum, Matt Kutcher, and Paul Rodney contributed to much of this project's historical grounding. Their work was funded in part by a University of Michigan Research Grant for Women Faculty. Heartfelt gratitude is due to the cheerful life support provided by the team that actually got the manuscript to press: Sondra Smith, Juliet Feibel, and our computer consultant, Pramit Nairi.

A year of work on this project was supported by the University of Michigan Institute for the Humanities. The staff at the Institute for the Humanities—Mary Price, Eliza Woodford, Betsy Nisbet, and Linnea Perlman—made my experience as the John Rich Fellow a pleasure, as did my fellow Fellows. The University of Michigan Office of the Vice President for Research and the Department of English supported one term of research leave, and a sabbatical leave from the university made possible another. The keepers of the flame at the Labadie Collection and the Clements Library at the University of Michigan guided me to key materials with singular deftness.

Earlier versions of chapters 2, 4, 5, and the conclusion have been published previously. Chapter 2 appeared in *ELH*, fall 1996; chapter 4 in *Re-visioning Romanticism: British Women Writers 1776–1837*, University of Pennsylvania Press, 1994. Most of chapter 5 was published in *American Literature* and reprinted in *Subjects and Citizens: Nation, Race, and Gender from Oroonoko to Anita Hill*, Duke University Press, 1995. Portions of the introduction and much of the conclusion formed an earlier version of "A Short History of Liberal Guilt," *Critical Inquiry*, winter 1996. Portions of chapter

6 appeared in *ELH,* fall 1996; the chapter also includes a small amount of material from "There and Back: Transatlantic Novels and Anglo-American Careers," in *The Past as Prologue: Essays to Celebrate the Twenty-Fifth Anniversary of ASECS,* ed. Carla Hay and Syndy M. Conger (New York: Published for the American Society for Eighteenth-Century Studies by AMS Press, 1995). Thanks are due to R. J. Matson for permission to reproduce his cartoon, "Neo White Liberal Guilt."

Karen Woollams held my professional life together for months on end. She and the rest of my colleagues at the Office of the Vice President for Research did not have much to say about the eighteenth century, but they have exemplified the spirit of interdisciplinary collaboration that has fueled this study.

To my mother, Mim Ellison, copious thanks are due for her ingenious ways of sustaining and surprising us.

Mark Creekmore is the not-so-secret hero of this book.

And finally, to Peter: Thank you for bringing up your mother. You're doing a great job. Keep it up.

INTRODUCTION

Someday Bridges May Have Feelings Too

The Weep Stakes

$\mathcal{B}$efore the 1992 New Hampshire primary, a front-page headline in the *New York Times* summarized the day's mood: "Democrats Offer Emotional Drama in New Hampshire: Humility and Passion Vie."[1] The *Times* is the consummate articulator of the politics of liberal masculine emotion in our time. The prestige of Whig sentimentalism lives on in its pages.[2] Thus I was not surprised to find even better news inside the science section of the same day's paper: "Someday Bridges May Have Feelings Too." Announcing the onset of "the age of 'smart' materials," a caption describes a "bridge that knows when it's hurting."[3] Materials that communicate their own stress soon will make the affective fallacy (our habit of attributing emotion to objects) technologically plausible.[4] "That would put a whole new slant on the expression, 'It's like talking to a wall,'" the writer concludes. This story about sensitive bridges, so near to the article on political affect, suggests how preoccupied we are with the itinerary of feeling. The politics of feeling places us in the latest age of sensibility. One day, I received further guidance from the local paper, this time from my horoscope: "Today you might resort to the unproductive luxury of emotionalizing." I have taken this suggestion to heart (where else?). In the process, I have tried to show, in a historical way, just how productive emotionalizing has been in the past—and the present.

This is a book of the 1990s, during which national and international politics increasingly turned on controversies over the value of empathetic reactions to representations of suffering. In the United States, the videotape of the beating of an African-American man, Rodney King, by Los Angeles police in 1991 might be the premier example of how images of trauma become tests of the public heart. But more typical of the nineties even than televised coverage of the 1992 Los Angeles riots, which followed the acquittal of the police officers charged with assaulting Rodney King, was the performance of suffering by politicians.

Representative Patricia Schroeder, now retired from Congress, was so struck by the extent of the news coverage of tears shed by public figures that she kept a "Tears File" of clippings on the subject. The articles tracking the American "Weep Stakes" included accounts of her own tears, shed as she withdrew from an incipient presidential campaign in 1987, and those of Edmund Muskie, during the 1972 New Hampshire primary.[5] The heavy political price paid by Schroeder and Muskie seemed to diminish during the 1990s. Everyone, it seemed, performed the intimate connections among sentimentality, gender, and politics. During the Clinton impeachment crisis in the fall of 1998, the president who had so effectively communicated vicarious suffering when witnessing others in pain suddenly occupied a position defined by the presence or absence of moral judgment, a different vocabulary altogether. He became the potential object of feeling rather than its subject. The sex panic of 1998 resulted from the ideological differences that formed the armature of the contest for sympathy throughout the decade. What are those ideological divides, and why do they matter to cultural historians? Economic arguments set forth in a neolibertarian "tough love" mood questioned the value of sympathy as embodied in a welfare state. When academics defended positions viewed as marginal or minor in character, the political right counterattacked, charging the professoriate with an overinvestment in the historical oppression of women and minorities—an overinvestment in victims. David Rieff's cover story in the October 1991 *Harper's,* "Victims All? Recovery, Co-dependency, and the Art of Blaming Somebody Else," stressed the links between victimology, political correctness, and college teachers.[6]

These attacks on liberal sentiment did not prevent the sentimentalizing of conservative politics. Conservatives themselves deployed "the culture of pain" to draw sympathy away from groups identified with liberal or radical causes (women, gays and lesbians, and racial minorities) and toward the unemployed white male, the crime victim, or the unborn, as in Pat Boone's antiabortion music video, "Let Me Live," in which he dreamed of infant voices that sang to him of experiencing life.[7] The former U.S. attorney general, Dick Thornburgh, pushed for the legal validity of victims' testimony and victims' rights in the judicial process, a program that has enjoyed considerable success. The Oklahoma City bombing trial of Timothy McVeigh showed the tight fit between the rhetoric of national well-being, the testimony of victims, and the death penalty. Conservative political culture displays as close a relationship between emotion and alienation as the political culture it opposes.

The project of this book is to investigate the cultural history of public emotion. This undertaking itself arises from a long-standing conjunction between civic claims and the language of sympathy. The current willingness of academics to address issues of emotion has been shaped by a national political mood that is both troubled and fascinated by a sentimental agenda. From within the atmospheric pressures of post–Cold War investigations of civil societies and public spheres, we are looking closely at past relationships between otherness and care, alienation and sympathy, empire and affect. At the core of these histories is the curiously absorbing figure of the sensitive man.

In his essay "Families and Prisons," former poet laureate Robert Hass broods over emotional, personal poetry about families. He speculates about why confessional poetry is peculiar to the United States and why it is subject to ridicule almost everywhere else in the world. He looks for a way to value this poetry without flinching from the fact that it could only be written in relative security in an internationally dominant political and economic culture. And in the process, he presents his own sentimental masculinity: "That feeling of pathos, the lump-in-the-throat feeling that shows up in movies about families like *Kramer vs. Kramer,* is at least one of the elements of an actual social bond, of a particular imagination of civility, morality."[8] This meditation on sadness carries Hass to the recent international history of victimized poets. Thinking about poets in prison—in Korea, Yugoslavia, concentration camps, the former Soviet Union—leads him to distinguish between "the history of literature" and "the history of courage." He does so in order to deprive poetry of any glamour deriving from victimization, especially any that would arise from an American poet beholding suffering from a distance. Hass offers a genealogy of pathos. He connects the pathos of children with romantic poetry; connects literary romanticism to romantic political thought, which "braided together our feelings about the abuse of power and the abuse of children"; connects political philosophy to "the middle class . . . and . . . mercantile imperialism"; and finally arrives at the Age of Sensibility and its still-embarrassing "tears and terror, sentimentality, and awe." Hass ends by committing himself to a poetry of personal suffering while at the same time understanding victimization in its full range of historical and international embarrassments.

Early in the essay Hass observes that he has arrived at the subject of "pathos and tenderness," of "familial feeling," through his effort to write poems about his mother. He follows the lead of two generations of postwar feminists, memoirists, and poets in making family memory public: "I have lately been trying with some difficulty to write . . . some of my childhood experiences. In my early childhood my mother was chronically alcoholic which filled my days . . . with instability, sorrow, and some terror."

Hass's essay is followed by a companion poem, titled "My Mother's

Nipples." The poem dramatizes the difficulty of finding a language for the mother's body, which is also the difficulty of finding a language for the child's feelings. It begins with the problem of memory and repression ("They're where all displacement begins") but quickly becomes a poem about a grown man's embarrassment. Ten voices perform variations on the theme of the mother's nipples, beginning with "The cosmopolitan's song on this subject" and proceeding through songs of the romantic, the utopian, the philosopher, the capitalist, the saint, the misanthrope, the melancholic, the indigenist, and the regionalist. These personae are painfully self-ironizing, until Hass shifts from his imagined cultural history of poems about "les nipples de ma mère" to a sequence of "memories" that sees him through to the end of the poem.

By the time the poem concludes his early dread of his mother has been transformed into a retroactive sympathy for her. Hass's fine-tuned embarrassment about the ethos of American confessional writing motivates his ethical attention to the history of authorial suffering in general. His embarrassment about "writing the child" is portrayed by his observance of his mother's body, the sign of her alcoholic abjection. Familial emotions fuse with the male writer's moral labor in writing about them and with the morality of international relations. Masculine sensibility, Hass shows us, cannot be separated from the family intimacy figured here by the mother's incontinent body, or from global culture, or from the poet's critical examination of both together.

Sensibility Studies

Sensibility in the Anglo-American political tradition started with the efforts of elite men to imagine political opposition and to understand political change. Sensibility becomes fashionable when men practice it— although they are not the only ones who practice it and although their practices have variable meanings. In these opening pages, I have used words like "emotion," "feeling," "affect," "sensibility," "sympathy," and "sentiment" in an impressionistic fashion, because my first order of business is to suggest the recent tone of civic life in the United States. But even as I write in a more analytical vein, I want to emphasize that what these terms have in common is much more important than what differentiates them from one another. As Adela Pinch remarks, "the many names for emotion travel as freely as the emotions themselves." I am oriented, like Pinch, to depictions of social relationships, to "transpersonal" domains, and to ideas of national and global systems within which emotion—however named—becomes part of historical perception.[9] One of the reasons why it is difficult to stabilize the meanings of terms like "sensibility," "sympathy," and "sentiment" is that they not only vary according to their usage in distinct historical contexts but also change as scholars seek an integrated understanding of emotion.

During the heyday of poststructuralist speculation in humanities departments, what Derrida called "theoretical emotion" was everywhere—in the overwrought citation from Nietzsche or Wordsworth, in theories of the ups and downs of feelings comprising the sublime, in the dizziness of the *mise en abîme,* in critical prose as performance art—everywhere, that is, except in the individual author, reader, or lyric speaker. Though subjectivity and agency are once more with us, in this respect poststructuralism prepared the way for current histories of the ways in which emotion is not coincident with the self, but "traveling" or "vagrant," as Pinch has observed, "located among rather than within people."[10] Selfhood and emotion have met in "the social performative," the domain of "rituals by which subjects are formed and reformulated."[11] In the nineties, even Derrida evokes the cultural history of masculine sensibility: "[T]he figure of the friend, so regularly coming back on stage with the features of the *brother* . . . seems spontaneously to belong to a *familial, fraternalist* and thus *androcentric* configuration of politics." Political crimes induce friendship's "complaint" or "forms of *grief* in which accusation mingles with mourning." Derrida now captures with uncanny precision the mood of masculine civic humanism "between these *imputable* crimes, between sentiments of guilt, responsibilities, compassions, testaments, and spectres: endless processions and trials."[12]

An emerging interdisciplinary conversation in the humanities and social sciences is advancing the view that emotion, including personal emotion felt to be inward or private, is a social phenomenon, though one not separable from bodily response. This was brought home to me several years ago, when I organized a two-week faculty seminar on the subject of emotion. The seminar accurately reflected the many subcultures of emotion studies. The distance between experimental cognitive scientists and sociocultural constructionists was obvious, sometimes irritably so. But, as June Howard—one of the participants—has argued, anthropologists, psychologists, sociologists, and neurologists are chipping away at the intellectual barriers between brain-based studies of cognition and culture-based studies of epistemology. As feeling and knowing converge, so, too, do culture and the body.

Howard shows that the contrast between authentic and inauthentic states of feeling, which traditionally distinguished "emotion" from reprehensible "sentiment," is obsolete. Instead of assigning sentimentality any specific referential content when "neither the socially constructed nor the bodily nature of sentiment seems to serve any longer to distinguish it from emotion in general," she proposes that we define sentiment as signaling a heightened awareness of emotion as an *issue:* "the ascription of sentimentality . . . [marks] a moment when the discursive processes that construct emotion become visible," making apparent the choice of "whether to yield to an emotion or to resist it." By saying that I am exploring the sentimental habits of our culture, therefore, I am referring also to the debates provoked by those habits: "Characterizing something as sentimental should open, not close, a conversation."[13] Emotion takes on the defining attributes of social life: it is gendered; it is old or young; it is associated with experienced individual and group identities; it partakes of national character; it assimilates landscapes, architectures, and other geographies. Never univocal or transparent, feeling inheres in the shapes and conventions of social and cultural life.

The eighteenth century witnessed the decisive popular fusion of sensibility and taste, so that emotional susceptibility was allied to aesthetic expression.[14] Despite its liquid quality, or perhaps because of it, sensibility became identified with particular scenes, plots, and characters. Jerome McGann concludes that the term "sensibility" clings to the early decades of the eighteenth century while "sentiment" has attached itself to a second, later phase. McGann wants to keep sensibility "the more primitive of the two," affiliated with instinct and the body, and to elevate sentimentality to "a sophisticated acquirement, a sympathetic understanding gained through complex acts of conscious attention and reflection."[15] I begin at a much earlier historical point than does McGann. And, while I agree that sensibility might be the earlier term, I do not think that its meanings are significantly different from those of Adam Smith's "moral sentiment" later on.[16] More importantly, I argue that sensibility and a host of other conditions were *always* sophisticated, reflective, and complex. A key historical shift occurred around 1713, but it has less to do with degrees of complexity or measurable changes in terminology than with the move away from defining sentiment in terms of transactions between socially equal persons and toward scenarios of inequality.

Literary historians sometimes distance themselves from sentiment in the very act of talking about it. By studying the "ideological work" that sentiment is performing in any given text or cultural milieu, the scholar allies himself or herself with ideology as the analytical term.[17] Sentiment is shown to have been a condition of lesser self-consciousness relative to the present, epistemologically superior interpretation of sentiment. Such strategies often imply that the authors of sentimental texts did not themselves understand sentimentality as a sociocultural negotiation. I do not wholly dispute the prevailing view of the ideological function of sentiment, that it represses the consciousness or expresses the unconsciousness of power relations. I believe, however, that much of the literature of sensibility exposes a complicated awareness of the human costs of national and imperial economies, as well as the knowledge that sensibility itself is a privilege. Sensibility is the *admitted* connection between speculation, mood, and power.[18] We still operate within sensibility, deprived of epistemological superiority toward our sensible or sentimental forebears.

I approach the literatures of sensibility and sentiment in the eighteenth century, therefore, as indices of the pain caused by political arrangements from which artists and intellectuals knowingly benefited but at the same time could not control. Sensibility is consciously bound up with the social management of sympathetic knowledge. Sentiment is not simply a taste for pathos. The ambivalent culture of vicariousness can reflect on itself.[19] The literature of victimization and pity can be knowledgeable about the market for pain and troubled by early modern forms of liberal guilt. And tenderheartedness is inseparable from the processes of political and cultural legitimation.

The effects fundamental to the genres of sensibility are organized by gender and race. Research on the culture of sensibility was put on its contemporary footing by feminist scholars who responded to the longstanding denigration of sentimental literature by women. The renovation of sentiment as worthy of our most complex thinking and teaching stands as an important accomplishment of feminist literary scholarship, gay and lesbian studies, and queer theory. The changing status of gendered sentiment in public life has induced our belated patience with sentimental fiction, perhaps, but scholars also forced the issue.

Scholarly work on sentiment has been a disproportionately American enterprise, carried out by American critics with reference to American literature. After foundational work by Carroll Smith-Rosenberg, Nancy Cott, and others, the polemical force of "emotion studies" emerged in Ann Douglas's critique of the market for sentimental culture and Nina Baym's exposé of "beset manhood" in academic attacks on women's sentimental literature. Jane Tompkins, a forceful advocate of sentimentality as a positive practice, replied vigorously to Douglas, but the work of

Cathy N. Davidson had the greatest impact on the literary landscape of the early national period.[20] The net effect was to make the American sentimental tradition politically interesting enough for its aesthetic practices to be worth serious academic consideration. As feminist studies labored throughout the 1970s and 1980s to stop evading differences between women, the critical understanding of sentiment underwent not just a thematic shift, but also a structural one. Faced with the role of sympathy in race and class relations, scholars found that it no longer made sense to be for sentimentality or against it.

Feminist critics are more committed than ever to the study of sentiment, now understood as an economy, a transaction, or a system. Karen Sánchez-Eppler's demonstration that nineteenth-century feminist sentiment and abolitionism meet in literary representations of the racially marked body provides one important model for such investigations.[21] Lauren Berlant's distillation of "the female complaint" in terms of its systemic contradictions offers another.[22] Eve Sedgwick's analysis of sentimentality in relation to homosexual discourses in a culture of straight male homosocial prohibitions gives us a third.[23]

A new generation of scholars is connecting gendered sensibility to the late eighteenth-century cultural politics of both national and diasporic identities. Dana Nelson poses the questions of how white women writers utilized sentiment "as an effective strategy to gain authorial advantage." She asserts that their newfound authority both supported "active intercession on behalf of the object of sympathy" and remained palatable for white middle-class audiences. Sentimentality, Nelson concludes, is "a mixed bag." Women who made careers as novelists could express cross-racial sympathy only in compromised ways, despite their efforts to "write beyond" the tearful endings of the genre.[24] Julia Stern's readings of "the potent middle ground of quasi-embodied expression" in early American texts go right to the heart of how women writers changed masculine conventions for talking about liberty. She demonstrates how female authors "[reimagine] the gendering of power" in scenes of burial and mourning.[25] When Laura Wexler insists that we face up to the "concrete social institutionalization" of sentimental culture, the actual "imposition of sentimental modalities on people" in schools, prisons, and hospitals, her skepticism is different mostly in degree.[26] Wexler is more exasperated than other critics, but the violence she stresses is a quality that they, too, build into models of sentiment's structural contradictions.

In *Cato's Tears*, clearly, I am participating in this rich scholarly conversation on American sensibility, even as I frame it in a larger Anglo-

American setting in order to connect it to an earlier history. I emphasize that masculine sensibility is part of the cultural inheritance of all Anglo-American eighteenth- and nineteenth-century intellectuals. Despite a growing number of good studies of manhood and masculinity that build on the fundamental transvaluation of sentimentality by feminists, the relationship between masculine and feminine sensibility has not been well understood. The dominant discourse of sensibility has never been decisively identified as a masculine political invention, nor have the consequences of this fact been explored. The strategies of female authors only make sense in the context of the early cultural prestige of masculine tenderheartedness. The literature of sensibility responds to the reorganization of masculine experience in an expansionist parliamentary culture.

The Man of Feeling

A friend sent me by e-mail part of the section on "Grief" from a book on eighteenth-century acting theory: "A girl collapsing in tears merely embarrasses the audience; a god or a hero, noble and elevated in bearing, who weeps despite himself, arouses the fear and pity essential to classical tragedy."[27] "I thought this might be grist for your mill," the sender commented. Grist indeed. The performance of weeping men on the eighteenth-century stage signifies the extent to which masculine emotion mattered.

Late seventeenth-century sensibility manifested itself in the civic prestige and mutual friendship practiced by men of equally high social status. The dilemmas of Whig masculinity turned on the problem of negotiating between the power of indifference, or emotional discipline, and the power of sensibility. Sensibility as a cultural ethos took shape in England significantly earlier than we once thought, as part of the culture of elite men with an affinity for republican narratives and parliamentary opposition. With the help of historians like Kathleen Wilson, who argues that politics was "a constitutive arena of culture," we are gaining a more finely tuned understanding of an oppositional ideology compounded of "mercantilism, nationalistic anxiety and libertarian fervor." The "powerful conflation of empire and liberty" was accomplished through more ambivalent masculinities than Wilson discerns, I believe, but she is certainly right to conclude that, across the social spectrum, "empire itself . . . construct[ed] gendered definitions of citizenship."[28]

These eighteenth-century developments are pertinent to the politics of liberal guilt in the 1990s. This is the case despite the fact that the meanings of both "liberal" and "guilt" are anachronistic when applied to that earlier age of sensibility. Liberal guilt feels to us like political failure or delegitimation, while eighteenth-century sensibility was a mode of political legitimation. The two are bound nonetheless by intricate histories capable of being specified or at least hypothesized. Putting a large frame around the culture of sensibility does not exempt us from studying the applications of vicarious pain in a particular time and place. But it does remind us that the present decade is not the first time that sensibility has been recognized as a signal cultural tendency because of its association with the civic life of men.

Over the course of the eighteenth century, the figures of Cato, Brutus, and other Roman men starred in scenes in which emotional reserve and sentimental display became mutually legitimating roles. Such philosophical characters helped a certain segment of British culture to renegotiate equality and inequality as earlier forms of clientage were breaking down and as the metropolitan aesthetic of global racial differences was taking shape.[29] Adam Smith's *Theory of Moral Sentiments* (1759), part of the core curriculum of liberal emotion, confirms the affective ideals of republican discourse. By 1759, Smith was working in the fully formed tradition that I survey in the chapters that follow.

The Theory of Moral Sentiments captures the ambivalence of masculine sensibility in its mixed signals about how the spectator is implicated in the sympathetic relation.[30] For Smith, the ideal manifestation of moral sentiment involves a dignified upper-class sufferer whose very self-control provokes his friends to vicarious tears.[31] He stages moral sentiment as a bond between elite males deeply but reticently involved in one another's humiliations and triumphs of self-discipline, large and small. These bonds belong to the neoclassical scenario of the Roman Stoic surrounded by his sympathetic friends. Fending off the temptations of downwardly directed sympathy, Smith tries to dismiss early modern liberal guilt as the erroneous teaching of certain "philosophers" who "have laboured to increase our sensibility to the interests of others":

> those whining and melancholy moralists, who are perpetually reproaching us with our happiness, while so many of our brethren are in misery, who regard as impious the natural joy of prosperity, which does not think of the many wretches that are at every instant labouring under all sorts of calamities, in the languor of poverty, in the agony of disease, in the horrors of death, under the insults and oppression of their enemies. Commiseration for those miseries which we never saw, which we never heard of, but which

we may be assured are at all times infesting such numbers of our fellow-creatures, ought, they think, to damp the pleasures of the fortunate, and to render a certain melancholy dejection habitual to all men. (139–40)

The Scottish thinker rejects feeling at a distance in favor of social near-ness. He does not hesitate to invoke the "whole earth" as a statistical measure in the next phrase, however. This suggests both that statistical inclusion can be used *against* emotional inclusion, and that the language of human connectedness (terms like "earth" or "humanity") is difficult to avoid when discussing benevolence:

Take the whole earth at an average, for one man who suffers pain or misery, you will find twenty in prosperity and joy, or at least in tolerable circumstances. No reason . . . can be assigned why we should rather weep with the one than rejoice with the twenty. This artificial commiseration . . . seems altogether unattainable; and those who affect this character have commonly nothing but a cer-tain affected and sentimental sadness, which, without reaching the heart, serves only to render the countenance and conversa-tion impertinently dismal and disagreeable. . . . Whatever interest we take in the fortune of those . . . who are placed altogether out of the sphere of our activity, can produce only anxiety to our-selves, without any manner of advantage to them. To what pur-pose should we trouble ourselves about the world in the moon? All men, even those at the greatest distance, are no doubt entitled to our good wishes. . . . But if, notwithstanding, they should be unfortunate, to give ourselves any anxiety upon that account, seems to be no part of our duty. (140)

Smith revives the rhetoric of anti-Puritanism to characterize the guilty liberal, the person overimplicated in others, as a sour killjoy and melan-cholic incapable of feeling "the natural joy of prosperity." Actually, these "whining moralists" with their overflowing feelings of "sentimental sad-ness" are fulfilling the Smithian program to excess: they are using their imaginations to "[ex]change persons and characters" with the suffering party, even though the victim is out of their direct social or moral reach.[32] But here Smith tells us that we do not need to suffer from sympathy for those "out of the sphere of our activity," "those at the greatest distance" from us, people who might as well inhabit "the world in the moon." His spatial metaphors activate social and cultural geographies, including those of colony, market, and empire. "The world in the moon" summons up all the eighteenth-century disciplines associated with such geographies, like mapping and astronomy. For the guilty liberal, being consciously included in systematic formations is the basis for the sense of implication or responsibility. For Smith, however, the productive virtue inherent in the system frees its knowing participants from having to share everyone else's unhappiness.

Such metaphors also imply the potential for distances to be technologically overcome. If we obtain detailed knowledge of the suffering of persons on another continent, if "miseries that we never saw . . . [or] heard of" come to be heard of and seen—that is, come to be reproducible—what happens to the overzealous sympathizer then? How fast should our sympathies outrun our agency? Will liberal guilt proliferate under expanded representational conditions? Does our changing understanding of our role in a global system of interdependence increase the legitimate range of duty? Are the Age of Sensibility and the Age of Mechanical Reproduction the same thing?

The moral embarrassment of the sensitive intellectual crystallized as a response to three historical factors: first, the racial politics of international mercantile and colonial power relations; second, a concept of the economy as a system that produced suffering for some and privilege for others; and third, cultural opportunities for the display of sympathy, especially sympathetic masculinity. The culture of late eighteenth-century Whig intellectuals in Edinburgh, including Hume, Hutchinson, Blair, Gibbon, and Smith himself—collectively, the Scottish Enlightenment—generated the period's crucial theories of economic, historical, metaphysical, and rhetorical operations. They crafted the culture of *systems* that is so important to the modern individual's feeling of being meaningfully related to remote locations and cultures. It should not surprise us, therefore, that this milieu should also produce the fictional paradigm of tenderhearted manhood.

A decade after the publication of *The Theory of Moral Sentiments,* another Scot, Henry Mackenzie, gave this period its title character in that classic of masculine sensibility, *The Man of Feeling.*[33] The novel includes a series of mini-narratives about sympathy extended downward on the social scale and outward to imperial venues. *The Man of Feeling* is fascinated not just by masculine equality but also by sentimental inequality. It accepts the pressure to emote across the empire rather than stoically to resist its sentimental opportunities. The 1771 publication of *The Man of Feeling* falls between the treaty of 1765, which gave the British East India Company administrative control of Bengal, and the Regulating Act of

1773, through which the British government intervened to make the appointment of a governor general subject to state control. More active government oversight would come with the East India Act of 1784, although direct rule was not assumed until after the Indian Mutiny of 1857–58. A mood of imperial momentum troubled by anticipatory doubt pervades the novel, at times with direct reference to India.

In a roadside encounter, Harley, the genteel Man of Feeling who ends up dead on a sofa, meets Edwards, a worn but stoical tenant farmer whom he had known as a youth. Once Harley and Edwards have recognized each other, Edwards tells his story. It is a generic tale of rural dispossession. A newly rich landlord hires a "London-attorney" for his steward.[34] The tenant is turned out of his farm onto a lesser holding, where his son, after an encounter with the justice's game-keeper, falls prey to a press-gang on Christmas Eve. The father bribes the sergeant to let him go in his son's place and ends up with British troops in India. This provides the setting for yet another tale within a tale centering on yet another stoical sufferer. Mackenzie's narrative links the economy of the British countryside to colonial relationships through the dynamics of sympathy.

The most striking aspect of this story is the way that Harley's response to the story of the merciful Indian who saved and was saved by Edwards is mediated by Edwards himself, the English farmer who is also the narrator. When Edwards and the Indian take turns caring for each other, victimhood seems less like something permanent or essential—less like racial or class inevitability—and more like a contingent status. At the same time, however, these disfranchised individuals, while granted considerable agency relative to each other, are placed at a clear social distance below Harley. I quote Edwards's narrative in full:

> "Amongst our prisoners was an old Indian, whom some of our officers supposed to have a treasure hidden somewhere. . . . He declared that he had none, but that would not satisfy them, so they ordered him to be tied to a stake, and suffer fifty lashes every morning till he should learn to speak out, as they said. Oh! Mr. Harley, had you seen him, as I did, with his hands bound behind him, suffering in silence, while the big drops trickled down his shriveled cheeks and wet his grey beard, which some of the inhuman soldiers plucked in scorn! I could not bear it . . . and one morning when the rest of the guard were out of the way, I found means to let him escape. I was tried by a court-martial for negligence on my post, and ordered, in compassion of my age,

and having got this wound in my arm and that in my leg in the service, only to suffer three hundred lashes and be turned out of the regiment; but my sentence was mitigated as to the lashes, and I had only two hundred. When I had suffered these I was turned out of the camp, and had betwixt three and four hundred miles to travel before I could reach a sea-port. . . . I set out, however, resolved to walk as far as I could, and then to lay myself down and die. But I had scarce gone a mile when I was met by the Indian whom I had delivered. He pressed me in his arms, and kissed the marks of the lashes on my back a thousand times; he led me to a little hut, where some friend of his dwelt, and after I was recovered of my wounds conducted me so far on my journey himself, and sent another Indian to guide me through the rest. When we parted he pulled out a purse with two hundred pieces of gold in it. 'Take this,' said he, 'my dear preserver, it is all I have been able to procure.'

"I begged him not to bring himself to poverty for my sake, who should probably have no need of it long, but he insisted. . . . He embraced me. 'You are an Englishman,' said he, 'but the Great Spirit has given you an Indian heart.'" (92–94)[35]

Edwards and the old Indian wept together in mutually self-sacrificing abjection that culminated in a moment of reverse orientalism: an Englishman has an "Indian heart." The scene confirms Homi Bhabha's observation that "the shadow . . . guilt casts on the 'object' of identification . . . is the origin of melancholia."[36] The question is, melancholia in whom? Juliana Schiesari has proposed that masculine melancholia was associated with cultural privilege as early as the Renaissance.[37] The Man of Feeling is the beneficiary of this legacy. Harley, a classic melancholic, now weeps with Edwards over the retelling of the earlier scene. This spectacle of the infinite regress of sentimental implication carries Harley, the privileged spectator, toward generalizations about foreign policy. Emotion causes Harley to become acutely aware of the tension between the British "native" or patriot and "the man," or universal human heart, within himself. The national and the international constitute a single relational phenomenon, and sympathy is central to the unending formation of the simultaneously local and translocal subject:

"Edwards," said he [Harley], "I have a proper regard for the prosperity of my country: every native of it appropriates to himself some share of the power, or the fame, which, as a nation, it acquires, but I cannot throw off the man so much as to rejoice at our conquests in India. You tell me of immense territories subject

> to the English: I cannot think of their possessions without being
> led to inquire by what right they possess them. They came there
> as traders, bartering the commodities they brought for others
> which their purchasers could spare; and however great their prof-
> its were, they were then equitable. But what title have the subjects
> of another kingdom to establish an empire in India? to give laws
> to a country where the inhabitants received them on the terms of
> friendly commerce? . . . You describe the victories they have
> gained; they are sullied by the cause in which they fought: you
> enumerate the spoils of those victories; they are covered with the
> blood of the vanquished!" (103)

Spoils covered by the blood of the vanquished: this is liberal guilt in late
eighteenth-century Britain. Harley's oration addresses the perceived conflict between mercantile and imperial interactions, the contiguity of wealth
and war, and the desire to keep trade distinct from conquest.

We can read Mackenzie's concluding paragraph on English imperialism in two ways. First, as pure ideology: trade and conquest are distinguished from each other in order to give a moral patina to their actual
connivance. Economic transactions appear benign and force looks reprehensible when, in fact, they are part of a single process of European
domination. Or, second, as *knowledge* of ideology: an epistemological moment in which the link between violence and material gain is understood
through the figure of the victim. This episode both obfuscates and admits
to the belief that British wealth is implicated in British torture. Mackenzie
might agree with Gayatri Spivak that "all of this comes accompanied by
large doses of liberal guilt about which I do not know what to begin to
say, but I'm sure you understand what the problem is." [38]

The *Whig* of Rome

*W*ith *Cato's Tears,* I enter the rapidly cohering interdisciplinary field of
"circum-Atlantic" studies in an attempt to change the terms of both feminist debates about sentimentality and assessments of republican ideology
by merging these two not always compatible endeavors. [39] I take on a large
subject: the politics of emotion—including the structuring force of race
and gender—on both sides of the Atlantic from the late seventeenth to
the early nineteenth century. *Cato's Tears* deals with drama, poetry, and
fiction and brings to light a number of texts that have not been substan-
tively discussed before or related to one another.

I trace the relationship between politics, sensibility, and masculinity
throughout the "long eighteenth century," starting unconventionally with

the English Exclusion Crisis of 1679–81 and ending in 1815 with the Tripolitan War, the first war involving the United States. The standard notion of the Age of Sensibility comprises the melancholy literature of the British man of feeling in the later eighteenth century. But in fact, sensibility begins much earlier and lasts much longer than that. Sensibility pervades a narrow stratum of Anglo-American culture as early as the Exclusion Crisis of 1679–81, which brought earlier republican attitudes to bear through parliamentary action. The first earl of Shaftesbury led the incipient Whigs in an unsuccessful attempt to force parliamentary control over the succession. The political drama of these years, particularly the genre of the "Roman play," developed well-understood codes of ideological affiliation. Aphra Behn mocked a familiar figure when she satirized the "*Whig* of Rome." [40] In chapter 1, "Conspiracy, Sensibility and the Stoic," I talk about gender in the political drama and verse of the Exclusion Crisis. Nathaniel Lee's *Lucius Junius Brutus* (1680), Otway's *Venice Preserved* (1682), and Dryden's *Absalom and Achitophel* show that the Roman republic plays a lead role in the ambivalent masculine culture intrinsic to political legitimation in the early parliamentary period. The republican ethos is not a character ("the classical republican") but rather a loosely orchestrated sequence of parliamentary sensations narrated through the foundational stories of imperial manhood.

Anthony Ashley Cooper, the third earl of Shaftesbury and the grandson of the first earl, provoker of the Exclusion Crisis, published his major essays as the *Characteristics* in 1711. He separates elite masculine friendship from conspiracy without forgetting the pleasures of conspiracy altogether. He is the philosopher of a high masculine sensibility that launders the factional passions of the early Whigs while modifying their emotional legacies for the Hanoverian era. The relationship between the two Shaftesburys thus replays—in a genteel fashion—the generational drama enacted in the Roman plays between the stern republican and the sensitive younger son or son surrogate.

In the Roman plays and their spin-offs in other genres, weeping men—especially the indifferent republican's tenderhearted son—circle around stoic Romans framed by an imperial, international setting. The Roman republic configures tensions between political decision and indecision, cultural centrality and marginality, law and tears. These texts foreground the need for impersonal law while accompanying its stern tones with the outcry of deep-feeling masculine subjectivity. Rome, therefore, provides a figurative shorthand for the ambivalent, gender-specific culture within which Whig political legitimation in the early parliamentary period was set. The pairing of stoic and sentimental men in these productions has had astonishing staying power, although the subsequent proliferation of other kinds of sensibility is equally remarkable.

Finding a cultural high ground for oppositional manhood—a practice other than conspiracy or faction—gave late seventeenth-century writers in this tradition their agenda. By the time of the death of Queen Anne and the installation of the Hanoverian monarchs in 1714, political parties had become almost normal. Republican scenarios were no longer the only narrative in town. At the point of transition, Addison's *Cato*—performed in 1713 and the subject of chapter 2, "Cato's Tears"—became the most politically significant drama of the century.

Cato features a sentimental African prince, Juba, as the romantic lead. Addison dramatizes an extended debate over the relative value of African and Roman cultures while telling the story of Juba's successful suit for Cato's daughter. The emotional life of the male citizen is represented as negotiating between the domain of civil sensibility where elite male bonding prevails and a more physical, "wild," or foreign condition. The category of race in the eighteenth century signified ethnicity, nationality, and tribe, as well as the ideology of color. In *Cato*, sensitive masculinity relies on cultural comparisons grounded in race in all these senses. Race becomes a figure for emotion; emotion makes racial distinctions. But most of all, race makes empire a setting for men in crisis. Similar dynamics shape Thomson's *Sophonisba* (1730), in which the title character, the Queen of Carthage, poses a complex Africanist challenge to masculine sensibility.[41]

Cato is still with us today, as I argue in the book's conclusion. In the intervening periods, "Cato discourse" has stood for individual liberty beholden to no one. As the signature of the citizen in Trenchard and Gordon's *Cato's Letters* of 1720–23, Cato represents the muse of antigovernment politics. He surfaces periodically throughout eighteenth-century poetry and in Smith's *Theory of Moral Sentiments;* he populates American revolutionary writings and is invoked by Barbauld in "An Inquiry into Those Kinds of Distresses Which Excite Agreeable Sensations" (1825): "The stern fortitude and inflexible resolution of a Cato may command esteem, but does not excite tenderness."[42] Chapter 12 of Royall Tyler's "The Bay Boy," an unfinished novel, offers a rollicking account of the "First Theatrical Representation in Boston," a surreptitious performance by "certain young clerks," at night, in a deserted shop, of Addison's *Cato*—a wry postrevolutionary memory of an older politics.[43] Noah Webster in the third volume of his reader recounts the heated dialogue from

Cato between Juba and Syphax, in which they alternatively mystify and deconstruct the worth of the Roman soul compared to African manhood. At least seventy-seven editions of Webster's reader appeared between 1785 and 1835.[44] In every case, the apparent persistence of "the classical republican" marks the repetition of the *system* of sensibility. Wherever Cato appears decked out in his stoic rigor, presented ironically or straight, sensitive masculinity hyperconscious of imperial and colonial frameworks resides nearby.

By the 1720s, we can discern a marked, rapid shift to a distributed mode of sensibility articulated by a more diverse population of writers. What has conventionally been defined as the late eighteenth-century Age of Sensibility is, in fact, sensibility's second act. As sensibility's social base becomes broader, its subject paradoxically becomes social *inequality*. Sensibility increasingly is defined by the consciousness of a power difference between the agent and the object of sympathy. The literary victim is typically marked by racial, social, or national disadvantages: the deep-feeling Moor, the dying Indian, the impoverished veteran, the slave, the vagrant. While writings featuring such characters underscore the pleasure in global prospects available mostly to white Anglo-American authors, they show that the nation also could be criticized as a corrupt system from which no one was exempt. The global geography of otherness leads to territories of emotion. North Africa and North America become zones in which non-European and European men meet in order to be glamorized as troubled sons and lovers experiencing crises of authority.

I use the term "republican" to refer to the characteristic masculine relationships in plays set in the Roman republic and in works that recycle all or part of that template. My vocabulary, however, does not conform to the usual distinctions between republican ideology and liberalism.[45] Masculine sensibility undergoes structural changes that correspond to some accounts of the movement from republicanism to liberalism. But masculine sentiment does not always translate into an argument about the end of republican and the beginning of liberal politics. If anything, the gendered history that I begin to offer here cuts across or even displaces these more familiar analytical frameworks.

Chapter 3, "The Deathbed of the Just," investigates how republican manhood merged with the second wave of sensibility—that is, sensibility located where we are used to finding it, in mid-eighteenth-century writing. Pathos-laden dramas of Native American encounters with Europeans are staged in London. This is the case with John Dennis's 1704 *Liberty Asserted*. The "conspiracy" of Pontiac was the subject of *Ponteach,* the 1766 printed drama attributed to the American Indian fighter, Robert Rogers. More importantly, the long-lived tradition of Roman plays infiltrates and is infiltrated by the poetry conventionally associated with sensibility. Edward Young, author of the 1745 *Complaint, or Night-Thoughts*, wrote *The Revenge*, a tragedy in the republican vein, first, twenty-four years earlier. "Unconquered Cato, virtuous in extreme" makes an appearance in Thomson's *Winter*, a poem begun well before his *Sophonisba*.

The relationships between *The Revenge* and *The Complaint, Winter* and *Sophonisba* depend on a transgeneric idiom of sensibility shared by drama, poetry, fiction, and nonfictional prose throughout the eighteenth century. The signature dynamics of affect in the literature of sensibility take the form of intersubjective relations that cross generic lines and, ultimately, lines of gender. The exquisitely sensitive stoicism of Lucrece in Nathaniel Lee's *Lucius Junius Brutus* recurs in the figure of Richardson's Clarissa, who is both tenderhearted and adamant in her stoical hold on suicidal liberty in the face of libertine aggression. The Man of Feeling, in Mackenzie's novel, dies as a result not only of sensibility but of the fatigue incurred in extending sympathy to myriad needy others while stoically refusing to speak his own romantic disappointment.

The strategies of female authors and the meanings of the feminine in the culture of sensibility make sense only in the context of this long pre-eminence of masculine tenderheartedness. Women writers who invested in sensibility often were motivated by the desire to enter into the powerful description of geographical and historical expanses—the big pictures of time and space—as a way of grappling overtly with public themes. The emergence of women writers in the arena of sensibility does not mean, however, that sensibility was at some point decisively "feminized." It is not clear that we know exactly what we mean when we talk about feminization. We rely on the term, I believe, because we do not possess a detailed history of masculine emotion. Critics point to sentimental, tearful, pathetic, or domestic male characters or authors as examples of "feminization" or "effeminacy." When certain genres are produced largely by women writers—the late eighteenth-century gothic novel would be one example—they are said to be "feminized," as well. I am skeptical of such uses of the term. But if, as I propose, sensibility with all the trappings—weeping, melancholy, suicide, self-pity, weakness, victimization, and sympathy—begins as a transaction that is insistently about parliamentary manhood, how do we interpret the protagonists' own admissions of effeminacy? For the enactment of extreme sensibility by men is described by themselves and other men as womanish.

The charge of feminine sensibility leveled by a man against another man does not represent the end of the story. The deep-feeling, fragile man of sensibility is thoroughly masculine, for his emotional nature is crucial to the drama of homosocial relationships. The style of his masculinity forces us to rewrite the literary history of gender. Male critics who tweaked women for their emotional excesses wrote at times in the pathetic vein themselves, read and admired the literature of sensibility, and, all told, were able to justify their own emotionalism while rejecting the emotional displays of women. A man could both have his sensibility, in other words, and despise it, too. The relationship between gender and sensibility is not symmetrical or transitive.

Claudia L. Johnson has come closer than anyone to taking seriously the deeply embedded cultural reality of sensitive manhood in late eighteenth- and early nineteenth-century Britain and to working in a sustained way from that premise. Her readings of Wollstonecraft and other women writers show the microeconomies of critique and revision that come into play in the politics of women's writing. She demonstrates precisely how stoicism became available for feminist appropriation. Johnson's history of masculine sensibility is quite different from my own, however. A number of modalities of masculine sentiment in the 1790s were construed by women writers as "archaic," as she argues. But this seems to me to be a somewhat restricted view of what had become a thriving, varied transcultural discourse. I am proposing that we view sentiment as a larger affair in which emotional volatility and emotional discipline are joined in strategically choreographed ways. If the older model of sensibility governing the relations of nervous equality among elite men and a few good women is understood to persist even as sensibility increasingly describes situations of inequality, then "competitiveness over the prized quality of sensitivity" involves greater political variety spread out over a broader array of instances than Johnson discovers.[46]

To illuminate the literary practices that organize this larger history of sensibility, I turn to the transatlantic "prospect poetry" of Anna Letitia Barbauld and Phillis Wheatley in chapter 4, "Female Authorship, Public Fancy." The works of Barbauld and Wheatley, each of whom published a volume of poetry in London in 1773, are self-consciously Anglo-American. Barbauld's anti-imperial critique of Britain relies on transatlantic and transhistorical comparisons. Wheatley maneuvers expertly between the attraction of Anglo-American political and religious ties and revolutionary patriotism, drawing on her slave status to speak as an expert witness on liberty. For both poets, sensibility is a form of affective hypermobility that allows the speaker to veer between the moods of power and weakness. Emotion is not just a personal matter in the poetry of Barbauld and Wheatley, however. At its peak, the energy of fancy opens up expanses of historical time and geopolitical space for the female poet. Consequently, fancy gives these writers the authority to address slavery and the politics of race.

In chapter 5, "Vagrant Races," I examine the onset of three American poetic careers. Sarah Wentworth Morton and Ann Eliza Bleecker, poets of the American Revolution and the Early Republic, compose emotional treatments of Indians in works that mark their entry into authorship. Their concerns are at once nationalistic and cosmopolitan. Morton's handling of the affectionate bonds between European and Indian men in her long narrative poem, *Ouabi*, urges the emotional potential for whites of virtuous and vanishing Native Americans. Bleecker's poems of maternal grief derive their emotional energy, by contrast, from her dread of Iroquois attacks in upstate New York. She surrounds these traumatic episodes with fancy-driven overviews of the regional landscape, the incipient nation, and the Atlantic theater. Philip Freneau's 1786 version of *The Rising Glory of America* speculatively rewrites debates about colonialism for the national era. His men's club of talking heads gives the reader a tour of theories of racial origins and comparative colonialism. In *The Rising Glory*, too, the mobility of emotions and perspectives dissolves the national ground, at the moment when stabilizing the country's geography would appear to be the American project. The nation is *fancied* into existence through the use of a global time line and a planetary overview. The importance of motion across cognitive and territorial distances persists in chapter 6, "Walkers, Stalkers, Captives, Slaves," where I connect veterans, vocations, and captivities. Charles Brockden Brown's *Edgar Huntly* (1799) is obsessed with Native Americans as a perturbation in white male closeness. Even more than Freneau's, Brown's national landscape is unnervingly porous. This novel makes the intimacies of masculine paranoia central to the meaning of race and land.

The United States was practicing internally forms of domination from which it had just extricated itself, while also striving for legitimacy abroad. This enterprise encouraged the recycling of colonialist aesthetics that we see in the works of Freneau and Brown. During the Tripolitan conflicts, captivity narratives by white Americans revive (without remembering) the North African setting of Addison's *Cato*. Royall Tyler's *The*

Algerine Captive (1797) links the protagonist's understanding of slavery to his discontinuous quest for a masculine vocation. Such texts investigate perceived degrees of personal and collective solvency, the price of the individual, and the humiliations of exchange. And they are tied—as orientalist writing had always been—to the aesthetics of emotion inherent in representations of race.

CHAPTER ONE

Conspiracy, Sensibility, and the Stoic

"Conspiring Virtue" and the Shaftesburys

*D*uring the Exclusion Crisis of 1679–81, the performance on the English stage of emotionally overwrought relations among men takes on a new cultural salience. Male homosocial bonds are defined by the interdependence of stoicism and sensibility. This affective structure builds on but also substantially changes the long-standing preoccupation with the Roman republic among elite, politically active Englishmen.

Conspiracy defined the mood of the Exclusion Crisis. The Popish Plot (1678) was concocted by the notorious Titus Oates and Israel Tonge, who drew up forty-three articles charging Jesuit conspiracies to assassinate Charles II and to foment attacks on Protestantism in England. Fueled by evidence of treasonous practices by the former secretary to the duke of York and by the murder or suicide of the justice of the peace who had deposed Oates, popular anti-Catholic feeling was inflamed, and those accused by Oates were tried and, in many cases, executed. The first earl of Shaftesbury, leader of the Parliamentary proto-Whigs, acted as "impresario" and publicist of the anti-Catholic forces.[1] The crisis-laden atmosphere induced by sequential conspiracies was inseparable from debates over the king's "just prerogatives" or "arbitrary power."

The Exclusion Crisis proper was triggered by the attempt by Shaftesbury's party to pass an act of Parliament regulating the succession. This act denied the Crown to the pro-Catholic, pro-French duke of York should Charles II die without legitimate issue, as was likely. Phillip Harth observes, "by magnifying the public's apprehensions of English Catholics at home and French Catholics abroad [the plot] gave the parliamentary opposition an opportunity to use those fears to win increasing majorities in the House of Commons, to focus them gradually on the prospect of a Popish Successor, and to create from them popular support for a confrontation with the Crown."[2] Week-to-week, Parliament witnessed the unfolding of challenges in the Houses of Commons and Lords; the judicial proceedings, imprisonments, and executions resulting from the Popish Plot and its successors, the Meal Tub Plot (1679), the Irish Plot (1680–81), and finally the Rye House Plot (1683); the provincial parliamentary campaigns; the mustering—and publication—of Petitions and Abhorrences; and the manipulation of sheriffs, juries, and crowds.

What is particularly interesting about this series of crises is the extent to which they operated culturally through the language of masculine feeling. Together, plots and parliaments changed the structures of masculine public life. This link between secrecy and legitimation invites us to think about conspiracy as a gendered practice and as an emotional one. On stage, of course, and in literary works, conspiracy—like soliloquy—is always public, and secrecy is always shared. A plot becomes moving and glamorous in a way that the antiheroics of actual conspiracies rarely are.

It is only by taking seriously the connection between the emergent party politics of the Exclusion Crisis and the link between conspiracy and sensibility in late seventeenth-century drama and poetry that we can address the question how sensibility became Whiggish. The relationship between Charles II and his recognized illegitimate son, the duke of Monmouth was represented as a sentimental drama. The king, the duke, and their followers enacted a suspenseful performance of the intricate negotiations among the principles of legitimate birth, political authority, filial and paternal affection, and the law. The first earl of Shaftesbury failed to manipulate the relationship between law and sensibility as well as the king did. Charles II's public response to his opponents, based on the security provided by his still-secret financial subsidies from Louis XIV of France, was increasingly effective. But when republicanism was represented in writings by authors of either party, it featured men in tears next to their stoical foils.

The third earl of Shaftesbury later became the speaker for the elite, tasteful sensitivity that marked Whig culture once factional crisis had yielded to tenuously normal parliamentary politics. In light of this fact, how should we portray the shift from the pragmatic handling of factional politics by Anthony Ashley Cooper, first earl of Shaftesbury, to the aestheticized homosocial Whiggishness of his grandson, the third earl, author of the broadly influential three-volume *Characteristics of Men, Manners, Opinions, Times* (1711, 1714)? [3]

Political drama and verse of the 1680s were organized around generational differences that are fundamentally differences between kinds and degrees of masculine emotion and agency. The literary treatments of intergenerational affection and violence by Lee in *Lucius Junius Brutus* (1680), Dryden in *Absalom and Achitophel* (1681), and Otway in *Venice Preserved* (1682) are structured by what Laura Brown has aptly called the "persistent analogy of pathos and republicanism." [4] These works illuminate the relationship between the work of the first and third earls of Shaftesbury. The third earl's urbane but affectionate manliness, set forth in *Characteristics,* remembers and modifies the role of the sensitive son in the politically charged literature of the Exclusion Crisis. *Characteristics,* typically viewed by twentieth-century scholars as sounding the opening chords of the Age of Sensibility, in fact is predicated on the unforgotten crises that led up to the Glorious Revolution.

Masculine relations within the family—of paternity, sonhood, and brotherhood—become fundamental to the nonfamilial bonds of men who are connected to one another through political parties, factions, conspiracies, and friendships. Seventeenth- and eighteenth-century political crisis tends to be framed in terms of the tension between familial and quasi- or nonfamilial types of affiliation, and it is in the *deviation from* family models that the ethos of masculine sensibility becomes so important.[5] Sensibility originates in the political and social importance of affinities other than blood, though it continually feeds back into family stories. Instead of the family, then, gender—masculinity—is the crucial term in linking politics to literature between the Exclusion Crisis and the death of Queen Anne.

In *Characteristics,* the third earl of Shaftesbury claims that "the sense of fellowship" is "natural." He asserts that conspiracy is natural, too. He first published *Sensus Communis: An Essay on the Freedom of Wit and Humour* in 1709, when the Whigs, if not exactly thriving, were becoming a legitimate part of the political scene. Here Shaftesbury examines the politics of exclusion, faction, plots and counterplots—the politics, that is, practiced by his grandfather, that founding Whig, the first earl. In doing so, he acknowledges the affectionate pleasures of combat and conspiracy as fertile ground for male bonding. Nowhere is "close sympathy and conspiring virtue . . . so strongly felt or vigorously exerted as in actual conspiracy or war," he observes. The reason? "[T]he most generous spirits are the most combining." In a fit of cultural nostalgia, the unsoldierly peer waxes eloquent on how men at war "delight . . . to move in concert, and feel . . . in the strongest manner the force of the confederating charm."[6] What follows is a social psychology of conspiracy.

Analogous to the affectionate communities made possible by war, there is, Shaftesbury notes, "in the way of peace and civil government, that love of party and subdivision by cabal." His own intermittently activist career in Whig politics conformed to factional affections.[7] For "sedition is a kind of *cantonising* already begun within the State," Shaftesbury explains, and "[t]o *cantonise* is natural." Invoking the traditional republican suspicion of big government and territorial bloat, the third earl remarks that "[v]ast empires are in many respects unnatural." He argues that "when the society grows . . . bulky . . . the affairs of many must . . . turn upon a very few, and the relation be . . . lost, between the magistrate and people." Systemic well-being can be aided by the emotional benefits of colonialism. For "powerful States," he implies, the advantages of "sending colonies abroad" include reviving the sense of lost community "at home." Lacking such global opportunities for otherness, men resort to political cabals: "The associating spirits, for want of exercise, form new movements, and seek a narrower sphere of activity, when they want action in a greater. Thus we have wheels within wheels" (76). Cabals thrive by offering the pleasures of homosocial collaboration:

> Nothing is so delightful as to incorporate. . . . And the associating genius of man is never better proved than in those very societies, which are formed in opposition to the general one of mankind, and to the real interest of the State.
>
> In short, the very spirit of faction . . . seems to be no other than the abuse or irregularity of that social love and common affection which is natural to mankind. (76–77)

For Shaftesbury, faction is an "abuse" of the natural appetite for civil community. The very fact that he can probe the positive pleasures of conspiracy, however, indicates just how far the Whigs have come since his grandfather's generation, when the term "faction" defined the extralegal standing of the opposition. To reflect on the social rewards of conspiracy marks the formation of a political culture in which party differences are normative, not deviant. Nowhere does Shaftesbury suggest that the exclusionist party of his grandfather constituted a conspiracy, but he everywhere reveals an awareness that under certain conditions all political "subdivisions" are prone to conspiratorial tendencies.

The third earl's urbane philosophizing measures the distance between the Exclusion Crisis and the reign of Queen Anne. It also provides an astute reading of faction as a masculine subculture. As an ethnographer of political practices that he can safely define as obsolete, the author of *Sensus Communis* finds the basis for gendered political continuity across Whig generations.

Shaftesbury makes it clear that politeness is an expression of masculine affection, and that the proper sphere of masculine affection is public—but not too public—life. Male affiliation requires public life, and serves it: "[W]here absolute power is, there is no public" (72). In public, the multiple pressures or "amicable collision[s]" of melancholic enthusiasm and cultural inequality create just enough inhibitions for wit (46). "'Tis the persecuting spirit has raised the bantering one," as Shaftesbury notes in one of his epigrammatic summaries of the relation between humor and politics (50). Liberty creates relationships that are social but not public. Because "politeness is owing to liberty," liberty is the necessary condition for "[p]rivate friendship," with the proviso that private friendship is closely allied with "zeal for . . . our country" (67). The "consent and harmony of minds," the "mutual esteem, and reciprocal tenderness and affection" at the core of manly friendship constitute what Shaftesbury calls "the liberty of *the club*"—the freedom that operates "amongst gentlemen and friends who know one another perfectly well" and who gather for conversation "in select companies" (53). If the third earl's writings underscore the difference between faction and the loyal opposition, they nonetheless conform to late seventeenth-century sensibility, which was predicated on the social equality of elite men.

Although he understands the motives of those who join cabals, Shaftesbury also defends those who take stands against them on the basis of their own principled individuality. An internalized standard of honor differentiates the gentleman from "the mere vulgar of mankind." This standard is nowhere more evident than in the behavior of "the voluntary discoverers of villainy and hearty prosecutors of their country's interest": "I know nothing greater or nobler than the undertaking and managing some important accusation, by which some high criminal of State, or some formed body of conspirators against the public, may be arraigned and brought to punishment through the honest zeal and public affection of a private man" (84). Is this a veiled tribute to the first earl of Shaftesbury, who—though hardly a "private man"—did heartily manage important accusations while prosecuting the Popish Plot? "The club" fosters the potential for civic heroism, it appears, and conspires on behalf of—instead of against—the public.

Lawrence Klein has argued that the third earl was "a political writer" whose "moralism, . . . deism, and . . . aesthetic interests were all harnessed to a political project." That project was "far from being an exercise in Whig radicalism," Klein asserts. Rather, it was "nothing less than the legitimation of the post-1688 Whig regime," which had "ushered in an era of gentlemanly culture." It is one of the signal contributions of Klein's study that he traces the emergence of eighteenth-century Whig politeness back through the third earl's own less polite politics of the 1690s, when he was allied with opposition Whigs of his grandfather's ilk who were decisively to the left of William's Court Whigs.[8] Unlike Klein, however, I regard *Characteristics* as continuous with, not antithetical to, the key affective configurations of the 1680s and 1690s. Since for the third earl politeness was inseparable from affection, and since affection was intrinsic to his understanding of the whole system of conspiratorial and anticonspiratorial politics, it is possible to construct a substantially different genealogy for the third earl's cultural claims than that proposed by Klein.[9]

It is clear enough that the third earl configured polite masculinity in a way that included his family's oppositional past. The first earl is literally grandfathered by the third into the genteel, legitimated Whig ethos emerging at the end of the reign of Queen Anne. This was no mean feat. "After 1688," writes J. R. Jones in his clearheaded history of the Exclusion Crisis, "those who called themselves Whigs explicitly repudiated [the first earl of] Shaftesbury's example. To them, in retrospect, he appeared to have been a dangerous incendiary," as well as a ruthless opportunist, as he indubitably was. Postrevolution Whigs honored Russell and Sidney, executed for treason in 1683 in the aftermath of the Exclusion Crisis, as martyrs put to death by a tyrant, but they would not acknowledge Shaftesbury as their political ancestor. However, Jones observes, "[l]ater generations disowned Shaftesbury, but they did not repudiate the principles on which the case for Exclusion, as well as the Revolution, rested."[10] In crafting his justification of the first earl's conspiracies, the third earl of Shaftesbury recaptures the key elements of the antityrannical republican pathos surrounding the executions of Russell and Sidney, a mode of masculine sensibility that had been expressed earlier in the political dramas of the Exclusion Crisis.

But what of the first earl himself? How can it be said that he had anything to do with masculine sensibility, such that affection among men becomes central to his family's political genealogy? I certainly shall not claim that the first earl of Shaftesbury ever represented himself as a sensitive man or was represented by others as being so. The first earl's political motives, language, and practices occasionally exhibit a commitment to moving others to passion but never set forth the claim that he himself was emotionally motivated. The first earl was unsentimental enough about his own class to be willing to make pragmatic cross-class alliances, effected by the discourse of adamant protestant nationalism:

> He alone maintained contact with and control over all sections of
> the party. . . . [H]e represented more clearly and fully than any
> other leader, then or later, the cardinal Whig principle that gov-
> ernmental power should be vested in those who possessed the

> greatest weight in society. His extensive Dorset estates, wide com-
> mercial interests (which included mining, money-lending, ship-
> ping, and colonial proprietorship), his legal connexions, and his
> intellectual interests . . . all gave him . . . influential contacts with
> every section of the upper classes. His avowed sympathies with
> the dissenters gave him additional influence, and he deliberately
> set out to approach the radical as well as the mercantile interests
> in the City.[11]

How, then, are we justified in linking the figure of the first earl to something called late seventeenth-century sensibility?

The first earl set in motion the coalescence of the eclectic "first Whigs"
into a political culture that found republican narratives useful in new
ways. He did so without being identified (or identifying himself) with the
figure of the Roman republican. The first earl is remarkably dissociated
from the emotion-expressing or emotion-inducing positions of the Com-
monwealth tradition. But antityrannical positions proved inseparable
from the crises of personal loyalty inherent in conspiratorial theatrics. In
the course of the Exclusion Crisis of 1679–81, consequently, the unsentimental earl brought issues of authority, deference, influence, and representation to a point of sufficient emergency that a contest for certain
forms of sensibility became a key feature of the literary culture of these
years. Strategies of masculine affection and postmonarchical institutions
evolved together. The link between sentiment and resistance was efficacious regardless of the personalities of specific political players.

A look at the relationship between fathers and sons, law and feeling,
in the cultural productions of the Exclusion Crisis shows that the emotional son is a recurring feature of Whig narratives of the rise and fall of
the Roman republic. One might think that the stoic leader would be the
most persistent character in these narratives, as it is later, once Addison's
Cato enters the spotlight. In the 1680s, however, the sacrificial figure of
the sensitive young man is what *Lucius Junius Brutus, Absalom and Achitophel,*
and *Venice Preserved* have in common. These works are preoccupied with
the national competition for the proper relation of principle to sympathy,
or of law to victimhood. Both Whig and Tory plays construct pathos-rich
cross-generational relationships that favor the sacrifice of the volatile son.

The Plot of Sensibility

*D*ramas set in the Roman republic or its modern correlatives, the republics of Venice and Florence, were universally understood to refer to

Whig opinions during the Exclusion Crisis.[12] Staged in December 1680, Lee's *Lucius Junius Brutus* was suppressed for its republican content by order of the Lord Chamberlain after at most six performances.[13] Lee's play was censored on 11 December 1680. The Exclusion Bill had been passed in the House of Commons on 11 November but defeated in the House of Lords four days later. In the first week of December, Lord Stafford, a Catholic peer, was sentenced to death in the Popish Plot. On 23 December, the first earl of Shaftesbury gave the address that was published on 31 December as *A Speech Lately Made by a Noble Peer of the Realm*. His survey of current conditions led him to conclude *"that we cannot trust the King."*[14] Throughout the fall of 1680, the Irish Plot was taking shape as a fully formed sequel to the Popish Plot, supported by the testimony of Shaftesbury's witnesses to a planned massacre of Irish Protestants. On 20 January, Charles II dissolved Parliament.[15]

The Junius Brutus plays that persisted from Lee's version through those by Gildon (1703), Bond (1733), and Duncombe (1734) center on the Roman father who seizes power as a just tyrannicide, becomes the object of patricidal plots, and extorts his favorite son's virtually suicidal death in the name of the restored republic. Negotiations with affectionate authority are fundamental to these plays, and that is why they are important to the development of the Whig sensibility articulated as argument in Shaftesbury's *Characteristics*.

Lee's *Lucius Junius Brutus* is dominated by three elements: confrontations between republicans and tyrants, displays of male homosocial affection, and sacrificial acts—namely the sacrifice of sons and daughters by fathers. The intimate relationship between antityrannical resistance and weepy masculine sensibility recurs in later expressions of republican affect with such regularity that this play comes to seem representative in kind if not in degree. Pathetic scenes in republican Rome are charged with the task of managing the tonalities appropriate to parliamentary masculinity. Our ongoing habit of associating liberal ethics with an emotional susceptibility to victimization and guilt attains its earliest Anglo-American articulation in late seventeenth-century settings like Lee's.[16]

I have referred to *Lucius Junius Brutus* as "Whiggish" in order to avoid calling Lee a Whig, which he certainly was not. In the context of the Popish Plot and the Exclusion Crisis, Lee moved briefly within classical republican discourses in order to explore the exigencies of parliamentary manliness. This is just one phase of an obsession with masculine disintegration that runs throughout Lee's career. And indeed, I do not want to imply that Whig conventions are the only arena for affective display. Pathos and sentiment wander freely through late seventeenth-century plays, crossing and recrossing party boundaries as they go, and complicating every political position with which they are associated.

As though it were a structural requirement, the drama of principled republican opposition produces the tears of the lovable male victim. The link between political action and the feelings such action produces, a link that involves separating these two functions by assigning them to different agents, forms the most significant of the binary structures generated within the play. Brutus's politics of system and Titus's politics of anguish suggest that law in one position produces sensibility in another, and vice versa. The Whig desire for political legitimacy is configured as a split between the idea of law and the sensations of sacrifice. If republican ideology comprises this entire complex of positions, then republicanism is tantamount to a politics that defines itself apologetically in the very process of performing its self-legitimizing gestures. This is precisely the paradox that Dryden will satirize in Absalom's speech to the English people in *Absalom and Achitophel* and that Otway will refuse to celebrate in *Venice Preserved*.

In Lee's version of the story, the son of the emperor, Tarquin, has just raped Lucrece. Her death precipitates Brutus's coup in the name of the senate. The younger Tarquin and his gang of monarchist rakes and libertines—including Brutus's nasty son, Tiberius—have preyed on the wives of senators and the Roman bourgeoisie (that fine anachronism). Brutus links marital fidelity to upward economic mobility, arguing that tyranny has taken the form of sexual predation and economic assault on the middle class.[17]

The rape of Lucrece—though not her mode of death—is refigured in attempted assaults on women in later republican plays, such as the near-rapes of Belvidera in *Venice Preserved* and Marcia in *Cato*. As Stephanie Jed rightly insists, the rape of Lucretia/Lucrece was "a paradigmatic component of all narratives of liberation" in the tradition of "republican freedom." Jed shows how Lucretia's body serves masculine political choice and becomes, culturally, "part of the rhetorical defense against tyranny": "Lucretia intends to set an example of how her male survivors should rebuild the broken, corrupted wall for the future and defend, once again, the barrier between the public and private domains." In Lee's play however, and others like it, we are left having to address the fact that Lucrece's effort to return to a chaste, private condition fails despite the victory of the republican cause. The mixture of civic and sexual passions replicates itself in Brutus's son, Titus, who represents the most high-minded type of the next generation of Roman men. Titus sacrifices himself in turn, suggesting that, while republican suicide may be linked to the desire for chaste thinking that is embodied in the virtuous woman, stoic rigor eager to impose clear boundaries between chastity and corruption is prone to sentimental subversion. While the disciplinary impulse is important in such dramas as *Lucius Junus Brutus,* Lucrece's suicide *clarifies* nothing. It drives men into a rage for just order that culminates in another ethically admirable sacrifice. What we remember is the recurring cost of republican law, not reinstated distinctions between public and private life.[18]

Brutus no sooner wins than he becomes the object of a counterplot, in which Tiberius enthusiastically participates. While Tiberius is plotting, Titus, his virtuous brother, secretly marries Tarquin's illegitimate daughter, Teraminta. Like most secret marriages in seventeenth-century plays, this one creates yet another layer of conspiracy. And like all conspiracies, such marriages foster both love and paranoia. Lee lavishes attention on the characterization of Titus as the hero of sensibility. Titus is all "sweetness," prone to weeping ("What, man? What, all in tears?" says Brutus) (2.279, 323). He possesses a "humble," "soft and melting temper" and a heart "brimful of tenderness" (4.428, 431, 421).

Titus's bodily condition—like that of Lucrece and Teraminta—comes in for luxuriant description. The metaphoric and performed display of bodily fluids—tears, blood, milk, and, in its conspicuous absence, semen—is the language of pathos for Lee, the incontinent theatricality of sensibility itself. The metaphors through which Titus and Teraminta refer to each other's bodies illustrate how hard it is to figure out where to place either of them, but particularly Titus, on some spectrum of masculine and feminine genders. Titus refers to his own maternal aspects in morbidly eroticized images of the breast, setting up a connection between sentiment and the male who is both motherly and infantile.[19] These figurations signify Titus's virtue and mark his temperamental difference from his father.

Titus and Teraminta take turns being the motherless baby and the bereaved mother, playing out a mother-son eroticism starkly opposed to the contest with paternal law: "O, Teraminta, once more to my heart," moans Titus, as he bids her farewell (2.518):

> Thus the soft mother, though her babe is dead,
> Will have the darling on her bosom laid,

> Will talk, and rave, and with the nurses strive,
> And fond it still, as if it were alive;
> Knows it must go, yet struggles with the crowd,
> And shrieks to see 'em wrap it in the shroud. (2.520–25)

These lines look ahead to the play's final scenes of Titus's trial before his father, in which Teraminta does "[struggle] with the crowd, / And shrieks" in protest of Brutus's incapacity for paternal fondness. But if, in those climactic moments, she construes Titus as the infantile corpse, herself as mother, and Brutus as part of the social crowd, her language also sustains the metaphor of Titus's maternity. Teraminta vows

> To murmur, sob, and lean my aching head
> Upon thy breast, thus like a cradle babe
> To suck thy wounds and bubble out my soul. (5.1.85–87)

The plural "breasts" reinforce Titus's "milky" qualities: "Come to my breasts, thou tempest-beaten flower" (3.3.171). His "breasts" offer a refuge for Teraminta, but then he shifts to fantasies of the sexual initiative that he desires but is never able to perform: "I'll smell thee till I languish, / Rifle thy sweets, and run thee o'er and o'er, / Fall like the night upon thy folding beauties" (3.3.174–76). Titus is certainly feminized, then, but his feminine qualities are so clearly reactions to encounters with paternal rigor that they have to be understood as deriving their meaning from male homosocial relations.[20] The sensitive male who alternates between the roles of mother, infant, and lover—the man who changes his mind—is a character generated by the anxieties of masculine political possibilities, or, as the case may be, impossibilities.

Jessica Munns believes that female characters are crucial to exposing the logic of masculine power She argues with reference to *Venice Preserved*, for example, that these women "speak from a different position, one which is rooted in the body and its pleasures, as in Belvidera's orgasmic speeches on love (5.249) (1.346)."[21] Munns invokes Cixous's model of "the female economy of the gift versus the male economy of thrift" and Irigaray's analysis of female pleasure in order to read the "common cultural inscriptions of woman" in late seventeenth-century drama.[22]

Although I find Munns's description of the critical force of female sexuality compelling, I confess to having doubts about the extent to which characters like Teraminta and Belvidera can be separated from the masculine project of republican drama. These figures seem to me to serve sensitive masculinity, rather than critique it. Teraminta and Belvidera, and their theatrical sisters, surround the sensitive young man with arias sung by moving women's voices. When joined with the speeches of one or more sympathetic men, their language helps to create a passional duration that pressures the fatherly law to yield to it. The father often stands alone, but the representative of male sensibility seems necessarily multivocal, choral, or codependent. So my view even of the magnificent women's roles in Lee's and Otway's plays is less sanguine, with respect to their feminist potential, than that of Munns.[23]

Enraged at Titus's marriage, Brutus reveals his "awful, godlike, and commanding" self, but in startlingly intimate ways (1.245). Brutus declares his authority over Titus through an embrace of enforced mimesis, precisely the kind of hug likely (for Freudians) to produce an ambivalent response:

> I like thy frame, the fingers of the gods
> I see have left their mastery upon thee,
> They have been tapering up thy Roman form,
> And the majestic prints at large appear.
> Yet something they have left for me to finish
> Which thus I press thee to, thus in my arms
> I fashion thee, I mold thee to my heart. (2.300–306)

In this version of parenting, maternity and nursing are bypassed in favor of the hands-on design of the gods and the imprint of the father. When the father's "heart" meets the son's "breasts," tears come to Titus's eyes, provoking a paternal reprimand: "Shake from thy lids that dew that hangs upon 'em, / And answer to th' austerity of my virtue" (2.308–9). The purpose of this "fashioning" is then revealed as Brutus makes Titus promise not to consummate his marriage, something he had looked forward to doing that very night.

Later, Tarquin's party, by threatening Teraminta with death, coerces Titus to join the conspiracy against Brutus. Titus spends the night with Teraminta, after all, but feels so guilty that he is seized with impotence that forces both affective and sexual withdrawal. We have Teraminta's word for this:

> Though in my arms, just in the grasps of pleasure,
> His noble heart, struck with the thoughts of Brutus,
> Of what he promised you, till then forgot,
> Leaped in his breast and dashed him from enjoyment. (4.355–58)

Titus tries too late to withdraw his signature from the list of conspirators. The conspiracy is discovered, and Brutus finds both sons implicated. With Titus's consent, the tone of which wavers between rapturous conviction and unhappy regret, Brutus finally sacrifices love to law and sentences his favorite son to death, along with the other conspirators. Everyone (critics included) is left wondering whether Brutus's rigor arises from monomania or integrity or from some combination of the two.

At the end of the play, lest Titus be too single-mindedly committed to the noble idea of his own sacrifice, Brutus gives him one last thing to be conflicted about. Brutus has sentenced Titus to die in the most humiliating possible way, not by the sword, but by the lictors' whipping and the "common hangman's" ax. The final scenes orchestrate the verbal and arterial outpourings of Titus and Teraminta. Counterpointing these arias of sensibility, Brutus experiences one last dubious fit of fatherly emotion. This moment is described by Brutus in an oddly qualified way—"I own thy suff'rings ought t'unman me thus"—and then he acts out what this obligation to be unmanned would entail: "To make me throw my body on the ground, / To bellow like a beast, to gnaw the earth, / To tear my hair, to curse the cruel fates / That force a father thus to drag his bowels" (4.556–60). Titus tells him to get up and consents to be whipped, as Brutus quickly recovers a mood of ecstatic rigor in the name of Rome.

In the last act, as in the first, the broken body of a violated woman is the somatic sign of republican rigor. The suicide of Lucrece catalyzed the republican victory over Tarquin at the beginning of the play. At the end, Teraminta enters disheveled and wounded after being tormented (in effect, raped) by "the mob," to which she is twice vulnerable, as a member of the tyrant's family and as an illegitimate member of that family. She displays her victimized condition on behalf of Titus, pleading for his life and testifying to his innocence. Then she protests his death sentence in tones more enraged and assured than any granted to Titus himself, as she joins in a delegation of other women trying to change Brutus's mind. That Brutus can withstand this moral claim for mercy after being moved by the moral necessity for justice after the violation of Lucrece is a measure of the virtue of the republic and its difference from tyranny. And the reason why the voices of the women are strong is that Titus is ambivalent and changeable. The point is less female strength, alas (would that it were so) than male weakness. Lucrece, Teraminta, and Titus are linked by their status as voluntary or suicidal sacrifices, and, as sacrifices, all three utter and provoke pathetic speech. But only Titus is ambivalent, and his ambivalence marks him as the center of interest, central *because* indecisive.

Why is the son defined as the locus of sensibility, the sentimentalist, the sufferer? The violence brought about within his own family by the liberator, Brutus, suggests that the ideology of liberty marks itself as guilty from a very early period. And in doing so, it appropriates for victimization a growing prestige or ethical clout. Plays in the Junian line generate sensibility as though engaging in an act of mourning over principle itself. According to the play's emotional economy, sensibility is the price paid by the republican family for its own appetite for impersonality. The ambivalence of the good son, therefore, articulates the tension between the system-serving and system-exposing capacities of sentiment based on the costly virtue of republican theory. Insofar as the son consents to suffer, the language of sensibility rationalizes rigor in the name of law and subjects patriarchy itself to constitutional principle. Insofar as the son protests or mourns the violence of extravagant impersonality, sentiment has self-critical efficacy, which redoubles the moral power of exclusionist positions. In permitting Titus to be executed, Lee makes sensibility fundamental both to legitimizing and to criticizing postmonarchical forms of power.[24]

Absalom's Complaint

*I*t is not surprising that Lee's play turns on plots of conspiracy and anticonspiracy. What is surprising is the extent to which it is preoccupied with the overwrought emotional state of its male protagonists. For the Tory position laid claim to manly sensibility, too. Dryden's *Absalom and Achitophel* satirizes the republican rhetoric of liberty, rights, and antityrannical exasperation in Absalom's speech to the people of England, an address that concludes with Absalom, King David's rebellious son, in tears. The link between sensibility and republican tenderness establishes a clear, though hostile, parallel to Lee's *Lucius Junius Brutus.* Dryden's poem similarly focuses on the son's entrapment by unscrupulous and cynical enemies of the legitimate rule of his father and on the drama of the son's divided loyalties.

In republican discourse, sensibility and stoicism line up on the same side, bound by the voluntary sacrifice of one to the other. Dryden's Tory irony, while it captures the essentials of this generational narrative, has a different purpose: it stresses David's paternal preference for leniency and his reluctant move toward discipline. In his role as poet laureate, Dryden shifts the accusation of tyranny away from the monarch by emphasizing the king's tenderness. In *Brutus,* the republican father risks lapsing into the partial policies of tyrants, so his legitimacy has to be proved by tough love. From the perspective of either side, however, crises of political legitimacy lead to a conspiratorial atmosphere in which masculine emotion—whether vented or contained—matters greatly to the outcome.

The biblical narrative of Absalom's revolt was grist for the mill of Restoration pulpit rhetoric long before the Exclusion Crisis, as Phillip Harth has recently shown. Restoration divines drew on Absalom and Achitophel, along with other Old Testament "rebels, seditionists, and usurpers," in annual anniversary sermons. These were delivered on 29 May, in thanksgiving for the restoration of Charles II and on 30 January, in national mourning for the execution of Charles I: "As long as the anniversary preachers continued to accommodate the Absalom story to the restoration of Charles I, David would completely overshadow Absalom and Achitophel as the protagonist of a drama in which the pivotal event was his triumphant return from exile, not the rebellion that preceded it." And David was characterized as affectionate, whether associated with Charles I whose "fatal mercy" was thought to have given his enemies the upper hand, or with Charles II whose "mildness" and "forgiving mind" Dryden had praised in *Astrea Redux*.[25]

Dryden's Absalom/Monmouth and David/Charles II are both defined by their ability to weep. The manipulative quality of Absalom's tearful delivery of his republican complaint is contrasted, near the end of the poem, to David's competing call for a different kind of tears. David confesses his "native mercy" and "tenderness of blood," pointing to the tension inherent in his double role: "So much the father did the king assuage." Oscillating between threat and regret, the King asks (in four lines added in 1682),

> But O that yet he would repent and live!
> How easy 'tis for parents to forgive!
> With how few tears a pardon might be won
> From nature, pleading for a darling son!

Unlike the republican father, the monarch dreams of yielding. "Poor pitied youth," the King sighs, consistent in assigning Absalom to the role of victim, but making victimization signify his son's defeat.[26]

Dryden satirizes the Whig plot according to which the restorer of the lawful republic is forced to sacrifice his own son in order to prove the impersonal justice of the state. After the modest reasonableness of a profoundly constitutional claim—"A king's at least a part of government"—David draws "the sword of justice" and dispenses with sensibility in favor of "necessary law": "Law they require, let Law then show her face" (977, 1002, 1003, 1006). As in Lee's *Lucius Junius Brutus*, the tension between stoicism and sensibility is played out in the relationship between father and son. Charles II as King David is far less stoic than Brutus. But in fact,

Charles II balanced fatherly indulgence with political hard-headedness. Early in 1680, he offered to forgive Monmouth's political transgressions on the condition that the duke either return to exile or supply the Crown with "information upon his compromising friends." Monmouth rejected both options, thereby moving toward open rebellion.

Absalom is preeminently lovable in *Absalom and Achitophel:* "none / So beautiful, so brave, as Absalom" (17–18). Absalom's "manly beauty" (22) both signifies his passionate temperament and justifies David's capacity for fatherly affection, as well as for the "exaggerated seminal potency" elsewhere assigned by Dryden to Charles II: [27]

> What faults he had (for who from faults is free?)
> His father could not, or he would not see.
> Some warm excesses which the law forbore,
> Were construed youth that purged by boiling o'er. (35–38)

Once Absalom is in the grip of Achitophel's—that is, Shaftesbury's—manipulations, the dynamics of sympathetic identification are subject to cynical political maneuver. Absalom bows "popularly low" to the people, and thus "glides unfelt into their secret hearts." He communicates sympathy for the crowd in order to elicit sympathy from it. He advances "with a kind compassionating look, / And sighs, bespeaking pity ere he spoke, / Few words he said; but easy those and fit, / More slow than Hybla-drops, and far more sweet" (689, 693–97). Absalom's speech is couched in the rhetoric of mourning over England's loss and his father's cruelty, self-pity for his own banishment, and sympathy, his gift to the nation.

A brilliant parody of republican rhetoric, the speech even features the climactic pathos of masculine tears. The sensitive son, who suffers on everyone's behalf—his own, his father's, and the country's—delivers the republican critique:

> I mourn, my countrymen, your lost estate,
> Though far unable to prevent your fate:
> Behold a banished man, for your dear cause
> Exposed a prey to arbitrary laws!
> Yet O! that I alone could be undone,
> Cut off from empire, and no more a son!
> Now all your liberties a spoil are made;
> Egypt and Tyrus intercept your trade,
> And Jebusites your sacred rites invade. (698–706)

Absalom's protest against "arbitrary laws," his defense of England's "liberties," and his expressed loathing of foreign influence sound the republican strains of Whig opposition. In his next breath, he turns on David "with reverence" in the standard Whig effort to dissociate the monarch, however faulty, from the principle objects of revenge: ministers, courtiers, and mistresses:

> My father, whom with reverence yet I name,
> Charmed into ease, is careless of his fame;
> And, bribed with petty sums of foreign gold,
> Is grown in Bathsheba's embraces old;
> Exalts his enemies, his friends destroys;
> And all his power against himself employs.
> He gives, and let him give, my right away;
> But why should he his own and yours betray?
> He, only he, can make the nation bleed,
> And he alone from my revenge is freed. (707–16)

The speech culminates in the proof of tears shed in the service of the political bonds forged through self-dramatizing victimization. And the great advantage of those tears is their legality. Tears are the king's son's constitutional weapon, says Absalom. Tears are the devices of Whig subversion, says Dryden, conspiracy's sentimental, false disguise. For the Tory poet, law sides with the monarch, who resists the siege of sensibility but pays a price—an *emotional* price, because the king is not a stoic—for doing so. Here is Monmouth's pathos, according to Dryden:

> ['] Take then my tears,' (with that he wiped his eyes),
> ' 'Tis all the aid my present power supplies:
> No court-informer can these arms accuse;
> These arms may sons against their fathers use,
> And 'tis my wish, the next successor's reign
> May make no other Israelite complain.' (717–22)

Absalom's tears are timed to communicate his lack of "present power," despite the backing of Achitophel and the sympathy of the populace. His weeping means something quite different from Titus's republican self-sacrifice. Titus finds agency in principled acquiescence to Brutus and the republic. Absalom delivers a *complaint*.

The complaint, Lauren Berlant proposes, involves "public testimony and witnessing." The embarrassments of complaint arise from the fact that the speaker has assumed that individual feeling is shared and therefore politically efficacious, only to end by lamenting the political limits of personal expression.[28] Absalom is reduced to abjection through the genre of complaint, the vehicle for self-limited opposition. But historically, Dryden's satire comes too late. The figures of sensibility and parliamentary resistance—Absalom and Achitophel, Monmouth and the first earl of Shaftesbury—have already combined in a productive cultural formation: the collaborative encoding of opposition and apology. The complaint is the genre of the political future. In the short run, Monmouth and Shaftesbury, in their different ways, lost to Charles II's successful representation of the Whigs as dangerous advocates of instability.[29] But thirty years later, with the third earl's *Characteristics* and Addison's *Cato,* such laments as Dryden parodies became canonical.

"I Never Loved These Huggers"

Absalom and Achitophel was published in November 1681. A week later, the first earl of Shaftesbury was released from Crown custody when a London jury returned a vote of "ignoramus" to the bill presented against him, blocking further prosecution. In an earlier stage of judicial proceedings, the Crown had revealed a document, purportedly found among Shaftesbury's papers, calling on Whigs to form an "Association" of "all true Protestants" in Parliament, "an Union amongst themselves . . . of mutual Defence and Assistance."[30] Otway's *Venice Preserved* premiered on 9 February 1682. The play thus coincided with the Abhorrence Movement, a carefully orchestrated Tory campaign of support for the king in "*Addresses* daily presented from several parts of *England,* in abhorrence of the late Damnable *Association* found in the Earl of *Shaftsbury's* Closet." The Abhorrence Movement was modeled on the Loyal Address Movement, which was itself a reply to the Whig campaign collected as *Vox Patriae* in April 1681.[31]

The November 1681 inquest was the last Whig victory of the Exclusion Crisis and the plots surrounding it, a "defensive" triumph followed by a progressive weakening of the cause.[32] Shaftesbury's narrow escape in November was fervently celebrated, and the inquest "proved to be the end of the Protestant Plot" provoked by the Irishman Edward Fitzharris. Fitzharris had been arrested for libeling the king and under pressure had turned against the Whigs. Fitzharris's testimony, published shortly before his execution on 1 July 1681, "first revealed to a startled public the treasonable conspiracy in which not only [Lord] Howard but the rest of the Whig leadership, including Shaftesbury would . . . be implicated."[33] The tide soon turned in favor of Charles as the Crown systematically created the conditions for Tory domination of the London courts and electoral apparatus. Parliament would not meet again until 1685, and the Whigs depended on parliamentary process for both legitimacy and agency.[34] The combination of no Parliament, Whig judicial disempowerment in the city, and an effective Tory propaganda machine sent Shaftesbury first into hiding, in September 1682, and then into exile in Holland, where he died in January 1683. Shaftesbury thus escaped the final Whig debacle, the revelation of the Rye House Plot in the summer of 1683, a Whig conspiracy to ambush the king and the duke of York as they returned from the Newmarket races.

Dryden's satire in *Absalom and Achitophel* had seen—or seen through—the Whigs' uses of sensibility, but the poem's impact did not lessen the cultural effectiveness of a young man's weepy ambivalence. Like Dryden, Otway was of a royalist temper.[35] Still, his drama of self-devouring conspiracies holds fast to the appeal of passionate masculine affection, even when affection is divorced from political integrity. Otway dissolves the typical roles of father, friend, and sensitive son so that mind-changing becomes the principal attribute of several characters, not just of the spectacularly embarrassed and dependent protagonist, Jaffeir. The play's contests between (and among) heterosexual and male homosocial loyalties foreground the dramatic interest of ambivalence itself as a political issue. But the rapid changes of loyalty that plotting induces in the Venetian republic—as in contemporary England—do not preclude manly embraces, however mortal.

Venice Preserved is notable for its double assault on Shaftesbury through two characters: Renault, who uses his conspiratorial privilege for an attempted rape of Jaffeir's wife, and Antonio, Otway's satire of sexual abjection in the notorious "Nicky Nacky" scenes. The impact of Renault's sexual treachery is greater than that of Antonio's debasement. Since the pragmatic efficiency of Renault is closer to Shaftesbury's real political persona, Renault's sexual opportunism combines with political opportunism to dramatize the self-cannibalizing nature of conspiracies. He is the one major character who never changes his mind and whose consistency is entirely unidealistic. Renault, whose sexual transgression sabotages the unity of the conspirators, is the one person who knows ahead of time that Jaffeir will betray the group. He is immune to emotional bonds. "I never loved these huggers," he remarks about Jaffeir's fraternal welcome into the conspiracy.[36] At the same time, Renault presides over a conspiratorial masculine subculture that is laden with affect. It is conventional to say that there are no virtuous positions left in *Venice Preserved*, once Otway has

de-idealized both Whig constitutional claims *and* state authority. But masculine tenderheartedness remains at the core of the story, in order to
recuperate some ground for masculine sincerity—if only as an object
of desire.

The relationship between Jaffeir and the soldierly Pierre is the crux of
manly affection in the play. Their friendship exhibits the standard republican preoccupation with the interdependence of sensibility and stoicism
that is played out between fathers and sons (or son-surrogates) in Lee's
Lucius Junius Brutus and Addison's *Cato*. Their on-again, off-again devotion
involves familiar discourses of ethical suicide and self-sacrifice from the
Roman plays, with Venice a well-understood variant on the Roman republic.[37] Because Pierre does not occupy the position of Brutus in Lee's
play or any number of other paternal stoics distributed throughout late
seventeenth-century tragedy, it is harder to discern the extent to which
he embodies republican principle. Nonetheless, the mutually generating
positions of stoicism and sensibility persist. The fact that they do reinforces the case I am trying to make for the cultural connection between
Whig emotionalism of the paranoid 1680s and its more familiar, later
forms.

Jaffeir hears the news of his personal downfall from Pierre, and when
he does, his tears provoke Pierre's indignant call to arms. With the connivance of his father-in-law, Jaffeir's property has been seized, dragged
into public view, put up for sale, and his family evicted from their residence. Jaffeir weeps, marking him as the sensitive and dependent member of the pair:

> I own myself a coward. Bear my weakness,
> If throwing thus my arms about thy neck,
> I play the boy, and blubber in thy bosom.
> Oh! I shall drown thee with my sorrows! (1.274–77)

Pierre directs Jaffeir to rage, not mourn, and to blame Venice, not
himself: "Burn! / First burn, and level Venice to thy ruin!" (1.277–78).
He is the representative soldier. A fellow conspirator greets the "dreadful" Pierre as "Mars!" (2.3.48–49). But the conversion of Jaffeir's failure
into his support for political conspiracy takes place only after Pierre has
told Jaffeir the story of his own erotic frustrations and their troubling
impact on his professional standing as a military man. Finding that the
"wretched old but itching Senator," Antonio, has been entertained by
his mistress, Aquilina, Pierre recounts how he "drove / The rank old
bearded hirco stinking home" (1.186, 192–93). Summoned to appear

before the Senate, Pierre had been "censured basely, / For violating something they call *privilege*." "This was the recompense of my service!" he protests, a betrayal that exempts him from future loyalty: "from that hour I think myself as free / To be the foe as ere the friend of Venice" (1.195–97, 202–3). Jaffeir and Pierre join in a duet that absorbs personal misfortune into republican critique, with its keywords of tyranny, slavery, justice, and the common weal: "In such a wretched state as this of Venice, / . . . all agree to spoil the public good," Jaffeir complains. Pierre concurs:

> Justice is lame as well as blind amongst us;
> The laws . . .
> Serve but for instruments of some new tyranny
> That every day starts up to enslave us deeper. (1.207–8, 212–15)

Pierre offers "blood or fortune" in assistance, but his real gift to Jaffeir is conspiracy itself (1.282). Belvidera will call on "Roman Lucrece" and "Cato's daughters" (3.2.8, 71) as her kindred spirits; Pierre invokes Brutus as his role model ("I mean that Brutus, who in open Senate / Stabbed the first Caesar that usurped the world") and others join in to reinforce this identification with the conspiracy of Roman assassins (2.3.52–53, 54–58). For Jaffeir to join the conspiracy requires Pierre's friendship, because he needs the soldier to vouch for him in order to be admitted into the plot. And conspiracy appears to him as an extension of friendship, a bond that both compensates for Jaffeir's expulsion to the economic and social margins of Venetian life and provides the opportunity for revenge on those who put him there. The word "friend" chimes throughout the seduction scene, when Pierre draws Jaffeir into the antisenatorial conspiracy. The relationship between the two expands to include the many friends of the incipient plot:

> *Jaffeir.*
>> A thousand daggers, all in honest hands;
>> And have not I a friend will stick one here?
> *Pierre.*
>> Yes, if I thought thou wert not to be cherished
>> To a nobler purpose, I'd be that friend.
>> But thou hast better friends, friends whom thy wrongs
>> Have made thy friends; friends, worthy to be called so.
>>   (2.2.63–68)

Just before introducing Jaffeir to the other conspirators, Pierre tells them, "I've brought my all into the public stock; / I had but one friend,

and him I'll share amongst you!" (2.3.113–14). The promise of a link
between the public good and the private friend is darkly echoed later by
Renault, when he pits conspiracy against brotherhood: "Though I had
one only brother, dear by all / The strictest ties of nature . . . / I'd . . .
hazard all my future peace, / And stab him to the heart before you"
(3.2.398–99, 405–6). The very spell of masculine intimacy cast by the
plotters, however, moves the new initiate to confess his ambivalence
about the political drive that propels conspiracy. Caught, in the subjunctive mood, between fraternal and marital affection, Jaffeir refers figura-
tively to "the rack" to which his ambivalence will ultimately doom Pierre:

> Oh Pierre, wert thou but she,
> How I could pull thee down into my heart,
> Gaze on thee till my eye-strings cracked with love,
> Till all my sinews with its fire extended,
> Fixed me upon the rack of ardent longing;
> Then swelling, sighing, raging to be blest,
> Come like a panting turtle to thy breast,
> On thy soft bosom, hovering, bill and play,
> Confess the cause why last I fled away;
> Own 'twas a fault, but swear to give it o'er,
> And never follow false ambition more. (2.3.228–38)

This, of course, is exactly what happens. Belvidera is nearly raped by
Renault. And this betrayal causes Jaffeir to obey her urgent demand that
he "Confess the cause" to the Venetian senators, even as he feels with
"Every step I move" as though he treads "upon some mangled limb / Of
a racked friend" (4.1.1–3). In act 1, Jaffeir wept on Pierre's "bosom."
Here Pierre's "breast" and Belvidera's "soft bosom" merge as though to
compensate through fusion for the conflict Jaffeir suffers between his loyalty to his wife and his loyalty to his friend. Like Titus in Lee's *Lucius Junius
Brutus*, Jaffeir's political instability is manifest in his taste for the roles of
lover, infant, and dependent friend. In their final scenes together, Pierre's
military stoicism first despises and then forgives Jaffeir's abject sensibility—for the price of his own execution and Jaffeir's suicide. This dynamic repeats the similar sequence in *Lucius Junius Brutus* of Titus's progress from abjection to honorable self-sacrifice under the stern judicial
gaze of his father. In the trial scene, Jaffeir, who characterizes himself as
kneeling before Pierre "With eyes o'erflowing and a bleeding heart"
(4.2.333), becomes a prototype of the "bleeding heart" liberal, a figure
that emerges historically from the union of republican rigor and republican affection.

Jaffeir abases himself before Pierre, speaking the language of "repentance," "supplications," and "submission" (4.2.177, 179, 202): "To thee I am the falsest, veriest slave / That e'er betrayed a generous trusting friend, / And gave up honor to be sure of ruin" (4.2.147–49). Jaffeir is berated by Pierre as a "whining Monk," as something subhuman, "nasty," and "loathsome" (4.2.180, 183, 193). Nonetheless Jaffeir urges Pierre to "take thy life on such conditions / The Council have proposed," provoking the incredulous reaction: "Life! Ask my life! Confess!" (4.2.212–13, 15). Jaffeir insists on humiliating himself in the name of friendship, refusing to leave Pierre even when cursed by him:

> Use me reproachfully, and like a slave,
> Tread on me, buffet me, heap wrongs on wrongs
> On my poor head; I'll bear it all with patience
> Shall weary out thy most unfriendly cruelty;
> Lie at thy feet and kiss 'em though they spurn me,
> Till, wounded by my sufferings, thou relent,
> And raise me to thy arms with dear forgiveness. (4.2.231–37)

Pierre points out that he has fallen for this pose once before, and lived to regret it. His "foolish heart took pity" on Jaffeir's "misfortunes" and "miseries," Pierre reminds him, and he "Relieved thy wants, and raised thee from thy state / Of wretchedness . . . / To rank thee in my list of noble friends" (4.2.248–52).

Yet paradoxically, when Jaffeir meets Pierre again before the scaffold and wheel in the execution scene, self-abasement does induce forgiveness and does permit a return to suicidal honor. Otway is relentless in his portrayal of Jaffeir's terminal embarrassment: "Crawling on my knees, / And prostrate on the earth, let me approach thee." But this time it has the desired effect. "Dear to my Arms," says Pierre, breaking down, "I cannot forget to love thee," and then, as the stage directions point out, "He weeps": "Curse on this weakness." Nothing is so moving as a stoic's tears, as Jaffeir's reaction duly registers: "Tears! Amazement! Tears! / I never saw thee melted thus before" (5.3.28–29, 35–36, 69–70). Jaffeir redeems himself by fulfilling Pierre's final wish, to kill Pierre with his sword, thus saving him from the disgrace of the rack. Then Jaffeir turns the sword on himself in a perfect dramatic realization of ambivalence.

In the play's closing moments, Belvidera goes mad and enters "distracted." The stage directions indicate that phantasms of Jaffeir and then of Jaffeir and Pierre together materialize before her: "Jaffeir's Ghost rises"; "Ghost sinks"; "The Ghosts of Jaffeir and Pierre rise together both bloody"; "Ghosts sink" (pp. 95–96). What are we to make of this gothic phantasmagoria at the last minute? Belvidera is in the grip of a hallucinatory desire for her husband, but her vision of him is followed by a second vision: "My husband bloody, and his friend too!" Seeing the ghosts sink, she tries to "dig, dig": "I have him! / I've got him." But her final cognition is of being dragged down to her own death by the two dead men together: "They have hold on me, and drag me to the bottom" (5.4.20, 23, 25–26, 28). This is a strange but not illogical ending for a drama that incorporates the norms of the Roman play on the model of Lee's *Brutus*. Conspiracy and constituted government are equally corrupt in the world of Otway's Venice, but conspiracy alone fosters affection between the stoic who sheds a few reluctant tears and the man of feeling who weeps copiously.

Venice Preserved can be read as one scene in the closing act of the Exclusion Crisis. But Otway's tragedy, despite its intimate connection to the events of 1679–81, had a future as well as a past. The third earl of Shaftesbury's *Characteristics* shows that this future finds no less complicated uses for masculine feeling. The persistent bond between stoicism and expressiveness in *Characteristics* dispenses with intergenerational narratives in favor of social and philosophical distinctions. This does not signify that intergenerational plots are obsolete. The formidable success of Addison's *Cato* and the persistent reputation of *Venice Preserved* attest to the ongoing interest of encounters between men marked by differences in seniority. But Shaftesbury's task in *Characteristics* is to craft an elite ethos defined relationally by skepticism or ridicule (aimed at the enthusiasms of other social orders), stoicism (performed for appreciative insiders), and affection (stoicism's earned supplement).

Shaftesbury defines sympathy as a consequence of contestation and idealizes the community of debaters. Intellectual resistance, the property of an educated and leisured class of men, is the basis for intimacy among its members. "To philosophize . . . is but to carry good-breeding a step higher," he writes (2.255). Stoicism and sympathy coalesce as the shared qualities of conversational peers, not as the contrasting values of older and younger men.

Skepticism becomes civic virtue in Shaftesbury's *A Letter Concerning Enthusiasm:* "'Tis only in a free nation" that men "give liberty to wit" (1.9, 15). "Ridicule," the most outspoken form of skepticism, counteracts the "melancholy" of enthusiasm (1.11, 12). Since "any affection" is "stronger . . . for being social and communicative," the excessive gravity of inflexible belief can escalate to "panic," defined as "passion . . . raised in a multitude and conveyed by . . . contact or sympathy" (1.13). Given the contagious energy of superstition, the equally social "freedom of raillery" is the only means to achieve harmony and temper (1.15). Stoicism signifies the philosophical temperament itself for Shaftesbury, another educated corrective to excessive belief. Just as wit is intrinsic to freedom, so temperament, or "temper of mind" is, too (2.44). Temperance, "this moral dame," is the mother or "political sister" of the more Amazonian "Lady Liberty" (2.44).

This celebration of temperance occurs in *The Moralists*, a Socratic drama of talking heads situated in the setting of an English country house weekend. At the heart of the quasi-pastoral *Moralists*, rhapsodies to nature and unabashed excesses of fancy are challenged, but nonetheless allowed, in the sequestered retreats of gentlemen. Theocles experiences a "fit" of rhapsody in the "the sacred groves," as Philocles ironically calls them (2.97–99). When Theocles "take[s] his leave of the sublime," he does so by proposing to depart from "these unsociable places whither our fancy has transported us"—to depart rhetorically, that is—and return to the "conversable woods and temperate climates" of everyday England (2.124). The mind that fends off fancy gains new and improved territories of self-possession (2.280). Shaftesbury posits a dialogic affection so temperate that the stoic ideal becomes compatible with sensibility without risking the excesses of either fancy or enthusiasm.

Characteristics argues so persistently against vehemence that, if read too selectively, it seems to argue against politics altogether. Shaftesbury does claim that clubbable skepticism, urbane public-spiritedness, "conversable" differences are free from the heated discourse of party. But at the same time, the assembled essays and treatises that make up *Characteristics* comprise a defense of the terms of the Whig code: liberty, stoicism, the civic good, freedom of speech, and self-possession. The third earl of Shaftesbury, in the end, celebrates political conflict when it can be restricted to the conversational domains where masculine affection flourishes. His writings mark both how far English politics have come from the era of conspiracy and faction, and how pertinent the emotional logic of the Exclusion Crisis could be, even for new generations of legitimate Whigs.

CHAPTER TWO

Cato's Tears

Black Surrogacy in British Plays

Addison's *Cato* (1713) and Thomson's *Sophonisba* (1730) make a spectacle of political cultures absorbed by the emotional dilemmas of empire. They dramatize, for British subjects, complicated Moors in an imaginary North Africa. Set within a politically divided, unstable Roman sphere situated in Mediterranean Africa, *Cato* and *Sophonisba* attest that strategic uses of postrepublican Rome fueled the development of important strands of British sensibility. Long an empire in that it conquered other peoples, this version of Rome was governed for the first time by an emperor at home, exhibiting the untidy connection between tyrants at home and outposts abroad. In the long eighteenth century in Great Britain, this connection is particularly generative of masculine anguish. The conflicts over political succession in which modern political agency develops imply an international arena—the total geography of diplomatic, military, and mercantile action. Race serves high culture as a way of signifying crises of identification and many degrees and kinds of power.

The specific eighteenth-century success of tender masculinity depends on a cast of political characters developed through conflicts over political succession. Succession is a drama enacted on an international stage. In *Cato* and *Sophonisba*, liberty, love, and suffering persistently combine in the figures of erotic aliens whose racial difference is also an emotional difference. As the early eighteenth-century politics of emotion takes shape, racial vocabularies are already habitual and telling.[1] At first glance, it appears that racial difference operates in these plays to distinguish Great Britain (as Rome) from uneasily subjugated cultures. In other words, it looks as though race is not yet internal to national identity, but functions to differentiate this nation from others. But the complexities of the dramas I examine in this chapter indicate that representations of race are also representations of sentiment. If racial discourse signifies traumas of personal identification and political loyalty, then race is already internalized, already subjective in British culture. Plots centered on the flash points of the Roman republic map out a zone of emotion that absorbs racial differences into subjectivity with astonishing facility. Roman North Africa becomes the terrain of the imaginary republican hero.

In this zone, North Africans behave as troubled sons and lovers experiencing crises of authority, and these crises induce British forms of sensibility. We can apply Toni Morrison's analysis of "black surrogacy" in American literature to the British situation. "[T]he thunderous, theatrical presence of black surrogacy," Morrison argues, a "real or fabricated Africanist presence," is "crucial to [white authors'] sense of Americanness."[2] If a British masculine political subjectivity is being fostered in the early eighteenth century through debates about the value of "Africa" and the figurative vocabularies that link color to cultural temperament, then Morrison's argument about "black surrogacy" applies to the earlier British case as well as to the later North American one.

"Africa" had several meanings in British plays as early as 1600, as recent studies of Renaissance drama have shown. Jean Howard's reading of Heywood's *The Fair Maid of the West, Part I* (1600–1604) probes the ambiguous status of North Africans in early modern English culture. Howard identifies the "rivalrous antipathy" between European nations in Heywood's play, then describes another kind of difference that prevails between the English and the Moors, a difference "seemingly more benign" because North Africans are not "overt enemies." Early travel writers and ethnographers, like their later counterparts, distinguished Muslim North Africa from sub-Saharan Africa on the basis of both culture and color. They also differentiated between "tawny Moors and black Moors" in North Africa itself.

The "vexed but well-established trade" transacted with North Africa in the sixteenth century had real cultural importance, then and later. The long-standing symbiotic relationship between trade and piracy in the North African Mediterranean created opponents comprising an array of mobile attackers sanctioned by the Barbary states, which impounded or detained English ships in port and gave rise to the well-understood trade in ransoming captives.[3] Taken together, these conditions gave "Africa" a particularly fluid cultural meaning in British plays. When North Africa is configured as the antithesis to or opposite of Rome, or Venice, or Britain, it becomes "Africa"—Europe's other—and Moors speak as, and for, "Africans." In other dramatic contexts, when North African characters refer to sub-Saharan Africans, it is important to discern the degrees of attributed savagery that become progressively greater as the interior of the continent is approached. The Moor, representative of sophisticated Mediterranean rim cultures, thus takes on some of the erotic possibilities of the mulatto in U.S. antebellum novels and is easily assimilated to sentimental or romance plots.

In *Cato* and *Sophonisba*, we find North African characters who catalyze debates about the problem of being "Roman," as well as about the problems of being "African" and male or, in one case, female. In these plays, set at the margins of a much-contested Roman empire, representatives of North African positions show the dominant culture to be prone to self-orientalizing tendencies. The staging of Roman and African styles of masculinity conveys Whig writers' preoccupation with other races as a way of representing the emotional dimension of politics in Britain. Masculine sensibility can be figured through race. The complex subjectivity of the man loyal to the idea of the republic is central to imperial narratives. The prominence of masculine feeling in these plays shows that the competition for political legitimacy, which is being carried out partially in and through dramatic performance, relies on the assertion of strategic ambivalence. Through racially specific discourses, British authors represent ambivalent sensations fundamental to the understanding of male subjectivity in public life.[4]

Orientalism was a family tradition for Addison. The playwright's father, Lancelot Addison, was chaplain to Lord Teviot at the British garrison at Tangier for eight years (1662–70). The port was acquired as part of the dowry brought by Catherine of Braganza when she married Charles II in 1662. Addison père published five books on the region, works that range from ethnographic observation to military chronicle: *A Brief Relation of the Present State of Tangier* (1664); *Account of West Barbary, or, A Short Narrative of the Revolutions of the Kingdoms of Fez and Morocco* (1671); *The Present State of the Jews; wherein is contained an Exact Account of Their Customs, Secular and Religious* (1675, 1676, 1682); *The First State of Mahumedism* (1678, 1679, 1687); and *The Moores Baffled; Being a Discourse Concerning Tangier* (1681, 1685, 1738).

There is no direct relationship between Lancelot Addison's publications on Tangier and the text of *Cato*. Addison substantially drafted the play, which was finished and staged in 1713, during his Italian tour and after the death of his father in 1703. Nonetheless, the British involvement in Tangier from the Restoration through the Exclusion Crisis suggests one reason why Moors, along with Romans, could become the vehicles of Whig republicanism in the early eighteenth century. The British possession and dispossession of the fort at Tangier is a minor episode in Restoration history, but one in which the relationship between national party politics and international relations is clear. Held by Spain between 1580 and 1643 before being repossessed by Portugal, Tangier came as the dowry of Charles II's Catholic queen and was associated, therefore, with the intricacies of diplomatic maneuver involving the Catholic powers, Spain and France.[5] For Charles II, Tangier was both expensive and convenient. The expansion and maintenance of the famous "Mole" (or pier) and the continual enlargement of the fort, combined with the staffing of a garrison under perpetual threat from Moroccan forces (who benefited from an ongoing trade in munitions with the British), were all costly undertakings—albeit ones that enriched most of the major players, Samuel Pepys among them. At the same time, the outpost in Tangier provided a substantial armed force under the direct control of the king.

During the Exclusion Crisis of 1679–81, when "the political principles that would become Whig orthodoxy after the [Glorious] Revolution" were being shaped, the double significance of Tangier as an object of royal expenditure and as the site of a standing army entered into the debates.[6] Charles needed money to sustain the shaky garrison, money that Parliament repeatedly used as a bargaining chip despite its recent strong support for maintaining the outpost. Citing the Catholic sympathies of the troops and officers at Tangier, Sir William Jones and others made new monies contingent on the passage of the Exclusion Bill. The bill was never passed; the funds were never approved. Charles could not hold onto Tangier, and in 1684 he ordered the Mole destroyed and the garrison evacuated.[7]

Juba's Self

*B*y the time *Cato* appeared, Whig legitimacy was confirmed, and with it the legitimacy of party politics in general. Addison had assumed an actively partisan role in England, editing the *Whig Examiner* and mediating between minor writers and party leaders.[8] His position as a partisan who successfully marketed himself as a moderate was well served by the popularity of *Cato*. This popularity, however, and Addison's reputation for suavity, depended on treating Cato as the hero of the play. It depended, in other words, on overlooking the relationship between republican motifs and the racial and sexual content dramatized through other characters. Arguably the most politicized drama of the century, *Cato* features a Numidian prince, Juba, as the romantic lead. The play stages an extended debate over the relative value of "African" and "Roman" culture while telling the story of Juba's successful suit for Cato's daughter. Addison draws on earlier Roman plays in depicting the emotional life of men close to power as a series of sentimental negotiations between family members or would-be family members. These often tearful scenes take the form of encounters between Roman rigor and a more bodily, wild, or foreign condition.

The play's original reception at the end of the reign of Queen Anne saw Whigs and Tories jostling each other to mark as their own an ethic of masculine disinterestedness (Cato).[9] The play's popular and critical histories reveal a long-standing lack of interest in the "African" characters, specifically the central figure of Juba. Juba is not erased in contemporary responses to the play so much as collapsed into a problem of genre—namely, the suitability of romance in the context of tragedy.[10] The minor interest in Addison's Juba is especially noticeable when compared to eighteenth-century audiences' investment in Cato himself, the indifferent father who makes other men weep and is subsequently canonized in political debate. In British literature of the next hundred years, and in the context of British North American resistance from 1750 through the Revolutionary War, neither literary commentators nor historians have discussed Addison's representations of North Africa, emotional masculinity, or sexual violence. Nor have they linked the historical prominence of *Cato* to its content: race, rape, and the spectacle of weeping men.

The definition of a Roman becomes dissociated from both place and race. With Cato's suicide, the Roman republic ceases to exist as a political entity and becomes an inducement to sentimental or vicarious positions.[11] Tears, shed seven times in *Cato* by men for brothers, fathers, sons, and friends, and only three times by women, make weeping a ritual of male bonding that combines shared feelings with civic virtue. Cato's family is shaped by the demonstrated commitment to public causes of its male and female members. Through the self-conscious imitation of this Roman civic-mindedness, Juba rejects his own African past. By the end of the play, Juba will marry into the Roman family after a series of successful imitations: Juba studies to imitate Cato and woos Marcia, Cato's daughter, who models herself after her father. At the end, Cato urges his surviving son, Portius, to "live retired" at his "paternal seat": "When vice prevails . . . / The post of honour is a private station."[12] But for Juba, who will be his posthumous son-in-law, Cato foresees a promising career in Roman public life.

The play's action is set in Utica (today's Tunisia), which in the Third Punic War had sided with Rome against Carthage. Nearby is Juba's country, Numidia, roughly the territory of modern Algeria. During the earlier Punic Wars, Numidia, too, had split from Carthage in order to support Rome. Both of these sites—Utica and Numidia—dramatize the difficult options faced by North African territories in the Roman world: the choice of being colony, ally, enemy, or some ambiguous combination of the three. As the empire hastens to conclude its victory, the key political and military figures converging on Cato and his family include Caesar, whose forces are gathering nearby; Juba, who has pledged to Cato what troops he can command; Syphax, the Numidian general who undermines Juba's command and eventually leads the Numidian forces over to Caesar; and Sempronius, a traitorous Roman senator who collaborates with Syphax.

Focusing on the failing resistance to Caesar allows Addison to zero in on the affective consequences of the as-yet decentered empire for the deep-feeling man. Both North African locations and Cato's republican cause gain their moral value from being outside Rome. The play moves toward an alliance between the Roman African, Juba, and the defeated Roman, Cato, in which the internalization of Roman virtue by North Africans depends on the temporary fragmentation of Roman authority. Cato's emotional power is inversely proportionate to his political success. He embodies the divorce between ethics and ambition that makes his party into a tender masculine family, and, in the process, reinforces the link between failure, manhood, and sentiment. This set of connections among morality, marginality, and tenderheartedness paradoxically provides the Whigs with a long-running legitimizing narrative. According to this narrative, political factions are transformed from conspiracies into positions critical of excessive ambition and allied with the national interest.

Juba transforms himself through a process of oedipal mimesis. "You long to call him Father," Syphax accuses him, and Juba admits that he loves Marcia because "*Cato's* soul / Shines out in every thing she acts or speaks" (1.4.97, 151–52). One of Cato's sons says to the other, about Juba: "Behold . . . / With how much care he forms himself to glory, / And breaks the fierceness of his native temper / To copy out our Father's bright example" (1.1.79–82). We learn that it was Juba's father's dying wish that his son follow Cato—a wish delivered in tears (2.4.7–15). The savage "Africa" invoked by Syphax in his attack on Roman values was obsolete or embarrassing even for Juba's father. By modeling himself on Cato in accord with his own father's desire, by striving to become Cato-like himself in order to marry Cato's Cato-like daughter, Juba performs a triple task of filiopiety while also renouncing Numidia.[13] Or rather, a lineage is created for the virtuous North African who takes upon himself the double task of criticizing savagery and of being son to a Roman father.

Juba's self-alienation provokes an insistent defense of "Africa" aimed at shattering Rome's fantasy of itself as a moral exemplar. This Africanist stance is undercut, however, because it is spoken by rapists and traitors. Two nasty rhetoricians protest Juba's decision to side with Cato: Syphax and Sempronius. Here it is appropriate to refer to Africa rather than North Africa because the dominant binary is Africa against Rome. The speeches of Syphax in defense of African autonomy and his attack on the logic of Roman virtue are undercut in advance by the fact that they serve his patently vicious intentions. Syphax delivers these addresses in the process of trying to convince Juba to betray Cato and kidnap Marcia. He embodies the equation between sexual and racial depravity. He defends Africa and criticizes Rome in terms of the appetites of the savage body, relying on the empire's crudest racial distinction. According to Syphax, Africa thrives on predation; and Rome, because it pretends to be philosophical, is corrupted by denying its own animality. Nonetheless, while Syphax's rhetoric rouses Juba to matching eloquence on behalf of Roman virtue, its ironic de-idealizing ruthlessness exposes Juba's will to believe in the most rarefied republican morality. Through Syphax's speeches, Africa accepts the predatory qualities attributed to it by Rome, as well as the slur of "Punic guile," and thus mirrors Rome's imperial prejudices.[14]

Syphax tries to win Juba away from Cato and back to an Africa whose savagery he recommends as a healthy response to the Roman ideology of virtue. Syphax resists Juba's sacrifice of Numidian loyalties to the Roman myth of public honor by exposing the savage genealogy of Cato's idealizations: "this almighty *Rome*," he argues, "was founded on a Rape" (2.5.44, 46). For Syphax, the rape of the Sabine women prefigures the impending onset of imperial corruption under Caesar. As Sempronius's own attempted rape of Marcia soon demonstrates, the analogy between political treason and sexual depravity still holds. Syphax describes Juba's former, more African self, the self to which he would recall him.[15] The Numidian general seeks to revalue the "barren rocks" and "burning sands" as the place of a fiercer masculine integrity than the Romans can muster: "there's not an *African* / . . . traverses our vast *Numidian* desarts / . . . / But better practices these boasted virtues" (1.4.16, 59–62).[16]

Linking "African" animal energy with male sexuality acted out in the spirit of the tiger hunt, Syphax recommends that Juba abduct and rape Marcia: "Give but the word, we'll snatch this damsel up, / And bear her off" (2.5.33–34). Reprimanded by Juba, Syphax exposes the genealogical origins of Rome and the consequent illegitimacy of Cato's claim to that "fine imaginary notion," honor:

> The boasted Ancestors of these great men,
> Whose virtues you admire, were all such Ruffians.
> This dread of nations, this almighty *Rome*,
> That comprehends in her wide empire's bounds
> All under Heaven, was founded on a Rape.
> Your *Scipio's*, *Caesar's*, *Pompey's*, and your *Cato's*,
> (These Gods on earth) are all the spurious brood
> Of violated maids, of ravish'd *Sabines*. (2.5.38, 42–49)

Juba responds with a critique of Africa in which he volunteers to civilize or to "break" his countrymen. He answers Syphax's first impatient accusations by juxtaposing the "wilds of *Africk*" to "the [Roman] Lords and Sov'reigns of the world": "Dost thou not see mankind fall down before them, / And own the force of their superior virtue?" (1.4.15, 12, 13–14). In response to Syphax's celebration of "*Numidia's* tawny sons" and "glowing dames" (1.4.19, 137), Juba defines the Roman mission as one that makes hunting yield to sociability—and this means homosociality. The mimesis elsewhere characterized as motivated by Juba's desire for Cato's approval is represented here as benevolent "discipline":

> A *Roman* soul is bent on higher views:
> To civilize the rude unpolish'd world,
> And lay it under the restraint of laws;
> To make Man mild, and sociable to Man;
> To cultivate the wild licentious Savage
> With wisdom, discipline, and liberal arts;
> Th' embellishments of life: Virtues like these,
> Make human nature shine, reform the soul,
> And break our fierce barbarians into men. (I.iv.30–38)

In this passage, "our fierce barbarians" means "myself," an African describing himself through the language of Rome (a Rome that, as I noted earlier, has been "imperial" for a long time although emperors are new to its domestic politics). Romans have precisely the effect of conduct books or moral essays on a global scale. They offer North Africa a classical version of the *Spectator*.

For the Romans, the debate between Africa and Rome signifies the conflict between "licentious" and "cultivated" liberty. Defying this view, Syphax exploits licentiousness as a means of exposing cultivation, for Roman cultivation leads, for Africans, to self-alienation. "What are these wond'rous civilizing arts," he demands,

This *Roman* polish, and this smooth behaviour,

. . . .

Are they not only to disguise our passions,
To set our looks at variance with our thoughts,
To check the starts and sallies of the soul,
And break off all its commerce with the tongue;
In short, to change us into other creatures,
Than what our nature and the Gods design'd us? (1.4.40–48)

Juba defends Cato because Juba is "severely bent against himself," Syphax
charges. He suffers from the continual embarrassment inflicted on him
by the behavior of his fellow Numidians (1.4.53).

What moves Juba to fall in love with Rome is the way Cato's transcen-
dence of sorrow calls forth compensatory emotion in those around him.
Juba's filiopiety—and he is exemplary but not alone in this—is elicited
by the void created by Cato's own sublime displacement of paternal affection away from sons and toward the state. Cato, too, is "severely bent
against himself," against all "natural" or familial feeling. Cato teaches the
Roman lesson of mildness and sociability, not by being mild or sociable
himself, but by causing others to be moved by the spectacle of his own
unemotionality:

Great and majestick in his griefs. . . .
Heavens! with what strength, what steadiness of mind,
He triumphs in the midst of all his sufferings!
How does he rise against a load of woes,
And thank the Gods that throw the weight upon him!
(1.4.78–82)

Cato's tears are shed in the famous scene where he rejoices dry-eyed
at his son's honorable death, then shows that it is more proper to weep
for Rome: "Behold that upright man! *Rome* fills his eyes / With tears, that
flow'd not o'er his own dead son" (4.4.96–97). This gesture signifies
Cato's emotional investment in the republic. But more importantly, it
refuses affection to sons in order to provoke the sons' own feelings for the
republic. Cato's stimulus has mixed results: one son earns his father's approval by dying in battle; the other is urged to retire from public life; and
only Juba, the assimilated North African son-in-law, is given a civic
future.[17]

Cato's power to inspire his sons' self-sacrifice puts the play squarely in
the tradition of the Junius Brutus dramas that proliferated from Lee's

version (1680) to Duncombe's (1734). These plays were centered on the Roman father who assumes power as a just tyrannicide, becomes the object of patricidal plots, and extorts his favorite son's virtually suicidal death in the name of the restored republic. The persistent relationship between paternal rule, political freedom, and the son's loving and guilty self-sacrifice, which organizes the Brutus and Cato plays, suggests that negotiating with affectionate authority is fundamental to the political culture of educated eighteenth-century men. It shows, furthermore, that "the classical republican" is not a figure but a plot, not a position but a relation.

As discussed in chapter 1, Nathaniel Lee's drama of masculine anguish, *Lucius Junius Brutus: The Father of His Country* (1680), zeroes in on the beginning, not the end, of the Roman republic.[18] But the pattern is the same. The son, or a son surrogate, is defined as the locus of sensibility, not just in the Brutus plays, but in *Cato*, in Thomson's later *Sophonisba*, and in many similar dramas. Sensibility is inseparable from ambivalence. If ambivalence is an unresolved conflict between two emotions, then this meaning certainly applies to the two central emotional conflicts in *Lucius Junus Brutus*: Titus's undecidable choice between his father and his wife, and the tension between praise and blame for Brutus's application of Roman law to the case of his favorite son.[19] Brutus's politics of system and Titus's politics of anguish—like Cato's impersonality and Juba's self-doubt—are arranged according to a strongly oedipal logic, by which law in one position produces sensibility in another. According to this reading, sensibility would be an effect of ambivalence. But ambivalence also appears to be an emotional state in itself. The sensibility attributed to Titus, Juba, and, in *Sophonisba*, to Massinissa, emerges as a preexisting temperamental susceptibility. It becomes difficult, finally, to decide whether ambivalence is the cause and sensibility the effect, or whether the reverse is true.

The advantage of understanding republicanism as a plot involving multiple positions is that we can separate characters from ideologies. If republican ideology is comprised of the entire complex of positions, instead of being vested wholly in the classical republican as an individual figure, then republicanism is tantamount to a politics that defines itself apologetically in the very process of legitimization. Ambivalent republicanism, furthermore, is inseparable from ambivalent imperialism experienced by the colonists and the colonized. As Ania Loomba observes, ambivalence is fundamental to dominant imperial or colonial discourses that are "heterogeneously composed [and] unevenly imposed."[20] These plays make a case for the importance of an emotionally fraught, racially inflected subjectivity in the early eighteenth century.

In Lee's *Brutus* and its clones, the transfer of authority is ethically grounded in displays of both disinterestedness and sensibility. The twist comes when paternal disinterestedness exacts sacrifices from the sensitive son or son surrogate. If not sacrifices of his very life, as in Lee's version, this entails suffering self-doubt and guilty feelings, like those undergone by Juba in *Cato*. According to the play's emotional economy, sensibility is the price paid by the republican family for its own appetite for impersonality. Legitimate political power cannot be generated dynastically from father to son. But in *Cato*, the situation is significantly altered from the outcome of *Lucius Junus Brutus*. Sentiment, attributed to Juba, the sensitive Roman African and son surrogate, looks like the future of politics, while the principled father kills himself. What lasts, throughout the tradition of republican plays, is the son's emotion and the father's indifference. The father becomes less violent toward the son—even, in *Cato*, letting him marry into the family—but the son's position is still defined by sentimental self-doubt. Insofar as the son consents to suffer, the language of sensibility justifies rigor in the name of law. Insofar as the son protests or mourns the violence of extravagant impersonality, sentiment criticizes authority—even "good" authority. The virtuous son's dilemma suggests that ambivalent sensibility is fundamental both to legitimizing and to criticizing postmonarchical forms of power.

In *Cato*, then, we find Juba divided between two states that correspond to the two realities of his past and present life. He inhabits the homosocial domain of civility and the equally masculine, savage, and foreign condition of his youth. The tension between these two conditions is played out within the person. North Africa is internalized in Juba's shame after Syphax treasonably commits the Numidian forces to Caesar. "I blush, and am confounded to appear / Before thy presence, Cato," Juba confesses. Asked what his crime is, Juba replies, "I'm a *Numidian*." Cato: "And a brave one too. / Thou hast a *Roman* soul." Although elsewhere Cato has complained of the barbarous conditions of Numidia, his argument here, for which his evidence is Caesar, is that Rome can be a state of mind: "Falsehood and fraud shoot up in every soil, / The product of all climes." Exonerated from a specifically Numidian shame, Juba still emphasizes the internal difference Cato's approval makes to him: "my ravish'd heart / O'erflows with secret joy" (4.4.40–43, 45–46, 52–53). Juba's ethical emotion acquires its dramatic charge, therefore, from just the experience of self-alienation that had been predicted by Syphax.

What does "Africa" represent in *Cato?* In a typical eighteenth-century fashion, the continent is characterized as racially and politically split. Juba, who in certain scenes embodies African qualities as though all Africans possessed them, elsewhere distinguishes between North Africa and sub-Saharan Africa. He refers to his father's alliances with the "Kings of *Africk*" from "foreign climes . . . / Behind the hidden sources of the *Nile*, / . . . on t'other side the Sun." He remembers their "black ambassadors" and recommends drawing on the strength of their "swarthy hosts." Cato turns down the suggestion, recoiling at the prospect of being compelled "like *Hannibal*" to "wander up and down, / A vagabond in *Africk!*" (2.4.23–28, 38, 43–45). North Africa occupies a liminal position. Relative to Rome, it synecdochically represents all of Africa, but when the sliver of Roman Africa occupied by Cato's forces is compared to the rest of the continent, it represents a cluster of nations and peoples assimilated into Mediterranean history and therefore available for imaginative use.

The question of what Africa signifies in *Cato* is complicated by Juba's "Roman soul" and by the savagery of the Roman senator, Sempronius, who is more corrupt than the corrupt African, Syphax. If representations of both Africa and Rome are structured by the contrast between savagery and cultivation, then Africa is a state of mind that can be embodied in either anti-Roman Africans or corrupted Romans. And Rome is a state of mind embodied in civil Africans or Roman republicans. The Roman characters are already in a vexed relation to any single notion of Rome, because Rome has no geographical or cultural center in a play in which Cato is in North Africa, Caesar en route to Utica, Pompey in Spain, the republic almost lost, and the imperial regime not quite established. Under these circumstances, Cato, the virtuous Stoic, is able to make others want to emulate him. This effect makes Rome permeable to people from other cultures through their own voluntary mimesis. More centrally, the tale of civilizing the "licentious savage" becomes the Whigs' troubled self-portrait. The univocal, indifferent father dies, succeeded by a more uncertain and more affectionate surrogate son. The inward turn of the play, in Juba's description of his own emotional state, locates republican ideals in the midst of sentimental self-alienation. The Roman transition from republic to empire is allegorized as the shift from trade to violence—a shift (or equivalence) that many eighteenth-century intellectuals wished they could revise (or undo). And this transitional state, finally, becomes the setting for masculine affection that elides the binary opposition between colonizer and colonized.

We can extend this argument by observing how the relation between racial difference and sexual violence in *Cato* shapes the confrontation of Juba, the Roman savage, with Sempronius, the savage Roman. Sempronius dresses up as Juba in order to rape Marcia, Cato's daughter. When Sempronius appears to abduct Marcia "dress'd like Juba, with *Numidian* guards" (as the stage directions specify), the play reaches a mimetic climax (4.2). Juba, who has defined himself all along as a cultural other who is trying to be the same, is faced with a parody of his own otherness. Sempronius, taking on the identity Juba is struggling to revise, snarls: "I long to clasp that haughty maid, / And bend her stubborn virtue to my passion: / When I have gone thus far, I'd cast her off" (3.7.14–16).[21] He treats his planned rape as a pleasurable assault on Juba's virtue as well as Marcia's (4.2.5–7). When Sempronius is disguised, predatory sexuality and racial difference appear to be fused, but because the apparently Numidian rapist is not Numidian, rape and race are sharply distinguished when the real Juba arrives on the scene: "death to my hopes! 'tis he, / 'Tis *Juba's* self!" (4.2.9–10). "Juba's self" kills his imitator, who dies, "disfigur'd in a vile / *Numidian* dress," complaining of his triple humiliation at the hands of youth, Africa, and woman (4.2.21–22). Juba is then treated to the spectacle of Marcia pouring out her love and admiration over the corpse she thinks is his. When he shows himself, she comments on the uncanny doubling of the scene: "Sure 'tis a dream! dead and alive at once! / If thou art *Juba*, who lies there?" (4.3.59–60).

If Marcia is at once an image of her father, an object of desire that motivates Juba's imitation of her father, *and* the reward for that successful mimesis, then exogamous love is bound up with homosocial relations and with a kind of mimetic incest. If Cato is the real object of Juba's desire, then the stories of cross-racial cultivation, of courtship, and of Cato's suicide are wholly connected. Wholly connected, despite the very entertaining objections of John Dennis to the "Romantick and incredible" intrusion of "the Amorous Passions" into Addison's "Nest of Stoicks."[22] In the transformation of Juba into a Roman, we witness the conversion of race into subjectivity.[23] Many sentimental writings of the eighteenth century follow suit. Men's tears express a masculine experience of public life that regards itself tenderly as savage, civil, and inescapably imperial.

"Ladies . . . Behold Your Cato"

*T*he recurrence of the mood of masculine doubt at the edge of empire in Thomson's *Sophonisba* (1730) confirms the logic of Lee's *Lucius Junius Brutus* and Addison's *Cato*. Thomson, a deeply Whiggish Scot dependent on the patronage of Charles Talbot, defined the English landscape for British readers in *The Seasons* (1726–30) and charted the progress of empire in *Britannia, A Poem* (1729) and *Liberty, A Poem* (1735). During the 1730s, Thomson gravitated to the opposition circle around Frederick Louis, Prince of Wales, while remaining on good terms with Talbot, by then Lord Chancellor.[24] The Prince of Wales became fond of *Sophonisba*, which the prince helped to revive as an unambiguous vehicle of political opposition, though it did not have this status when first performed. It is worth noting that the Prince of Wales was observed cheering with the opposition at a performance of *Cato* in 1737, and that new dramatizations of the story of Junius Brutus appeared in 1733 (by Bond) and 1734 (by Duncombe).[25] That a story formed from intersecting tales of cross-racial encounters, imperial aggrandizement, and female patriotism should be the bearer of civic prestige reveals the complications within what we might call oppositional high culture.

The play opens late in the history of a fight over the succession of African thrones in which Rome has intervened. Carthaginian forces are about to face a Roman army in battle. Sophonisba, Queen of Carthage, is married to Syphax, King of Numidia. Years before, Sophonisba had married him on the basis of public policy considerations. He cherished a gratifying hatred for the Romans and a vehement loyalty to Carthage that matched her own. Sophonisba, indeed, stands precisely for the absence of ambivalence. Syphax is a tyrant at home, if a patriot in his defiance of Rome. When she married Syphax, Sophonisba gave up her romantic attachment to Massinissa, called "the Numidean Roman" because of his alliance with Scipio.[26] Massinissa was driven from his throne by Syphax, survived an ordeal in the North African wilds, and now, backed by Scipio, leads the army that challenges Carthage.

Syphax loses the battle to Massinissa. With Scipio due to arrive as Rome's political representative, Sophonisba confronts her worst fear, life as a Roman captive ("detested thought") (1.1.4). The laws are conveniently such that her marriage to Syphax is nullified after his capture on the battlefield. In the course of several scenes with Massinissa, she reinspires his passion, despite his determination not to be swayed, and arouses his sympathy for her national cause. In a reversal of the gender roles that prevail in *Antony and Cleopatra, All for Love,* and other plays in the love-or-glory genre, she chooses glory and he chooses love. He quickly marries her in the hope that once she is his wife, Scipio will not make her parade through jeering crowds in the streets of Rome.

Everyone has a hunch that Scipio will not yield to this romantic logic, and, in fact, they are right. He lavishes quasi-paternal affection on Massinissa in a reaffirmation of the homosocial bonds that Rome represents but makes it clear that he considers capturing Sophonisba to be the point of the whole expedition. In short, he will not be dissuaded from delivering her up to the Senate. Massinissa, as he has promised to do earlier, sends Sophonisba a bowl of poison which she gladly drinks in order to avoid this fate. Despite his previous defense of Roman consistency, Scipio repents his hard-line position, but Massinissa arrives with news of this too late to save Sophonisba and then stabs himself.

Sophonisba reworks many of the thematic and structural features of *Cato*. As in *Cato*, the romantic lead is a royal North African. The fact that this character is a woman accounts for the most significant deviation from Addison's precedent. The queen takes Carthage as her love object, "a whole collected people" (4.2.154). Sophonisba defines herself as committed to public life and cedes romance to the conflicted male sentimentalist, Massinissa. Massinissa's filial admiration for the perfect consistency of Scipio closely parallels Juba's effort to model himself on Cato, while Scipio bears out the association of Stoicism with paternal authority. In both plays, the younger African male is marked by an extreme emotionality that the Roman mentor paradoxically counteracts and rewards.

The question of how race relates to gender hinges largely on the meaning of Carthage, not only in this text, but in the long tradition descending from the *Aeneid*, in which Dido's Carthage represents a feminine diversion of Roman progress. This view is encapsulated in the response of Massinissa's advisor, Narva, who links "fatal Punic guile" with the "boundless witchcraft of ensnaring women" (2.1.24–25).[27] Faced with Roman captivity, Sophonisba invokes her Carthaginian predecessor: "My soul/ . . . will indignant burst from a slave's body, / And, joined to mighty Dido, scorn ye all" (2.1.57–58). This eighteenth-century version of what I call the "Carthage Syndrome" links the racial difference of North Africa with feminine power. Then it positions both as collaborating in a critique of tyranny, ultimately ineffective but nonetheless moving.

Carthage, like Utica, is shifty as a signifier of racial difference. It is frequently unclear how "black" Thomson's Carthage is. When he wants to emphasize black skin, he makes the "gloomy Lybian" the opposite of the white Roman. Carthage becomes most nonwhite, most racially "other" relative to Rome through references to Massinissa's youthful sojourn in its wild landscape (a wilderness evoked in *Cato* as Juba's place of origin, as well). North Africa is characterized by its fauna—"the serpents hiss and tigers yell" (1.3.42)—and by the animality of the land itself, with its "impending rocks . . . paths abrupt . . . deep-swoln torrent . . . devouring flood" (1.1.84–95).

But North African qualities are also communicated through the equally wild loyalty of Sophonisba. In his preface, Thomson claims that emotional fluctuations caused by changes in Sophonisba's status give the play its structure: "[The story] is one, regular, and uniform . . . and yet affording several revolutions of fortune; by which the passions may be excited, varied, and driven to their full tumult of emotion" (p. v; see also 4.1.2–8). Drawing on the association of North African geography with wildness, energy, and freedom, Thomson marks the North African couple as emotionally unstable, both individually and together. Massinissa, in the grip of a weakly internalized Roman ethos, perceives North Africa as a condition of mental apocalypse and regards subjectivity as a wilderness:

> O save me from the tumult of the soul!
> From the wild beasts within! . . .
> The monster brood to which this land gives birth,
> The blazing city and the gaping earth;
> All deaths, all tortures, in one pang combin'd,
> Are gentle to the tempest of the mind. (1.5.6–14)

Sophonisba tries to sever the link between North Africa and emotional anarchy in order to define Carthage as liberty, Rome as slavery. Like Syphax in Addison's *Cato*, she strips away the Roman mystique: "Romans are the scourge / of the next world," operating under "the smooth dissembling mask / Of justice . . . as if slave / Was but another name for civilized" (3.3.71–75). The character of Scipio—the "mask of justice"— negatively reinforces the association between Moors and emotion. Scipio is the antithesis of variable passion. In Scipio's big scene with Massinissa in act 5, he conflates Roman civilization with consistency itself and suggests that its opposite is "savage nature," the North African condition: "From savage nature / 'Tis patience that has built up human life, / The nurse of arts! and Rome exalts her head / An everlasting monument of patience" (5.2.29–32). Later, predicting that the senators will demand Sophonisba's captivity, he reiterates the equation of Rome with emotional discipline:

>   fate itself
> Is not more steady to the right than they,
> And, where the public good but seems concern'd,
> No motive their impenetrable hearts,

Nor fear near [nor] tenderness, can touch: such is
The spirit that has rais'd imperial Rome (5.2.242–47)

Against Scipio's Roman steadiness are ranged the emotional extremes of
Sophonisba's love-hate relationship with Massinissa and, particularly, of
Massinissa's own internal conflict.

Once cultural and racial differences have been joined to emotional
flux under the geographical rubric of North Africa, and once all these
terms have been juxtaposed to Rome, we are left wondering whether race
has been negated in *Sophonisba* by its status as a trope for emotion. Has
sentiment absorbed race, as in *Cato?* The short answer is yes. But in order
to address the connection between race and sensibility—and thereby to
unfold the long answer—we have to more systematically consider the
question of gender. The gender structure of the play involves two configurations: first, the characterization of Sophonisba as both nonfeminine
(a "female patriot") and hyperfeminine; and second, sentimental masculine friendship enacted in the name of bourgeois domesticity in the scenes
between Massinissa and Scipio.

"Ladies . . . behold your Cato," declares the epilogue to *Sophonisba*,
"By a Friend. Spoken by Mrs. Cibber." (9). Sophonisba, like Cato, speaks
of herself as the defender of "public spirit"; unlike him, however, she
simultaneously defies both romantic love and Roman stoicism (1.4. 125;
epilogue, 15). She embodies a feminine patriotism perceived by others as
an admirable mania. Massinissa is distressed that she entertains only a
single emotion, "that all-controuling love she bears her country" (2.1.15).
He collaborates in defining female patriotism, which keeps Sophonisba
in a state of "too much rage" (1.1.27–28), as pathological excess. In fact,
however, it is Massinissa's romantic and sexual passion, "the triumph
of excessive love," that becomes embarrassing, to himself and others
(3.3.165). Sophonisba's public spirit makes her both Roman and the antithesis of Rome: "not a Roman burns with nobler ardor, / A higher
sense of liberty than she" (1.4. 120–21). At the same time, the liberty she
defends is feminine and uncultivated. Hope, says Sophonisba, "Fled, with
her sister Liberty . . . / . . . to some steep wild, / Some undiscover'd
country, where the foot / Of Roman cannot come" (1.3.36–39).

If Sophonisba gives voice to the rhetoric of liberty, she also represents
a distinctly feminine commitment to political agency, which is juxtaposed
to stereotypes of conventional femininity. "It is not for the daughter of
great Asdrubal / . . . to pine in love," she exclaims, "like a deluded maid;
to give her life, / And heart high-beating in her country's cause, / To

mean domestic cares, and idle joys" (1.1.60–67). In a more fully developed critique of domesticity, she grounds her public vocation in the "passions":

> Think as you list of our unhappy sex,
> Too much subjected to your tyrant force,
> Yet know that all, we were not all, at least,
> Form'd for your trifles, for your wanton hours.
> Our passions too can sometimes soar above
> The household-talk assign'd us, can extend
> Beyond the narrow sphere of families,
> And take great states into th' expanded heart. (4.2.93–100)

Syphax, her listener, responds: "A female patriot!—Vanity!—Absurd!" (4.2.108).

For the female hero, passion is sensibility gone public and political, but for her male foil, passion is politics gone wrong. Massinissa refers to passion as "tyrant love" (5.2.74), the uncontrollable desire for a woman that feminizes the male lover in his own eyes: "thou hast melted down my stubborn soul / To female tenderness" (3.3.204–5). Thomson was no feminist and he did not celebrate a female patriot for the good of women. One has to conclude, then, that female heroism derives its cultural value here from the fact that it can be represented as exotic and doomed. Sophonisba's anti-Roman suicide is as civic-minded as Cato's quintessentially Roman death. She is even granted—in spite of her sex and in spite of being African—a distinctly Stoic prestige. She is an antagonist worthy of Rome.

Massinissa, as committed to extremism as she, kills himself, too. But before he does, he is allowed to validate the way that sentiment can be admirable if it strengthens homosocial bonds. Massinissa recalls something like falling in love with Scipio. To his "panting soul," Scipio was "Resistless . . . like a descending God" who "snatched me from the Carthaginian side / To nobler Rome" (2.1.43, 8–11). When Sophonisba accuses Massinissa of having been "seduc'd" by Scipio, she echoes his own account of the event (2.2.84). Massinissa and Scipio confirm their affection when they cry together at the very moment that they renounce womanliness. Massinissa, trying to meet Scipio's manly Roman expectations, equates his passion for Sophonisba with the feminine wilderness: "Thro' what enchanted wilds have I been wand'ring? . . . I am in a desart." Scipio urges him to "shake off this effeminate disease; / These soft ideas, which seduce thy soul, / Make it all idle, weak, in glorious, wild."

At this point, Massinissa weeps—"I am a child again"—which so moves Scipio that he weeps, too, describing his reaction as valid because masculine: "Tears oft look graceful on the manly cheek . . . Lo! Friendship's eye / Gives thee the drop it would refuse itself" (5.2.209–210, 227–29, 267, 270–72). This is what Eve Sedgwick refers to as the "sacred tears of the heterosexual man." [28]

Earlier in the play, foreshadowing Scipio's tears in this scene, Narva tells the story of Scipio's sentimental response to the pleadings of a female captive in New Carthage—Spain. The woman wept, "the Roman legions languish'd," and Scipio experienced the melting moment of sensibility. But upon reuniting the woman with her husband, freeing them both and restoring the man's lands and crown, Scipio named his price to the husband: "In return / I ask but this. When you behold these eyes, / These charms, with transport, be a friend to Rome" (2.1.94, 128–31). The emotion elicited by a weeping woman precipitates a transaction between men. The favor of domestic bliss—the refusal to rape—effects a political change of heart praised by Narva in the retold story as the essence of masculine friendship. Men can take civic pride in "languishing" over a woman, as long as the sentimental response ends up aligning all the men, now affectionately bonded, on the same side.

In *Sophonisba*, there are losers but no villains. The audience is asked to admire both Scipio and Sophonisba, both the charitable virtues of imperial filiopiety and resistance in the name of liberty. In order for both Scipio and Sophonisba to be admirable, Sophonisba's accusation of Roman tyranny has to coexist with the Roman claim to represent a reasonable liberty. Thomson does not have to relinquish the legitimacy of Sophonisba's critique of Rome. Her arguments retain their persuasiveness while leaving Scipio untainted. Carthage—feminine, passionate, racially different, and entrepreneurial—represents anti-authoritarian liberty as sufficiently exotic to be contained, after a tragic pang, within a rational empire.

The most untenable position in the play is that occupied by Massinissa. He is forced to choose between Scipio and Sophonisba, between fraternal loyalty and erotic passion. Massinissa's ultimately useless attempts to introduce some difference between public and private life only emphasize the fact that he is the character least able to maintain this distinction. Loving both Sophonisba and Scipio, he invests in the separation between eros and power. By assigning the two ideological antagonists to the categories of private and public, he tries and fails to sustain both relationships. Massinissa thus dramatizes the process by which race becomes a metaphor for other differences. As the North African who accepted Rome's autocracy over other North Africans, he signifies the dramatic fate of this "zone of emotion." In the tradition of *Othello*, North Africa is a territory of racial difference susceptible to romance. It fosters a condition of undecidable empathy that circulates, with manifold variations, through the literature of sensibility.

"Playing a Part in *Cato*"

*T*he cultural persistence of *Cato* itself or material related to it in later works shows the future of republican sensibility. These examples suggest both how politically variable the recurrences of republican tenderheartedness were, and how successfully integrated into the long history of sensibility this very particular ideological configuration would become. The first instance is the relationship between Addison's *Cato* and Trenchard and Gordon's *Cato's Letters* (1720–23; collected 1724), a relationship strengthened later when both works—powerfully conflated with each other—enjoyed a remarkable vogue in the American colonies just prior to and during the Revolutionary War. The second example, Adam Smith's homage to the figure of Cato in *The Theory of Moral Sentiments* (1759; 6th ed. 1790), shows how durable the performance of stoicism is as a mark of masculine superiority—and how consistently this performance is experienced by other men as a tear-jerker. The third configuration—one in which racial difference is very much on display but in which classical republicanism almost, but not quite, vanishes—appears in relation to the character of Juba in Maria Edgeworth's *Belinda* (1801). This example advances us to a period when sensibility and antislavery positions had become thoroughly identified with each other. Looking at these three intertwined lines of descent together gives us a new and more balanced view of just what linked neoclassicism and sensibility well into the nineteenth century.

Trenchard and Gordon's *Cato's Letters* appropriates the rhetoric of republican opposition but diverges from the Roman dramas I have discussed by blurring the interplay between the Stoic Roman and his sons. *Lucius Junius Brutus, Cato,* and *Sophonisba* define a political orientation by probing the morally attractive ambivalence stimulated by Cato's performance of Stoic consistency. *Cato's Letters* rejects ambivalence altogether in favor of exasperation. At the same time, the masculine, tough, and irritable persona of *Cato's Letters* is obsessed with the threat of government conspiracies. An atmosphere of alarmed intransigence is here carried forward from the Exclusion Crisis and the stresses of the 1690s into new political circumstances. But in contrast to other modalities of republicanism, Trenchard and Gordon's writings aspire to oppositional legitimacy only. This is fundamental to the kind of masculinity they represent, defined by a fierce insistence on the individual's property in himself and on nationalism located exclusively in such proprietary subjectivities. Their revulsion fueled by the spectacle of public corruption during the South Sea scandal, the authors of *Cato's Letters* want to put both money and arms in the hands of the citizen. Possessive rage equates public institutions with tyrannical decadence and despises both. As I will argue at greater length in the conclusion, it is not surprising that the latest libertarian tribute to Trenchard and Gordon—the Cato Institute, in Washington, D.C.—displays its tough-mindedness by fetishizing personal property and by habitually accusing any commitment to governmental institutions of sentimental error, liberal conspiracy, or both. It is the ambivalence of the sensitive man, so deeply interwoven with narratives of the Roman republic, that is being expelled by Trenchard and Gordon in *Cato's Letters*—in the name of the republic.[29]

    Cato's Letters and *Cato* were transatlantic texts. Both were widely read in the North American colonies in the first half of the eighteenth century.[30] But if the name of Cato is the signature of the oppositional citizen, the dramatic figure of Cato encapsulates the narrative of sacrifice. Addison's *Cato* was acted in the colonies from its first recorded staging in Charleston in 1735 to its more frequent performances, beginning around 1750, by colonial and English professional companies, culminating in its peak years in the 1760s and 1770s. The play entered deeply into iconic self-dramatizations of George Washington, Patrick Henry, and Nathan Hale. Their identification with the character of Cato himself is palpable. Two plays were performed after the winter of 1777–78 at Valley Forge; one of them was *Cato,* attended by Washington on May 11, 1778. Patrick Henry, in his famous peroration, asked: "Is life so dear, or peace so sweet, as to be purchased at the price of chains and slavery? Forbid it, Almighty God! I know not what course others may take, but as for me, give me liberty, or give me death!" Henry thus appropriated Cato's trademark phrase, "It is not now a time to talk of aught / But chains, or conquest; liberty, or death" (2.4.79–80) and sanitized the implications of the traitorous Sempronius's speech: "Gods, can a Roman senate long debate / Which of the two to choose, slavery or death!" (2.1.24–25). Nathan

Hale's dying words, "I only regret that I have but one life to lose for my country," repeated Cato's transcendent disinterestedness as he gazes upon the body of his son Marcus, who has died in battle: "What pity is it that we can die but once to save our country" (4.4.81–82).[31] Hale thus casts himself as both the self-sacrificing son who emulates, *avant la lettre,* his father's principled suicide and the appreciative paternal commentator on such a death.

The most telling swerve away from an identification with Cato in fact reinforces the way in which the old republican Stoic has tended to thrust Addison's other characters—especially the African ones—into the background. In 1758, when Washington, then twenty-six, was serving under General Forbes during the Seven Years' War, he wrote to Mrs. George William Fairfax from the front: "I should think our time more agreeably spent believe me, in playing a part in Cato, with the company you mention, and myself doubly happy in being the Juba to such a Marcia, as you must make." The author of the article that recuperated this piece of information identifies Addison's Juba only as a "soldier"; like Washington himself, the twentieth-century critic elides the fact of Juba's Numidian difference.[32] By the 1790s, when the new republic was having trouble with Barbary pirates—tensions which would lead, in 1801, to Jefferson's Tripolitan War—Juba's homeland matters a good deal and reappears in stories of Barbary piracy and Algerian capture. By this time, too, "Juba" had become a stock figure on the American stage—the dancing, dandified slave who would later be the centerpiece of scripts such as *Juba: An Ethiopian Opera, in one scene* published in New York by the Happy Hours Company in 1874 as one of one hundred items in its "Ethiopian Drama" series.[33] But during the revolutionary period itself, the combined intransigence and pathos of the white American, or "Roman," citizen dominated the echoes of *Cato* in the public rhetoric of politically active men.

Adam Smith, whose *Theory of Moral Sentiments* substantially preceded the American Revolution in its first edition (1759) and followed it in its sixth and final edition (1790), shares the American revolutionaries' investment in Cato's stoic performance. The best victim, Smith believes, "fixes his thoughts . . . upon . . . the applause and admiration which he is about to deserve by the heroic magnanimity of his behaviour."[34] Like Nathan Hale, Smith's Cato enacts emotional self-control for the sake of his posthumous reputation.

Cato materializes in the midst of Smith's emphatic claim that the

normal witness to the suffering of others exhibits only a "dull sensibility" (1.3.1.12, 47). By contrast, we experience our own afflictions so intensely—they make "so violent an impression"—that self-control is a
struggle (1.3.1.14, 49). The emotional triumph of Cato lies in the fact that
his own willed "insensibility" coincides with the natural moderation of
feeling in the spectator:

> Cato, surrounded on all sides by his enemies, unable to resist
> them, disdaining to submit to them, and reduced, by the proud
> maxims of that age, to the necessity of destroying himself; yet
> never shrinking from his misfortunes, never supplicating with the
> lamentable voice of wretchedness, those miserable sympathetic
> tears which we are always so unwilling to give; but on the con-
> trary, arming himself with manly fortitude, and the moment be-
> fore he executes his fatal resolution, giving, with his usual tran-
> quillity, all necessary orders for the safety of his friends; appears
> to Seneca, that great preacher of insensibility, a spectacle which
> even the gods themselves might behold with pleasure and admi-
> ration. (1.3.1.48)

Having lauded Cato for treating himself with the coolness of the on-
looker, Smith immediately changes his account of the spectator's response in order to show how sublime degrees of deliberate insensibility
in the sufferer tend after all not to provoke corresponding insensibility in
others, but rather, to generate an unusual strength of sympathy. Here
Smith describes the phenomenon of how Stoics like Cato cause other
people to weep:

> We are more apt to weep and shed tears for such as, in this man-
> ner, seem to feel nothing for themselves, than for those who give
> way to all the weakness of sorrow. . . . The friends of Socrates all
> wept when he drank the last portion, while he himself expressed
> the gayest and most cheerful tranquillity. (1.3.1.48)

Smith dwells on the social embarrassment of tears (1.3.1.46–47). But
in an earlier portion of section 1, he describes the appropriately mini-
malist mode of masculine emotion in terms that look forward to his
vignette of Cato. Here Smith makes understandable Cato's several tears,
shed for Rome:

> we reverence that reserved, that silent and majestic sorrow, which
> discovers itself only in the swelling of the eyes, in the quivering

of the lips and cheeks, and in the distant, but affecting, coldness
of the whole behavior. (1.1.5.3, 24).

Smith writes as a connoisseur of both history and theater. The fundamental narrative of republican masculinity as represented in eighteenth-
century Roman plays persists: Stoicism and sensibility provoke each
other, and the republican hero earns his cultural keep by justifying other
men's tears.

What happens, then, when a woman reads Adam Smith's book and
uses her claim to rational sensibility to justify her cross-racial sympathy?
The most direct fictional transformation of Juba comes in Edgeworth's
Belinda (1801). The cultural memory of Addison's hero is repressed, for
this Juba is modeled on accounts of slave performances. The name of
Juba, like that of Cato, comprised many meanings. "Juba" was the name
of historical Numidian rulers who both opposed and were educated by
Rome, and of a city in the Sudan; it is the Bantu word for peanut; it was
a slave term for leftovers from the white table; and, beginning around
1790, it referred to a particular form of African-American slave dance,
the Juba. Edgeworth identifies the slave with the dance.[35]

Actually, there are two Jubas in *Belinda*. One is the stereotypically low
character of the slave or servant of Belinda's Creole suitor, Mr. Vincent,
a Jamaican planter. The other is Vincent's dog. Dog and slave (or former
slave) are paired throughout as the objects of their owner's affection; indeed, Mr. Vincent is unable to decide which he likes the most:

> "Juba is, without exception, the best creature in the universe."
> "Juba, the dog, or Juba, the man?" said Belinda, "you know,
> they cannot be both the best creatures in the universe."
> "Well! Juba, the man, is the best man—and Juba, the dog, is
> the best dog, in the universe," said Mr. Vincent, laughing, with
> his usual candour, at his own foible.[36]

The figure of Juba comprises the social freedoms accorded to low comic
types, but these are charged with Edgeworth's nervous pathos. With the
blessing of his employer, Juba marries a white woman, Marcia, the virtuous daughter of "industrious tenants . . . reduced to misfortune" (230).
For sentimental-comic lovers at the bottom of the social spectrum, race is
no barrier to romance. Juba's association with song and dance is dramatized in the genre scene of Juba and Marcia's wedding. The song he sings
while accompanying himself on the "banjore" combines superstition with

"the most touching expression of joyful gratitude." In the 1810 edition of *Belinda* in the British Novelists series, however, the interracial marriage was excised in response to hostile criticism (xxv), a striking instance of authorial ambivalence.

Juba's appearances in *Belinda* are governed by their metonymic contiguity to manifestations of Belinda's sensitive liberal rationality. She embodies the combination of reason, reading, and sensibility that rescues Juba from the psychological torments of a manufactured apparition (243, 207–10). White genteel British sentiment continues to be bound up with the figure of the African, and the African, now thoroughly deromanticized, continues to mediate romance. The connection is established through familiar streams of cultural consciousness:

> her ladyship now turned the conversation from Juba, the dog, to Juba, the man. She talked of Harriet Freke's phosphoric obeah-woman, of whom, she said, she had heard an account. . . . She spoke of Juba's marriage, and of his master's generosity to him. From thence she went on to the African slave trade, by way of contrast, and she finished precisely where she had intended, and where Mr. Vincent could have wished, by praising a poem called "The dying Negro", which he had, the preceding evening, brought to read to Belinda. (329)

The utter inappropriateness of the unladylike and conniving Mrs. Freke is established by the trick she plays on Juba and—when she calls to apologize for this—by her expressed dislike of Adam Smith's *Theory of Moral Sentiments*, of which Belinda approves. To show just how insensitive she is, Edgeworth allies Mrs. Freke with Wollstonecraft's critique of the way delicacy "enslaves" women: " 'I hate slavery! Vive la liberté' cried Mrs Freke—'I'm a champion for the Rights of Women' " (216). Mrs. Freke's limitations are exposed by her feminist appropriations of liberty, hyperbolic falsifications of her role as the slave's tormentor. Belinda, meanwhile, who admires Smith—and represents a rational femininity modeled on late eighteenth-century masculine sensibility—befriends Juba and cures him. Her cure is the outcome of emotional intelligence; it mercifully applies a comparative understanding of belief systems. She heals the servant by exposing his religion as false.

This conjunction between racial difference, the defense of sensibility, and the courtship plot, though its relationship to eighteenth-century Cato discourse is attenuated, shows precisely why we need to understand this discourse as a cluster of narrative or dramatic relationships rather than as a stable republican ideology or as "the classical" republican embodied in a single character. Cato discourse comprises not a discrete set of beliefs or attitudes, but a recurring arrangement of positions defined by the interdependent presence and absence of gendered sentiment. The variability of these positions in different works and, in particular, the shifting role of race in relation to them suggest that sensibility's long life arises from the ongoing cultural pertinence of affection experienced as public crisis, of public crisis experienced as affection.

CHAPTER THREE

The Deathbed of the Just

Cato in Retirement

The theater of masculine sensibility provided the means to reflect on citizenly desire in a parliamentary state.[1] The Roman plays had an afterlife. *Lucius Junus Brutus* or *Venice Preserved* pervaded long stretches of literary culture that scholars have regarded as having little in common with Roman or quasi-Roman dramas. Sensibility as seen on the English stage continuously entered into the cultural practices of the British Atlantic. Sensitive manhood emerging under the conditions of multiracial empire pervades both eighteenth-century plays and the poetry of sensibility. The poetry of melancholia and retreat sustained an ongoing conversation with an overtly ideological dramatic tradition.

In starting to trace the metamorphoses of Cato in the previous chapter, I suggested that the emergence of later idioms of sympathy did not erase the oppositional allure of sensibility performed in liberty's name. In order to look ahead to the future of Cato discourse, I traced a path through later works in several genres. I will now backtrack in order to investigate more fully how drama in the Roman mode related to eighteenth-century poetry. This will provide a starting point for an account of the generic fluidity of passionate cosmopolitan masculinity and lay the foundation for the discussion in later chapters of sensibility's shifts across gender positions.

The poetry that drew on the language of sensibility was receptive to the crisis-charged masculinity of the stage Stoic and his circle of teary compatriots. We find no decisive rejection of republican conspiracy dramas as we move into the eighteenth-century decades that are habitually identified with the ethos of sympathy. What we find, in fact, is the energetic recycling of masculine national and *international* fantasy across genres, careers, and political orientations, to modify Lauren Berlant's term—"national fantasy"—for the dynamics of "images, narratives, monuments and sites" through which "national culture becomes local" or embodied.[2]

This chapter ranges from *Liberty Asserted*, an Indian drama of 1704 by the Englishman John Dennis, to *Ponteach: or the Savages of America, A Tragedy*, wrongly attributed to the American military figure, Robert Rogers, in

1766. I take up poems occupying the interval between Thomson's *Winter* (1726) and Gray's *Elegy* (1751). This chapter, therefore, engages the period during which the Age of Sensibility is conventionally thought to occur.[3]

In the Roman plays and their descendants, urbanity negotiates with catastrophe to articulate civic feeling in the midst of local or international violence. These negotiations are helped along by the fact that "theater was . . . a forum in which national stereotypes were constructed and perpetuated with a vengeance."[4] In verse settings, the Roman hero may make a mere cameo appearance in an allusive vignette, or else the situation of the poem's speaker and his friends is laden with civic meanings conveyed through gestural or verbal cues. Still, what looks like interiority, rural sanctuary, or domesticity in the poetry of sensibility is often a highly coded claim to serious world citizenship.[5] It is a claim that locates the thought of racial difference in the associative twists and turns of the long poem.

Eighteenth-century plays help us to read eighteenth-century poems by providing a key to the logic that connects reflection to gender and nation in poetic contexts. But the plays cannot simply be *read into* the verse. The transactions binding sensibility to stoicism tend to assume a provincial location. The perspective is that of Cato's surviving son, the one he advises to retire from public life. The provincial viewpoint becomes cosmopolitan, however, and incorporates both the nation and the world. Provincial distances in the long poems of sensibility thus recuperate elements of the Roman plays into the spatial and kinetic relations of verse.[6] At the same time, the poems retain overt, if compressed, political narratives and public characters. Some of the century's most influential poets explored sensibility in both drama and verse. They knew that national issues, thrashed out on the London stage, could move into ambitious long poems and then back, on occasion, to the theater. Each of these transpositions involved subtle changes in meaning.

The connection between the poetry of sensibility and dramas that trade in retroclassical themes appears in Thomson's dramatic engagement with "the Carthage Syndrome" in *Sophonisba,* staged in 1730, and in his poetry of the immediately preceding period. In 1726, Thomson published *Winter,* the earliest, and paradigmatic, book of *The Seasons. Winter* helped establish a popular model for eighty years of English verse in which a fanciful subject speaks among vivid landscapes. Between the revisions of *Winter* and the rest of *The Seasons* that accrued for twenty years,

Thomson wrote *Sophonisba;* two other long poems, *Britannia* (1729) and *Liberty* (1735); and several more tragedies.

The figure of Cato appears in early editions of *Winter*. Cato material-izes in the company of Timoleon, "that attemper'd Heroe, mild, and firm, / Who wept the Brother, while the Tyrant bled," and of "*Scipio,* the humane Warriour, gently brave."[7] Cato is summoned, according to the poem's associative logic, to the protected masculine core of house-hold life, a domestic altar to the republican idea. The speaker celebrates the pleasure of reading the classics in an interior room, the "deep retire-ment" amenable to masculine sociability. The "friends" here are virtual ones, classical authors: "Thus . . . would I pass / The winter-glooms, with friends of pliant soul." Contemplating this course of reading leads the poet to an exercise in vicarious civics. He honors the "race of heroes" of "virtuous times," including "Unconquered *Cato,* virtuous in Extreme."[8] By the final 1746 edition of *The Seasons,* the space devoted to Roman heroes had grown considerably; it includes the "sternly sad" Lucius Junius Brutus, the "public Father who the private quell'd."[9] As John Barrell observes, "Private friendship may thus be a private virtue, but it is the private virtue peculiarly exhibited by 'the public Soul' of 'Patriots, and of Heroes.'"[10] Reading about Cato occupies the speaker's winter months as a form of imaginary transhistorical male bonding and en-hances the civic meaning of the domestic environment. The republican reference tacitly establishes masculine cultural difference within the gen-teel rural household. If this marks the onset of a domestic ideology for men, then it is an ideology that arrives cloaked in the intimate patriotism of the republic.

Thomson's *Summer* (1727) raises the ghost of Cato once again, but this time the fantasy is different. Africa provides retirement of another kind, an exotic but stark refuge for the enemies of tyrants. It is Cato and Liberty who have "retired," in this instance, *to* the sun-drenched wasteland of republican tough love, not *from* the city to the country or from the wintry landscape to the hearth:

> E'en here, into these black abodes
> Of monsters, unappall'd, from stooping Rome
> And guilty Caesar, Liberty retired,
> Her Cato following through Numidian wilds:
> Disdainful of Campania's gentle plains,
> And all the green delights Ausonia pours;
> When for them she must bend the servile knee,
> And fawning take the splendid robber's boon.[11]

The aging Cato, caught between the "black abodes" of monstrous Africa and the "stooping" Romans who have acquiesced to Caesar amid the "green delights" of Italy, forms part of the allusive shorthand of *The Seasons*. Speculation on the tension between retirement and political action knits together the city and the country even as it drives them apart. The reflective subject identifies with the defiant libertarian and escapes the futility of both "winter-gloom" and "stooping Rome." In the process, civil liberty and domesticity collaborate in a literary tradition in which reproductive life provides a sanctuary for masculine moods. Rendered with varying degrees of compression, such scenes migrate across the century from drama to verse, from the stage encampment to the literary cottage and back again.

In Love with Liberty

*I*n February 1704, a year after Addison first conceived of a play on the subject of Cato and almost a decade before that play embodied the most deeply felt sensations of its political moment, John Dennis's *Liberty Asserted* was staged at Lincoln's-Inn Fields. This proved to be a successful work by an independent author of Whiggish loyalties better known then and now for his critical writings.[12] Dennis sets the fraught masculine spirits of the Roman-style play in the midst of the imperial and tribal conflicts of North America's "middle ground."[13] *Liberty Asserted* had a good run, benefiting from the swell of national feeling following Marlborough's victory at Blenheim in August 1703. The first crushing defeat of the French by a British general in two generations, Blenheim was a turning point in the War of the Spanish Succession—a conflict intertwined with changing Indian alliances and French and British policies in North America. Dennis blasts the French in his preface while showing them considerable tolerance in the play itself. *Liberty Asserted* achieves a high pitch of nationalist sensibility by placing the contest between the French and the British and the fluctuations of Native American diplomacy within the confines of a multiethnic, multinational family.

Dennis was one of the first to shape republican narratives to the geopolitics of North America, though he could and did build on seventeenth-century Indian plays set in South or Central America and the Caribbean.[14] With no apparent investment in historical accuracy, his play nevertheless captures several important realities of the confluence of the Huron-French and Iroquois-English alliances.[15] More significantly, the cross-national, cross-racial friendship between a pair of virtuous, affectionate men is tested against fierce maternal adherence to the national identity of the father.

The "Dramatis Personae" of *Liberty Asserted* reveals the blend of historical and generic elements in Dennis's play. Frontenac (1620–98), the governor of New France, is a character firmly located in the recent past. Frontenac presided over French success in "King William's War" of 1689–97, the play's historical milieu and a branch of the European War of the Grand Alliance settled by the Treaty of Ryswick in 1697. The portrayal of Frontenac's love life is wholly imaginary, however. The names of Miramont and Beaufort, the high-minded exemplars of ideal French and English manliness respectively, are straight out of Restoration comedy. The Native American characters are from different tribes—the Iroquois, the Hurons, and a tribe referred to as the Angians (*CW* 1 : 323). The Native Americans have names that sound like stage Turks or Moors: Ulamar, Zephario, Arimat, Sakia, and (even more implausibly), Irene. Dennis plunks complex North American material into a ramshackle version of the sentimental Roman conspiracy play. Captivity, intermarriage, and European primogeniture explain concealed or confused identities. *Liberty Asserted* shows that the Roman play and colonialism are made for each other. The Roman drama that pits reproductive against homosocial relations, and sets both against abstract law, could tell a story set in any contested terrain.

Dennis's drama is nationalistic, virulently anti-French and anti-Jacobite, and supportive of Queen Anne and the Tory Marlborough. Characteristically reminding his audience that his writing is independent of any political party, Dennis insists that *Liberty Asserted* is not "a Party Play." His goal, he says, was to write for "ev'ry person in *England,* excepting those who are wishing for a French Government or contriving to bring it in" and "to animate our *English* against the *French*" (*CW* 1 : 321–23).[16] Dennis's fierce defense against the anticipated charge of party bias reveals the vexed role of sentiment in the claim to public virtue. Dennis is the critic who would later complain that in *Cato* Addison's Stoics are insufficiently stoical, and that Cato, Juba, Marcia, and the rest "play the whining Amorous Milk-Sops" when they should be displaying "the undaunted invincible Resolution of an admired Assertor of Liberty." Insofar as Stoics are supposed to be impassive, they are poor candidates for tragedy, he would argue with reference to *Cato.* Insofar as they are passionate about freedom, they should not be making love (*CW* 2 : 49–55).

But Dennis's own interracial drama has a happy ending, justifying the mixture of patriotism and romance. "This Play" is not "writ for a Party" because its "Design . . . is to make Men in Love with Liberty," he writes. How? "[B]y shewing them that nothing can be more according to Nature." "Mr. *Lock*" has already proved this to the learned, but Dennis's demonstration, aimed at "ev'ry Understanding," relies for proof on "the most Tender of all Sentiments which Nature has implanted in the Minds of Men, and that is, the Love of their Children" (*CW* 1:321). To late twentieth-century readers, the resort to family values as the litmus test of citizenship and as the sign of universal intelligibility is instantly recognizable. The party of parents is the nation itself:

> The Party . . . that this Play was writ to oblige, are all those who have any concern for their Country, their Religion, their Relations, their Friends and their Children; and the Party it was writ against, are all those who care not one farthing for any or all of these. (*CW* 1:321)

The characters that Dennis presents, however, are no advertisement for untroubled domesticity. Geopolitical conflicts are intensified by being compressed into the narrow space of the family. The play tells the story of Sakia, a Huron woman who secretly married and had a child with a French officer. He vanished before she was handed over to the Iroquois with others of her people. During her twelve years in captivity, Ulamar, her son, has been assimilated to Iroquois ways. Since the Iroquois are allies of the English, Ulamar can enter the charmed circle of British masculine bonding in the Roman mode. Beaufort is a thoroughly unambivalent British officer whose passionate transnational friendship for Ulamar, whom he describes as "sent express from Heav'n / To civilize this rugged Indian Clime" (9), is fueled by an idealized vision of what Britain stands for.[17] Both Ulamar and Beaufort are in love with Irene, daughter of Zephari, an Angian. The Angians form one of the Iroquois "nations"; thus they are friends of Britain and enemies to the French and their Huron allies. Irene is awarded by her father and a council of British and Iroquois leaders to the bravest man, deemed to be Beaufort. Knowing she loves his friend, Beaufort nobly disclaims his marital privilege. Because friendship is only possible in the pure absence of coercion, liberty and manly affection signify each other.

The rest of *Liberty Asserted* consists of delayed revelations of racial and national identities. Sakia, Ulamar's Huron mother, holds nothing back in staking the claims of race and blood through emotional blackmail, complaint, secrecy, and rage. But her claims unfold slowly in a way that allows the doubled identities of European nation and allied Native American

tribe to torment everyone in turn. For the first half of the play Sakia tries
to sabotage the marriage of Ulamar to Irene on the grounds that this
match will pit Ulamar decisively against his Huron heritage. She speaks
on behalf of not only the oppressed Hurons but also the French, to the
point of disclaiming her own maternity: "my Son, who thinks himself a
Huron / . . . / No Huron is, nor of Canadian kind; / . . . he descended
of a Christian Sire, / . . . / French is his Nation, *Miramont* his Name"
(1.5.21–29). Sakia finds herself trapped in her knowledge of the layers of
false consciousness brought about by cross-racial love and feigned, then
real, captivity:

> In secret *Miramont* and I were match'd,
> And thrice three Years in Bonds clandestine liv'd;
> In secret too I brought forth *Ulamar;*
> And for three Years in private was he nurst,
> And five I bred him with me as my Slave,
> By *Miramont* presented to my Father,
> And then your Angians made us real Captives. (1.5.57–63)

Sakia had sworn to her husband, Miramont, that "when my Ulamar arriv'd to Manhood, / I ne'er would wed him to an Indian Maid" (1.5.123–
24). Ulamar's betrothal to Irene provokes Sakia's maternal curse on them
both in accordance with that vow. Sakia, who emerges as the defender of
one native people against another, also has to block her son's Indian romance on behalf of his unknown French blood.

Just as Addison's Juba will identify with Rome as the domain of universal reason, Ulamar has internalized British values, above all the belief
in "the Dignity of Human Nature." He calls Angia "my country" because
it bears the British seal of approval:

> For ever blest be that eternal Pow'r
> That gave me a human comprehensive Soul,
> That can look down upon all narrow Principles.
> For every brave Man's Country is the Universe,
> His Countrymen Mankind, but chiefly those
> Who wish the Happiness of all the rest,
> And who are friends to all their Fellow Creatures:
> And such are all the brave Iroquois Tribes,
> Such are th' unconquer'd English, free themselves,
> And loving all who actually are free. (2.2.48, 21, 35–44)

Told by his mother that "among the French too thou might'st find
Relations," Ulamar assumes that she uses the word "Relations" in a figu-

rative Enlightenment sense: "'Tis true we . . . all descend from one eternal Sire" (2.1.79–81). It takes Sakia's long maternal complaint in Act 3 over her condition as "a mournful Widow and a Slave" to convince Ulamar to suppress his idealistic loyalties and to work for a "solid peace" with the French-Huron alliance:

> From thy dear Father I have long been torn
> And kept a mournful Widow and a Slave
> In insupportable Captivity,
> Disconsolate, forlorn, and desolate
> Among my Barbarous and Insulting Foes . . .
>
> . . . .
>
> Thou hast refus'd to dry thy Mother's Eyes,
> But prov'st a cruel and a bitter Child to me,
> Untouch'd by all my Grief, umov'd by all my Love. (3.1.153–
> 57, 162–64)

Ulamar, the Iroquois, the French, and the Hurons come to terms when the French concede that their recent aggression arose from "a rash private act" by a French officer lusting after Irene. Only the British paragon, Beaufort, will have none of it, accusing Ulamar of giving in to an equally rash private impulse in yielding to his mother. Ulamar has imitated the worst of European culture, the finicky Beaufort charges:

> Ay, This is what has Captivated *Europe,*
> When their Domestick Interest most prefer
> Before the Weal and Honour of their Country,
> Tho' private good on publick Weal depends,
> And he who for his House betrays his Country,
> Betrays his Family, Betrays his Children,
> All his Posterity to shameful Ruin,
> And makes them Poor, Precarious, Abject, Base. (3.6.21–28)

Beaufort and Ulamar's friendship breaks up on the shoals of a debate about family values and public policy. Miramont betrays the truce and attacks Ulamar on the detested orders of the French king. Ulamar is reluctantly condemned to death, and he and Irene argue—in the best tradition of neoclassical drama—over who ought to commit suicide first. What no one knows until the last minute is that Miramont was the name of a younger son. In one of the miraculous transformations made possible by continental patriarchy, when he inherited the estate his name changed to Frontenac. Finally Frontenac, whom Sakia has known as Miramont, and Sakia, whom Frontenac has known as Nikaia, come face to face, clarifying who is who. Frontenac dispenses with the royal orders with a flourish: "Ha! / Perish all Tyrants; and their black Commands!" (5.7.66–67). A moderate French revolution takes place in Canada, as Frontenac, Ulamar, and Beaufort join in a Whiggish triumph over "Lewis" and "the wretched *French*," who "For Fifty rowling Years . . . / Have to their Tyrants Sacrific'd their Sons" (5.8.12–13).

The cross-racial, transatlantic nuclear family is reunited through the complex politics of the French and British empires and their Indian allies. Masculine sensibility is concentrated in the son whose typically ambivalent role is doubled: his Huron French parentage represents one international alliance; his Anglo-Iroquois friendship and romance represent another. He needs to effect a quadruple alliance to stay alive. The potential for parricide (he keeps saving the Frenchman he thinks is his father) and for suicide (he faces sacrificial death under French law) have to be fended off continuously. Often fantastic, the play still acknowledges the reality of captivity and assimilation. But within the magical domain of dramatic brotherhood, imperial inequality is translated into equality: Ulamar, the native, is raised up in order for Beaufort to have a friend, but in such a way as to amplify the torments of mixed race, mixed loyalties, and mixed feelings.

I have stressed the conventions that Dennis's play shares with *Lucius Junius Brutus*, *Cato*, and *Sophonisba*. But it has just as much in common with Sarah Wentworth Morton's long poem, *Ouabi; or, the Virtues of Nature* (1790), on which I focus in chapter 5. Morton was a member of an elite Boston family, an avid supporter of the American Revolution, an opponent of slavery, and a defender of Native Americans. Her poem concerns a love triangle comprising a pair of Illinois lovers, Ouabi and Azakia, and a fugitive European, Celario, whom they encounter amid hostilities between the Illinois and the Hurons. The story is bracketed off from the history of European expansion in North America. There are no French or English officers roaming the woods, only a single melancholy white man. Nonetheless, Celario is a literary cousin of Ulamar and Massinissa: he embodies republican virtue by suffering no abatement of his affection to both his mistress and his friend. The character caught between multiple national or ethnic loyalties expresses longing for the reconciliation of civic and heterosexual love. His conflicts are layered one upon the other in a hyperbole of emotional torment. The fact that such predicaments are narrated or performed in drama and verse for a century or more suggests that this transgeneric practice forms part of an Anglo-

American international fantasy within which both British and American national subjectivities coalesce.

"Great in Ruin"

*E*dward Young's renowned book-length poem, *The Complaint: or Night-Thoughts on Life, Death, & Immortality,* published in stages between 1742 and 1745, is a genuinely insomniac production.[18] *The Complaint* represents the high-water mark of eighteenth-century nocturnal masculine sensibility in the mode of *penseroso* piety. Young's pathos was already evident in his *A Poem on the Last Day* (1713), which exhibits a taste for tombs, night, and melancholia.[19] But Young's absorption in the deathbed of the virtuous man also descends in some measure from his tragedy, *The Revenge,* successfully staged in 1721. Preceding *The Complaint* by more than twenty years, *The Revenge* zeroes in on the emotional nexus of male friendship and mourning. A variant of *Othello,* the play focuses on a vindictive, racially marked, and subjectively injured protagonist. Young joins Othello's African identity to Iago's resentful position, eliminating the role of the sensitive native except as a means of deception. Despite Young's reliance on the full repertoire of dramatic conventions associated with civic value, this tragedy is populated by men obsessed with themselves, not with the general good. In *The Revenge,* Young is less interested in liberty or citizenly ethics than in masculine self-absorption. This reflexive preoccupation is not an expression of mere vanity, however. The stoic position becomes a moment, phase, or mood, rather than being embodied in a person. There is no Cato, Brutus, or Scipio in *The Revenge,* only a triangle of men who take turns being controlled, enraged, abject, and mournful. The ideal of disinterestedness and stoic rigor is voiced repeatedly but is not assigned to any single character.

The action is set in Spain, six years after the Spanish victory over the Moors. Despite the derivative feel of the plot, it is based on the story of an actual murder committed in Spain and recounted by John Hughes in *The Guardian* in 1713.[20] The protagonist is Zanga, whose identity as a Moor includes religious, racial, and territorial dimensions.[21] Zanga's origins partly resemble Juba's in Addison's *Cato.* But whereas Juba's Moorish father admired Rome and desired his son's Roman education, Zanga's royal Moorish father fought the Spanish, giving his son a legacy of resistance against "Proud, hated *Spain!*" (2.1.172). All the fragile male contestants in *The Revenge* are consumed with honor as the essence of masculine well-being, and assaults across status lines are insupportable. Zanga is most enraged not over his capture in battle by the Spanish general, Alonzo, or the death in combat of his father at Alonzo's hands, but by Alonzo's thoughtless blow, an arbitrary abuse of the slaveholder's absolute power.

Alonzo's best friend is Don Carlos, whom he has freed from Moorish captivity. Carlos celebrates how, in victory, Alonzo's "godlike Arm / Has made one Spot the Grave of *Africa*," and Alonzo reciprocates: the "cruel Chains" binding Carlos "Inflam'd me to a Rage unknown before" (1.1.217–18, 222–23). While Carlos "groan'd in Bondage," he "deputed" Alonzo to be his "Advocate in Love" to Leonora (1.1.88–90). Inevitably, Alonzo and Leonora fall in love. Heterosexual love competes with masculine friendship, as Carlos learns:

> I love fair *Leonora* . . . .
> Yet still I find (I know not how it is)
> Another Heart, another Soul for thee.
> Thy Friendship warms, it raises, it transports. (1.1.225–28)

Yet precisely because Alonzo gave Carlos "Liberty and Life," the pure disinterestedness of male friendship does not permit Alonzo to ask for Leonora in exchange: "it so resembles a Demand, / Exacting of a Debt, it shocks my Nature" (2.1.148, 151–52). Alonzo and Carlos are locked together in a phobic reaction to inequality. Leonora, given perhaps the quintessential line of eighteenth-century sensibility, "I shall blush to Death" (1.1.377), weeps with Alonzo over the conflict between their love for each other and their loyalty to Carlos, a conflict that they agree will kill them.

Zanga, like Iago, plans his vengeance in strict accordance with the protocols of mutual manly affection. He vows "to persuade / *Alonzo* to request [Leonora] of his Friend, / His Friend to grant—then from that very Grant, / The strongest Proof of Friendship Man can give, / . . . to work out a Cause / Of Jealousy" (2.1.83–88). Zanga calls on Alonzo to sacrifice Leonora to virtue's standard in the Roman fashion of "doing Right in stern Despight to Nature" (4.1.405–9). In the end, Alonzo waffles, Leonora kills herself, and Zanga exultantly reveals that he, the Moor, is the author of Alonzo's phantasmic torments. Zanga, who has turned the Roman ethos of stoical sacrifice into a call for murder, draws on the lexicon of liberty, nation, and race in his moment of triumph:

> Let *Europe* and her palid Sons go weep,
> Let *Africk* and her Hundred Thrones rejoyce.

> O my dear Countrymen! Look down, and see,
> How I bestride your prostrate Conqueror!
> I tread on Haughty *Spain,* and all her Kings. (5.384–88)

In Young's career, tragic drama and the poetry of sensibility are shaped by common motives: masculine friendship amplified by emotional self-absorption, stoic virtue in the grip of fatality, and the performance of freedom worth weeping over. In *The Complaint,* the poet unfolds his "philosophy of tears." If "to feel is to believe," then religious reflection and emotional self-investigation inspire not just a philosophy, but a mental archaeology of tears:

> Hast thou descended deep into the breast,
> And seen their Source? If not, descend with me,
> And trace these briny Riv'lets to their Springs.[22]

The Complaint was written under the impetus of three deaths in Young's immediate family. "Thy shaft flew thrice" (1.213) striking Narcissa, Lucia, and Philander, code names for Elizabeth Lee, Young's stepdaughter, who died in 1736; his son-in-law Henry Temple, who died in 1740; and his wife, the former Lady Elizabeth Lee, who died in 1741. *The Complaint* evokes an apparitional wasteland, "*Woe's* wide empire," where suffering calls forth "generous Sorrow" (1.291, 300). In the course of Young's sustained *momento mori* in response to the experience of serial deaths, the poet's closeness to his son-in-law becomes the occasion for a dramatization of the emotional logic of masculine friendship. The elegy for Henry Temple, or Philander, zeroes in on that Anglo-Roman specialty, the "*Deathbed* of the Just" (2.615). This scene compresses and revives the homosocial ethic of Roman plays, carefully extracted from the framework of imperial geopolitics.

Night 2 of *The Complaint,* "On Time, Death, and Friendship," is devoted to four subjects: *"Time's wondrous price, / Death, Friendship,* and *Philander's final Scene"* (2.16–17). The poet mourns Philander because the heart of their friendship was the social discourse that has saved Young from thoughts that "Stagnate," rust, or form a "learned scum" on the surface of the mind's "standing Pool" (2.466, 482, 486–87). Manly conversation and perambulation shaped a therapeutic friendship, the antidote to the mind's self-referential excess:

> How often we talk'd down the Summer's Sun,
> And cool'd our Passions by the breezy stream?
> How often thaw'd, and shorten'd Winter's Eve,

> By Conflict kind, that struck out latent Truth;
> Best found, so sought; to the *Recluse* more Coy! (2.447–55)

A young man is mourned by his grief-stricken mentor: "I lov'd him
much; but now I love him more" (2.596). Not surprisingly, such feelings
lead the speaker to the mortal scene itself, because tenderness between
men can be earned by the spectacle of a brave death. I say *spectacle* advis-
edly, since the scenic challenge begins as a test of poetic mettle but concludes as a dramatic accomplishment.

> Man's highest Triumph! Man's profoundest Fall!
> The *Deathbed* of the Just! is yet undrawn
> By mortal hand. (2.614–16)

Performed in the "Chamber where the Good Man meets his Fate,"
the drama transforms Philander, first, into a living "Lecture," and then
into a republican hero whose self-sacrifice defeats the tyrant, death
(2.631, 647). Cato's stoical suicide modulates here into a death from
which violence is excluded and in which the aura of virtuous agency
alone is retained. This scenario is profoundly gratifying to the poet's desire to amaze himself. Philander's "shrine" doubles as a "temple" for the
poet's "theme" as the charisma of the stage Stoic is imported into the
poetry of psycho-religious meditation: "Is it his Deathbed? No; It is his
Shrine,"

> The Chamber where the Good Man meets his Fate,
> Is privileg'd beyond the common Walk
> Of *virtuous* life, quite in the verge of Heaven
>
> .   .   .   .
>
> If sound his Virtue; as *Philander*'s sound.
> Heaven waits not the last moment, owns her Friends
> On this Side Death; and points them out to men,
> A Lecture, silent, but of sovereign Pow'r!
> To Vice, Confusion; and to Virtue, Peace. (2.629, 631–33,
> 644–48)

A line or two later Philander's majestic virtue carries us from the poem
into the realm of Roman tragedy on the British stage. Like all true antityrannical exemplars, Philander is "Great in Ruin"—like Rome itself—
and "closes with his fate" in a display of stoical agency that makes other
men weep:

> *Virtue* alone has Majesty in Death;
> And greater still, the more the Tyrant frowns.

. . . .
His Comforters He comforts; Great in Ruin,
With unreluctant Grandeur, *gives*, not *yields*
His Soul Sublime; and closes with his Fate.
How our Hearts burnt within us at the Scene! (2.649–51,
672–75)

In *The Complaint,* there are very few gestures toward the nation or the civic realm. Even in Young's writings for the stage, the state is not the issue. Death, not Caesar, is the tyrant in *The Complaint,* though a hint of sacrificial loss clings to the young man who dies before the older one. Retirement has a geographical dimension—*The Complaint* is a deliberately provincial poem—but mostly Young retires into a certain kind of expressive time. The experience of serial death within the family and the flood of words and thoughts associated with that experience engage the moods of reading and writing in repetitive affective cycles: "I loved him much, and now I love him more." In 1719 Young had reported on Addison's deathbed scene. The poignancy of the moment is not lost on Young's biographer:

Addison . . . died in peace. The history is well known: how on his deathbed, "life now glimmering in the socket," he sent for his stepson, the Earl of Warwick, forcibly grasped his hand and softly said, "See in what peace a Christian can die." And this story comes from Young.[23]

"*Ponteach* I Am, and Shall Be *Ponteach* Still"

*I*n 1759, General James Wolfe is said to have recited a poem on the eve of his victory over Montcalm at Quebec—the eve of his own death. In the account of this performance we find again the familiar link between the poetry of sensibility and the tenderhearted hero in the company of his affectionate followers. This time, they are joined together in a real action, though one stylized both at the time (assuming the episode occurred at all) and in retrospect:

[Wolfe's] ruined health, the gloomy prospects of the siege, and the disaster at Montmorenci, had oppressed him with the deepest melancholy, but never impaired for a moment the promptness of his decisions, or the impetuous energy of his action. He sat in the stern of one of the boats, pale and weak, but borne up to a calm height of resolution. Every order had been given, every arrangement made, and it only remained to face the issue. The ebbing

tide sufficed to bear the boats along, and nothing broke the silence of the night but the gurgling of the river, and the low voice
of Wolfe, as he repeated to the officers about him the stanzas of
Gray's "Elegy in a Country Churchyard," which had recently
appeared and which he had just received from England. Perhaps,
as he uttered those strangely appropriate words.—
    "The paths of glory lead but to the grave,"
the shadows of his own approaching fate stole with mournful
prophecy across his mind. "Gentlemen," he said, as he closed his
recital, "I would rather have written those lines than take Quebec
tomorrow." [24]

Francis Parkman narrates Wolfe's performance of Gray's *Elegy* in the
Harvard historian's *The Conspiracy of Pontiac* (1851). In his nonfictional version of the eighteenth-century conspiracy drama, Parkman pauses to
celebrate Wolfe's exquisite masculine sensitivity and taste in reciting the
quintessential poem of sensibility, set off by stoic bonding in the imperial
interest. Parkman's rhetoric in this scene reminds us that the readers of
the 1850s still entertained an unchecked passion for manly pathos in the
civic vein.

The figure of Wolfe harks back to the quasi-Roman themes hinted at
in Gray's link between "glory" and "the grave." Elsewhere in the *Elegy*,
too, the republican tradition of Hampden, Milton, and Cromwell is
evoked in the image of the citizen-farmer who, "with dauntless breast /
The little Tyrant of his fields withstood" (57–58). Perhaps even more telling is the less defiant quality of melancholy affection bestowed upon the
nameless "Youth" in "The Epitaph." If *"Melancholy mark'd him for her own,"*
he was nonetheless generous and "sincere," emotionally delicate but not
antisocial (120–21). The juxtaposition of "tear" and "friend" as adjacent
end words miniaturizes a culture of tears (or of the single tear) as proof of
male homosocial affection: *"He gave to Mis'ry all he had, a tear, / He gain'd
from Heav'n ('twas all he wish'd) a friend"* (123–24). This tear is not shed for
the friend, but for the poor recipients of the Youth's emotional *"bounty,"*
who are collectively personified as *"Mis'ry."* Nonetheless, the tear of pity
authenticates in the domain of social inequality the sensibility that takes
the form of friendship when it operates in the realm of social equality.

The poetically minded General Wolfe serves as a foil for the title char-
acter of Parkman's history, Pontiac himself. Parkman depicts the Native
American leader as the embodiment of conspiratorial destructiveness. In
Parkman's account, Pontiac manages to exemplify *both* the literary figure

of the ruthless conspirator, like Renault of *Venice Preserved* ("I never loved these huggers") *and* the Africanist Syphax of *Cato,* defender of his race:

> Among all the wild tribes of the continent, . . . [c]ourage, resolution, address, and eloquence are sure passports to distinction. . . . it was chiefly to them, urged to their highest activity by a vehement ambition, that [Pontiac] owed his greatness. He possessed a commanding energy and force of mind, and in subtlety and craft could match the best of his wily race. But, though capable of acts of magnanimity, he was a thorough savage, with a wider range of intellect than those around him, but sharing all their passions and prejudices, their fierceness and treachery. His faults were the faults of his race; and they cannot eclipse his nobler qualities. . . . Revenge, ambition, and patriotism wrought upon him alike, and he resolved on war. (183, 186)

Parkman's conspiracy narrative features stories of native superstitions and gothic nights spent in "rough clearing[s] . . . illumined by the blaze of fires . . . casting their deep red glare upon the dusky boughs of the surrounding forest, and upon the wild multitude" (197). Pontiac is cast as "the Satan of this forest paradise," "the patriot hero," "champion of his race," and an exemplar of the "savage mind"—all on the same page (217).

"Parkman created a Pontiac to fit his dramatic needs," argues Richard White, "a chief to symbolize a people" in "a fundamentally racial struggle." In fact, White observes, as an historical event, "Pontiac's Rebellion was almost the reverse of the ultimate racial showdown Parkman imagined." With this more modest view of the rebellion, Pontiac has been reconceived by recent historians as "but a local leader." At the time, though, Pontiac was a larger-than-life figure. The British "magnified [his] power" and "made Pontiac the key to the peace that eluded them," until he was endowed with "nearly superhuman status." By 1768, Pontiac "was both the most famous Indian in the *pays d'en haut* and a man without a home."[25] As a *British* legend, the eighteenth-century Pontiac hovered between the character of the cultural outsider as Machiavellian villain and that of the doomed republican.

If British diplomats mythologized Pontiac even as they negotiated with him, Major Robert Rogers (1731–95), author of or consultant for some of Parkman's sources, approached the subject differently. Rogers gives a favorable account of Pontiac and a critical one of Europeans in North America, but challenges only British methods, not British goals.

Rogers improvised an opportunistic transatlantic life that sandwiched a few years of writing between the two halves of his career as soldier and explorer in British North America. *Ponteach,* a tragedy based on Pontiac's resistance or "rebellion," has always been attributed to Rogers, though he was almost certainly not its primary author. Published (but not performed) in London in 1766, the play juxtaposes the rhetoric of the conspiracy drama and low comic scenes exposing the crimes of French and English traders and settlers against the Indians. Rogers has been kept alive in cultural memory by military historians and reenactors fond of Kenneth Roberts's fictional *Northwest Passage* (1937), which recounts the adventures of "Rogers' Rangers" during the French and Indian Wars. A good fighter, Rogers tried to surf the political currents of the mid-eighteenth-century North Atlantic without much success. His career is worth a digression, for it shows precisely how imperial defense and administration could sanction cultural entrepreneurship.

Born in New Hampshire, Rogers joined the army in 1755 and commanded nine companies of rangers by 1758. He attacked and nearly wiped out the Indians of Saint Francis, Quebec, and in 1760 supervised the surrender of Detroit by French forces. Briefly pausing to marry Elizabeth Browne in 1761—his absences and failures to provide support are cited indignantly in her divorce petition of 1778—Rogers fought in the Cherokee War in North Carolina and returned to Detroit in 1763.[26] He quickly ran into the longstanding antipathy of the newly appointed General Gage, who refused to pay him on the grounds that he had been a volunteer, contravening Sir Jeffery Amherst's previous orders. At home in New Hampshire and unable to participate in the 1764 military campaigns, he speculated on tracts of land that were rendered worthless when the Crown awarded these areas to New York.[27] Rogers arrived in England in 1765.

In London, Rogers submitted a petition for a multiyear expedition to seek a northwest passage, proposing a budget of 32,000 pounds. He published in that same year two books on America at his own expense: his *Journals* and the more popular *A Concise Account of North America,* which contains an unusually sympathetic treatment of Native Americans. Both projects were probably assisted by Nathaniel Potter, an American minister whom Rogers had met in Boston, and also the prolific Dr. John Campbell of London.[28] While in London, Rogers accepted Benjamin Franklin's offer of recommendation; gained some favor through Charles Townshend (of the unpopular Townshend Acts), whose brother had died by his side; and was presented at Court.

Although in 1766 he was given the command of the British fort at Michilimackinac in northern Michigan, Rogers's luck proved ephemeral. Gage had him removed from the post and court-martialed in Montreal on charges of fiscal irresponsibility. Acquitted, he returned to England until 1775, when he arrived back in North America on the eve of the Revolution, probably to recruit supporters for the expedition. As Rogers traveled throughout the colonies during the next year, he was suspected of being a spy and confessed to being "exceedingly chagrin'd at my present Situation." He joined the British army in America in 1776, and his wife's divorce petition of 1778 refers to this act of disloyalty in tones that suggest that it was the last straw for their relationship. In 1780 Rogers sailed for England, where he died in London many years later.[29]

Elizabeth Rogers's petition throws the masculine world of transatlantic passage and cross-continental mobility into sharp relief. The exasperated voice of the *femme couverte* accuses Rogers of abandoning her for years on end, without making provision for her support, and of leaving her without the legal means to do business or to "change her situation":

> The last time your Petitioner saw him, which was about two years since, he was in a situation—which, as her peace and safety forced her *then* to shun & fly from him—so Decency *now* forbids her to say more upon so indelicate a subject. He has since joined the Ministerial Army—and so put it out of his power—even should he incline ever to return to this Town or to her again.[30]

The document thus concludes with Elizabeth Rogers's humiliation and embarrassment at her husband's unmentionable choice of national affiliation.

Ponteach or the Savages of America, A Tragedy appeared anonymously several months after Rogers had left London for America. It is a play inspired by a book review. The reviewer of the *Concise Account* for *The Critical Review* had praised Rogers's portrait of "the emperor Ponteack," remarking in the tones of a theatrical connoisseur that Pontiac "would appear to vast advantage in the hands of a great dramatic genius." The play was duly written—by someone—and attributed to Rogers, although he never represented himself as its author. *Ponteach* is a hybrid work, drawing on Rogers's *Concise Account* and on generic tragedies of conspiracy and patriotism. Having sparked its composition, the reviews had no use for the play. *Gentleman's Magazine* greeted its "scalpings and gore" with "abhorrence and disgust."[31] *The Monthly Review* deemed it "one of the most absurd publications of the kind that we have ever seen." It was a "great pity," opined the *Monthly* reviewer, blaming Rogers, "that so brave and judicious an officer should thus run the hazard of exposing himself to ridicule . . . in turning bard, and writing a tragedy." [32]

The play is absurd. But it is also telling. *Ponteach* combines bitter depictions of treacherous white hunters and traders with the motifs of British tragedies in the Roman style. Forty years after the staging of Dennis's *Liberty Asserted,* tragedy in the Roman vein still served in London as a vehicle for the exemplary Indian. This figure had long been conflated with the doomed republican and descended as well from the neoclassical glamour of the suffering native heroes in Dryden's *Indian Emperour* (1665) and Behn's *Oroonoko* (1688). Rogers's *Ponteach* emerges in the same historical moment as Wolfe's recitation of Gray, and as Gray himself—a long moment in which the language of Roman civic tragedy drapes stoic heroes, even contemporary ones.

Ponteach's position relative to the British is not unlike that of Cato facing Caesar's domination. Like Cato and Junius Brutus, Ponteach has two sons. This may be a matter of biographical accuracy, but it also conforms to the familiar tragic pattern: the sensitive, virtuous civic-minded son is duped and assaulted by the bloody-minded, nihilistic plotter. [33] Pontiac's life would have provided an impressive enough tragic death for the play, had it been written after his assassination by Peoria Indians in 1769. [34] The play's language even points toward such an outcome: "Better to die than be a Slave to Cowards . . . / Better to die than see my Country ruin'd." [35] But the play must deny Ponteach a hero's death in order to conform to well-known contemporary facts. At the same time that it repeats the conventions of the Roman republican tragedy, *Ponteach* becomes a vehicle for a bitterly farcical exposé of British greed, cynicism, and out-and-out Indian hating. The Indians are assigned the rhetoric of tragedy, while the British speak in crude colloquialisms.

The European characters include two traders (McDole and Murphy), two hunters (Honnyman and Osbourn), three "Governors" (Sharp, Gripe, and Catchum) and two garrison commanders (Colonel Cockum and Captain Frisk). The names alone are sufficient to convey the despicable behavior of the entire English contingent, motivated almost without exception by pure greed. The traders chortle to one another "That it's no Crime to cheat and Gull an *Indian*" and share trade secrets concerning rum and trick scales: "A thousand Opportunities present / to take advantage of their Ignorance" (1.1.29, 48–49). The hunters vent their frustration at being prevented from chasing "the savage Herd where-e'er they're found" and are inspired both by revenge ("They kill'd my Father and my eldest Brother") and by sheer loathing: "I abhor, detest, and hate them all, / And now cou'd eat an *Indian's* Heart with Pleasure" (1.2.25, 32–33, 38–39). These antisentimental predators despise in particular the Indian *complaint,* the language of protest arising from the experience of suffering. The "Complaints / Of Wrongs and Injuries, and God knows what" voiced by Ponteach on behalf of his people provoke the military men to curse the "damn'd bawling *Indians."* The complaint, indeed, is the vehicle of Ponteach's sovereign claims (1.3.1–3).

The English governors finally provide evidence in favor of the libertarian habit of blaming not the king but the king's ministers for the corruption of the state: "Here are we met to represent our King / And by his royal Bounties to conciliate / These *Indians* Minds to Friendship, Peace, and Love. / But he that would an honest Living get / In Times so hard and difficult as these, / Must mind that good old Rule, Take care of One" (1.4.1–6). The governors accordingly divide among themselves two thirds of the thousand pounds' worth of presents sent by the Crown to the Indians in order to "reconcile their savage Minds to Peace" (1.4.23). Later in the play, when Honnyman and his wife and children are captured by the Ottawa, the English hunter admits that he himself has brought torture upon his family. Honnyman, his wife greeted as "You Tygress Bitch! You Breeder up of Serpents!" by the nastier of Ponteach's sons, laments the absence of native sensibility: "Their brutal Eyes ne'er shed a pitying Tear; / Their savage Hearts ne'er had a Thought of Mercy." But Honnyman weeps repentantly, "unman'd" as he confesses, "I murder'd many of them, / And thought it not amiss." His wife registers appropriate moral horror and concedes, "we die as guilty Murderers" as "just Heaven's Vengeance / Pursues our Lives." Honnyman appeals to the Ottawa's "secret Pity" and "tender Passion" and Ponteach ultimately spares the woman and children, though not in a sentimental manner. Honnyman, however, is shown dying from *"various Instruments of Torture"* in the scene that so offended *Gentleman's Magazine* (4.3.76, 4.4.10–11, 56, 73–74, 84–86, 139–40, 190–200).

The figure of Ponteach, not always attractively or consistently, represents the values abandoned by the depraved English. These principles are couched in the familiar language of libertarian ideology: respect for national and individual rights, diplomatic integrity in negotiations between sovereign countries, the honor of the kingly station, representing the public good, and the pursuit of liberty to the point of just vengeance. Ponteach, unlike his republican predecessors on the English stage, has not defeated a domestic tyrant in the name of law and due process. His critique of tyranny rather takes the form of a small country's national defiance of massive imperial coercion. He expresses Indian pride, even an extreme haughtiness, as the essence of royal character: "Know you whose Country you are in? / . . . / This Country's mine, and here I reign as King" (1.3.2–5). Not surprisingly, Ponteach's speeches deploy a thoroughly European vocabulary of legitimation. The Ottawa war song, a stage direction specifies, is sung to the tune of "Over the Hills and Far Away" (3.3, p. 65). Ponteach aims "to secure / Our Country, Kindred, Empire, all that's dear, / From these Invaders of our Rights, the *English*" (2.2.38–40). Knowing full well that the British sovereign "like a God sits over all the World," he speaks the language of "Subjects" and "Redress," stirs up "patriot Shame" in the hearts of "ye Sons of antient Heroes," and claims his "Right to Empire" and his status as an "Ally" not a "Vassal" (3.1.126, 1.4.211–12, 3.3.49, 2.1.37–38).

Ponteach's major oration before the "Indian *Senate-house*" during the war debate culminates in the idioms of civic ideals that justify his more imperial claims: "Wrongs like these are national and public, / Concern us all, and call for public Vengeance." It is precisely in this speech that a British ethnographic fantasy of Native American life is set forth, a fantasy already lit by the pathos of "impending Wretchedness and Shame":

> Better to die than see . . .
>
> . . . .
>
> Myself, my Sons, my Friends reduc'd to Famine,
> Expell'd from hence to Barren Rocks and Mountains,
> To curse our wretched Fate and pine in Want;
> Our pleasant Lakes and fertile Lands usurp'd
> By Strangers, Ravagers, rapacious Christians. (3.3.88–89, 30, 21–28)

The conventions of British republican dramas define the figures of Ponteach's two sons as well. Like Titus and Tiberius in Lee's *Lucius Junius Brutus*, one, Philip, represents cruel cynicism given over to ruthless vengeance; the other, Chekitan, embodies the ethical sensibility that prefers romance to war. "Peace has its Charms for those who love their Ease," Philip sneers, "But active Souls like mine delight in Blood" (2.1.73). He mocks his brother's effeminacy: "Thou always wast a Coward, and hated War, / And lov'st to loll on the soft Lap of Peace. / Thou art a very Woman in thy Heart" (2.2.198–200). True to form, Philip conspires murderously against his father and his brother in order to sabotage the Indian alliance. Discovered in his treachery, he is killed by Chekitan, who then kills himself in despair at Philip's murder of his lover, Monelia.

The whole point of the sensitive son is undercut, however. The usual purpose of the contrast between the treacherous and the innocent sons is to provide a wrenching emotional test for their father, the republican hero who has successfully defeated the tyrant and reinstated the rule of law. The pairing of brothers poses the question: Will that law be applied impartially to the willful plotter and to the unwitting conspirator, his victim—that is, to the vicious and virtuous sons alike? Because Chekitan is not tricked into conspiratorial activity and because Ponteach is never forced to discipline him—thus proving his commitment to law over sentiment—the purpose of this plot device is mostly lost. Ponteach appears momentarily in the familiar role of the suffering father who disciplines his woe in order to devote himself to public values:

> Ye that would see a piteous wretched King,
> Look on a Father griev'd and curs'd like me.

But then he resolves: "'Tis not a Time to Grieve. / For private Losses, when the Public calls" (5.5.28–29, 34–35). He talks the talk of the stoic father but does not exercise sufficient agency in the death of his sons to acquire the charisma of a Cato or a Lucius Junius Brutus.

The play is not just poorly written. Its awkwardness results from the effort to combine the habits of republican drama and the truth of Pontiac's historical conflict with the British and Native American groups. At the end of the play, these contradictions come to the fore. Ponteach has lost the military contest, and therefore cannot speak as the grimly virtuous, stoic, and public-spirited Roman-style hero who will rule justly though he has lost his sons. Nor—bound as the play is to contemporary facts—can Ponteach commit suicide in the face of British victory. In his closing speech, addressed to the land itself in the absence of surviving followers, Ponteach displays the heroic temperament divorced from its home territory. He is denied the stoic choice between just rule or suicide, and consequently is fated to repeat, at ever-greater removes, the Indians' last stand:

> Ye fertile Fields and glad'ning Streams, adieu;
> . . . .
> I am no more your Owner and your King.
> But witness for me to your new base Lords,
> That my unconquer'd Mind defies them still;
> And though I fly, 'tis on the Wings of Hope.
> Yes, I will hence where there's no *British* Foe,
> And wait a Respite from this Storm of Woe;

> Beget more Sons, fresh Troops collect and arm,
> And other Schemes of future Greatness form;
> *Britons* may boast, the Gods may have their Will,
> *Ponteach* I am, and shall be *Ponteach* still. (5.5.87, 93–102)

Ponteach utters an elegy for lost territory and hegemony that divorces sovereignty from character. "*Ponteach* I am, and shall be *Ponteach* still," he concludes, but, like Cato, his "unconquer'd Mind" is consigned to the perpetual motion of exile. Unlike Cato, he cannot transform exile into moral victory through suicide. His mental motions, borne on the "Wings of Hope," allow us to glimpse a failed attempt to bring off the increasingly conventional linkages among sensibility and imagination, failure, eloquence, and Indians. The suffering Native American transcends his pain and stoically masters it by exerting mental energy. But by surviving, this individual almost becomes the object of sympathy.

CHAPTER FOUR

Female Authorship, Public Fancy

From Deathbed to Death Song

"*I*nvention is perhaps the most arduous effort of the mind," declares Judith Sargent Murray in "On the Equality of the Sexes" (1790). Claiming the arts and public life for women, Murray answers her own rhetorical question: "Is the needle and kitchen sufficient to employ the operations of a soul thus organized? I should conceive not." [1] Fancy is a female "creative faculty," specializing in "continual variation," "playfulness," "exuberance," and "prolifick imagination." Fancy is both a point of entry into the public culture of sensibility and a device for mapping power relations within the space and time of that culture. Fancy is crucial to the gendered poetics of race in the long eighteenth century, and it is worth moving carefully from one body of poetry to another in order to establish why that is so.

The works explored in the previous chapter are bound together by the scenic language of civic elegy shared across lyric and dramatic genres from 1704 to 1766. If we pause to look back over these texts and over the long span of time that they encompass, we discern the high standing of sensibility in writings by educated white men sixty years before Richardson's *Pamela*. We see how the story of Cato—the Stoic amid his sensitive sons and followers—was periodically resurrected. Cato's cameo appearances conferred legitimacy on the ambivalent emotions of an educated and usually Whiggish identification with the British metropolis. The master plot of the republican hero proved to be extraordinarily accommodating, extending not just to other Romans or their functional equivalents in tragic drama but also to the deathbed or graveyard scenes of eighteenth-century poetry by men.

But melancholia was not just associated with masculinity. It was also thoroughly conflated with the imagined subject of the internationally self-conscious nation and its margins. The literary history of eighteenth-century masculine pathos was demonstrably inseparable from the racial imagination of a colonial and imperial culture. Sensitive subjectivity could be represented as either British (or Roman, or European) or Native American (or African, or Arab). The attribution of deeply felt suffering to racial "others" was critical to the dissemination of sensibility after the

Treaty of Utrecht in 1713. Racial, ethnic, and national differences became efficient vehicles for translating sensibility into narratives of inequality. The ideological malleability of sentiment, as a relationship available to conservatives, liberals, and radicals of the right and the left, relies on the ubiquity of race. Race and empire, then, are key factors in the story of how sensibility becomes central to the historical vision of women poets.

That sensibility is a transaction, not a character type, is never more clear than the way in which it is distributed on both sides of interracial encounters and portioned out to the dying man, or his friend, or both. The whole encounter is charged with the intimate tension of social equality—equality that often registers the struggle to invest narratives of cross-racial imperial relationships with the legitimizing rhetoric that evokes friendship between peers. Sensibility inspired by manly death joins empire to elegy. This is especially important in the close connections in eighteenth-century literary texts between elegy and Indians. The British fascination with the Native American "death song" fused the lyric mode with the figure of the "vanishing Indian." The violence of European occupation is rewritten as conveniently voluntary deaths or removals undertaken by native inhabitants themselves. The literary Indian suffers or elects his (or occasionally her) own death, and the song that bears his spirit forth blends stoicism with pathos—especially when sung during torture.

The Indian death song thrived among British and Euro-American poets in the late eighteenth century, and a rigorous study of the genre's origins in response to early ethnographic feedback from traders and missionaries would certainly yield even earlier examples. Literary death songs were composed by female poets about male Indians and by male poets about female Indians. They formed part of a cluster of lyric types that include Indian songs other than death songs and lyrics that rely on the persona of the Indians' white captive. Hester Thrale Piozzi recorded Anne Hunter's "North American Death Song, Written for, and adapted to, An Original Indian Air" in her journal in 1782.[2] This is the well-known and much-circulated song of Alknomook performed by the female lead in Royall Tyler's drama of the Early Republic, *The Contrast*, having apparently made its way from London to New York.

Hunter's lyric expresses Alknomook's defiance under torture, and his pathos-laden refusal to speak the language of pain or lament. The refrain is a series of variations on "the son of Alknomook will never complain." The son of Alknomook reminds his Indian enemies of his ruthless exploits against them, but the song ends with gestures of filiopiety, friendship, and stoicism rewarded:

> I go to the land where my father is gone,
> His ghost shall rejoice in the fame of his son:
> Death comes like a friend to relieve me from pain;
> And thy son, O Alknomook, has scorned to complain.[3]

In the 1802 preface to *Lyrical Ballads*, Wordsworth recalled his interest in tracing how "maternal passion" "cleave[s] in solitude to life and society" when composing his 1798 poem, "The Complaint of a Forsaken Indian Woman." For Wordsworth, "maternal passion" is a form of affective projection, a social expression of fancy that is receptive, as this lyric shows, to the genre of complaint. This poem arose, Wordsworth explained, from having read "with deep interest" Samuel Hearne's *Journey from Prince of Wale's Fort in Hudson Bay to the Northern Ocean* (London, 1795). The speaker of the poem, "unable to continue" her journey with her "companions," is left to recover or die, as Wordsworth's ethnographic note states. She oscillates between stoicism—"No pleasure now, and no desire. / Then here contented will I lie! / Alone, I cannot fear to die"— and mourning her parting from her "poor, forsaken Child":

> I should not feel the pain of dying,
> Could I with thee a message send;
> Too soon, my friends, ye went away;
> For I had many things to say. (lines 18–20, 65, 47–50)[4]

Wordsworth's poem shows the close affiliation of the deathbed scene and the figure of the Native American with the power of fancy. A favorite form of eighteenth-century lyric action, fanciful thinking or meditative projection is compatible with loss as well as with the pleasures of appropriation. The exotic vignette of the North American wilderness and the activity of fancy join forces, for example, in Charlotte Smith's *Elegiac Sonnets* of 1797 and 1800. Two of the sonnets turn on conceits derived from captivity narratives and other accounts of the North American wilderness. In Smith's "Sonnet LVI," "The Captive Escaped in the Wilds of America," the "breathless Captive," disoriented and terrified by "the war-whoop howl" in the distance, is shaken by every motion of the forest that "Speaks to his trembling heart of woe and death." The sestet introduces the image of a light at the end of the tunnel: "far streaming, a propitious ray" emanates from "some amicable fort." At the last minute—in the last line—and with a crucial "As," we learn that this has all been an elaborate conceit. The saved captive represents the English-woman's gratitude toward her friend: "He hails the beam benign that guides his way, / *As I*, my Harriet, bless thy friendship's cheering light" (emphasis added).[5] Danger becomes figurative, not literal, and the protagonist turns from a man into a woman. The speaker, it turns out, has worked herself up to a gothic fantasy of capture, escape, pursuit, and rescue.

"America" is the setting for a similarly overwrought mood—a mood in which racial images float to the surface of the mind—in Smith's "Sonnet LXI," "Supposed to Have Been Written in America." The sonnet is a precursor of Poe's "The Raven," tracing the speaker's hysterical reaction to the call of an "Ill-omen'd bird." The state of "shuddering fancy" yields the image of a susceptible Native American, signifying the speaker's powerful imagination of exotic scenarios and also drawing on the Indian as a trope of pathos. The bird is heard by "the Indian" as well as by the speaker, and this phantasmic Indian, too, is overcome by the "Dark dread of future evil":

> O'er my sick soul thus rous'd from transient rest,
> Pale Superstition sheds her influence drear,
> And to my shuddering fancy would suggest
> Thou com'st to speak of every woe I fear. [6]

These lyrics by Hunter, Wordsworth, and Smith show how both male and female poets absorb the cluster of related terms that includes the Stoic, the Man of Feeling, and the Indian. They also reveal how a poem can slip from a commitment to the discourse of Whiggish civic sensibility to the condition of fancy, gothic atmospheres, and complaint. The slip occurs by way of elegy, for "the deathbed of the just" is genetically related to the literary "death song." Fancy forms a key part of the aesthetics and politics of sensibility. It represents subjectivity that is at once ungrounded—liberated from or deprived of territory—and mobile, committed to ambitious itineraries through international space and historical time. As a motion of escape and mastery, fancy lends itself to complex ambitions for public-minded poets of both sexes and of different races. As such, it plays a crucial role in the fundamental reorientation of sensibility to the needs of global culture. In order to understand the shifty politics of aestheticized emotion, I will focus in this chapter on recurring connections among race, melancholia, artfulness, and empire—all in relation to gender and the career of the woman poet. Because fancy is at the heart of this cultural matrix, I will emphasize the ways in which this faculty performs the management of sensibility.

"Sovereigns of the Regions of Fancy"

*B*y the late eighteenth century, fancy was well established as an inferior but therapeutic faculty. Definitions of fancy catalog verbs for operations performed on images and ideas: associating, collecting, combining, embellishing, mixing.[7] According to the usual explanations, fancy treats experience, including feelings, as material that can be managed but not transformed. It draws unsystematically on the processes of intellectual sorting that comprise the methodologies of the early modern human sciences. When accelerated, these pleasurable and empowering mental acts give fancy its dynamic structure. Fancy's rapid substitutions, in turn, give it its ephemeral or "airy" quality. As pure motion from one image to another, it claims no substance of its own, despite the materiality of the particular representations in which it deals.[8]

Recent studies of late eighteenth- and early nineteenth-century poetry have started to frame the period's aesthetic terms by historical contexts. This tendency has allowed critics to see "arrested violence" in the picturesque; to see in beauty a feminine reflection on imperial time; and, in my own contribution to this development, to see fancy as a way to negotiate tensions between high art and industrializing England.[9] But however well prepared, we are still not quite ready for fancy to flourish in the poetry of sensibility. For fancy appears to be exactly the antithesis of pity, the opposite of melancholia induced by collective guilt and systematic contamination. Fancy enjoys mimicry, the exotic, nomadism, displacement, strangeness, and hybridity. According to many characterizations of fancy, it typically dissociates these motions from their historical environments and manipulates the stuff of culture with facility and enjoyment. A purportedly victimless kind of imagination, fancy nevertheless enters into the texts of sensibility both as an antidote to melancholy and as a condition allied to pathos.

As a form of motion, fancy's spatial or geographical dimension connects it to the poetics of the prospect. The view from mental heights induces fancy to stage "the magnitude of prospect a rising empire displays" and then to entertain visions of imperial time ranging from elegy to celebration, from apocalypse to panegyric.[10] In these historical or geographical prospects, fancy meets politics. The mental trajectory of the fanciful poet dramatizes an engagement with historical process. Situated in retirement but ascending to survey international or even cosmic change, these speakers often rely on the conventions of the poetry of rural retreat in order to launch a more inclusive perspective. Panoramas of the progress of empire and of poetry, the big pictures of civilization's ebb and flow, bring into fancy's view vignettes of the national or racial other. And with the appearance of a stereotypical sufferer, fancy modulates into sensibility directed toward the alienated figure of the slave, the Indian, the oriental, the poor, the homeless, and—persistently combined with all these other identities—the female.

The texts of sensibility register the awareness of a political connection between pleasurable emotion and real suffering. In the tradition of literary victimization, melancholy combined with otherness leads to art. Indeed, we know that liberty, love, and suffering are invested so persistently in figures of the other by Anglo-American and European writers that such figures come to stand for emotion itself, while the specifically racial difference of the alien subject correspondingly diminishes. The mode of reflective address that reaches beyond the local situation to international subject matter and cosmopolitan audiences is as important to the dynamics of sensibility, therefore, as the pathos surrounding its familiar types of victims. The activities of "fancy," "reflection," "meditation," and "imagination" structure the reader's progress. While these choreographies of invention play a part in many poems that have nothing overtly to do with race, they are bound up even then with the speaker's desire to conceive a world and to move actively within it. The prospect typically furthers the quest for a reading audience or for critical respect earned by taking on public matters, including evangelism, abolition, and the early anthropology of Native Americans. In the geography of prospect and forest, therefore, fancy fuses imperial and lyric consciousness. In this imaginative economy, it is possible for the sensitive, fanciful poet to protest—against slavery, war, and religious intolerance—but it is by no means inevitable.

Fancy is available in different ways for male and female poets. Writing in the *Massachusetts Magazine* of March–April 1790, Murray conflated imagination and fancy in order to make a case for female mental power: "[S]uffer me to ask in what the minds of females are so notoriously deficient, or unequal. . . . The province of imagination hath long since been surrendered up to us, and we have been crowned undoubted sovereigns of the regions of fancy." [11] Some male writers, especially those who subscribed to a more familiar, romantic theory of the imagination, considered fancy a form of slumming, a trivial recuperative interlude with children, animals, the working class, and women. But for many writers of both sexes (Freneau, for example, and, later, Shelley), fancy retained the vertical, almost sublime associations implied by the phrase flight of fancy. Fancy became one idiom of authorial ambition by virtue of its metaphors of ascent and expansion. It could also serve the language of collective aspiration, including ambivalent or oppositional aspiration.[12] What, then, are the affinities between fancy and specific political content?

It would not be hard to organize this chapter like the preceding one, which connected drama in the Roman republican tradition to the eighteenth-century poetry of sensibility. Female intellectuals, like their male contemporaries, admired British Roman plays. Republican tragedy signifies cultural seriousness for Anna Letitia Barbauld in her early poem, "Corsica" (1773); for Judith Sargent Murray in her essays, "Panegyric on the Drama" and "Observations on the tragedies of Mrs. Warren" (1798); and for Mercy Otis Warren in her verse play, *The Sack of Rome*.[13] I stay focused on poetry, however, in order to introduce the category of fancy. Taking fancy seriously expands our understanding of the repertoire of sensibility over a long stretch of literary history. Because fancy is a mode in which gender dynamics are unabashedly overt, it allows us to examine the negotiations by female authors with masculine sensibility in politically serious poetry by women.

Anna Letitia Barbauld's first verse collection and Phillis Wheatley's only volume of poetry were both published in London in 1773. Both volumes were fostered or subsidized by sophisticated transatlantic cultural networks: in Barbauld's case, by the community of intellectuals centered in English Dissenting academies; in Wheatley's, by the Methodist circles of her Boston owners, the Countess of Huntingdon (her English patron), and evangelist George Whitefield, whom she eulogized. The idioms common to the poetry of Barbauld and Wheatley—specifically fancy—point to a broadly disseminated literary vocabulary that connects the growth of female authorship to racial politics.

Fancy in "Transatlantic Realms"

*B*arbauld's poetry demonstrates the way fancy can lead both to and away from questions of public policy. In many instances, her sensibility is more reflexive than social. What is other to the self takes the form of transcendental or descendental motion, an altered state of consciousness, the spirit's own spatial or temporal prospects. In "A Summer Evening's Meditation" (1773), the relationship between fancy and sympathy is narrated by a contemplative female speaker. Impelled by fancy's vertical energy, the speaker rises from the "green border of the peopled earth" past Jupiter's "huge gigantic bulk" and beyond to "the dim verge, the suburbs of the system," where Saturn presides "like an exiled monarch." [14]

In other poems by Barbauld, the structure of meditative action matches the drama of historical vision. Fancy brings before the reader vignettes of slavery, trade, and cultural transmission. In "A Summer Evening's Meditation," however, fancy leads lyric subjectivity through the cosmos in search of its own powers and limits. Here fancy finds vistas that connect it to epic aspiration through a resemblance to Milton's tours of space. But such extravagances, even in the poetry of retirement, link fancy to the history of Europe's geopolitical prospects, as well. There is a clear correlation between cosmic place and power relations: Jupiter is central and dominant; Saturn is dethroned and suburban, in the long-standing negative sense of "the suburbs." Even more striking than the political geography of center and suburb are the implications of another term, "the system." For sensibility is bound up with notions of interdependent structures and economies, the circulatory systems that no liberal author feels able to escape.

The culture of vicariousness includes experiences—of desire, projection, and substitution—that complicate the whole spectrum of subject positions. We are tempted to consider a writer like Barbauld to be almost within the system, while a writer like Wheatley is marginal to it. But, as R. Radhakrishnan has observed, both "mobilizing the inner/outer distinction" and choosing "radical relationality" pose problems for the late twentieth-century scholar.[15] We can extend this dilemma backward. The dynamics of eighteenth-century sensibility rely on the logic of center and margin while simultaneously incorporating both positions into a relational field.

"A Summer Evening's Meditation" dramatizes an encounter between the poetry of contemplation and the poetry of prospects. Fancy emerges from a fostering nocturnal environment to undertake a prospective mission. Such endeavors derive in part from Thomson's poetry of British prospects and polite indolence; they also descend from *Paradise Lost*, where elevated surveys are prophetic or satanic.[16] The action of "A Summer Evening's Meditation" centers on the figure of Contemplation. Emerging from her grotto, Contemplation directs the poet/speaker, who has already narrated the displacement of Apollo by an "impatient" Diana, to gaze on the night sky. "With radiant finger," Contemplation "points / To yon blue concave swelled by breath divine." When her "unsteady eye . . . wanders unconfin'd / O'er all this field of glories," the speaker describes the "spacious field" of starry "hieroglyphics" as a "tablet" that has been "hung on high / To public gaze." Human viewers are characterized collectively as the "public" that looks upon "the Master." The Master's directive specifies a required attitude: "Adore, O man! / The finger of thy God." The public, then—including the speaker—is defined by its distance from and attraction to elevated power. And in this gesture, the female poet refuses to be idiosyncratic by virtue of her sex and joins the general, or public, culture. Contemplation needs the authority of the celestial text in order to create a spatial arena vast enough for the subjective expansion that follows. The upward wanderings of the "restless and dazzled" eye require the "blue concave swelled by breath divine" (9, 23–24, 28–34).

But this vertical thought is followed by the downward gaze of maternal stars, "pure wells / Of milky light," "friendly lamps" that "light us to our home." The speaker is almost back where she began, in Nature's "thick-wove foliage," Contemplation's "lonely depth / Of unpierc'd woods." Down here the proper language is not the hieroglyphic text spread before the public eye. Despite the stars' mediation, the speaker, instead of intensely looking, is "[i]ntensely listening": "the raised ear . . . drinks in every breath" and hears nature's praise in the voice of silence itself and a "tongue in every star that talks with man." The starry tongues, perhaps, constitute a counterpublic to human viewers. "Wisdom mounts her zenith with the stars" and we expect the speaker to ride along. Deep space and deep time are now interior to the subject, however, or, in Barbauld's phrase, interior to "the self-collected soul":

> At this still hour the self-collected soul
> Turns inward, and beholds a stranger there
> Of high descent, and more than mortal rank;
> An embryo God; a spark of fire divine,
> which must burn on for ages, when the sun
>
> . . . .
> Has closed his golden eye. (36–39, 18–20, 46–49, 52–59)

This passage marks another surge of agency. Masculine fire is taken into the female subject. In this annunciation scene, the meditative faculty turns inward to behold an alienated self-image. The soul is pregnant with itself. But this fiery selfhood has to be a "stranger" of "high descent" in order to give the speaker genealogical access to the "ages." This strange son, the soul's soul, enables a passionately speculative episode.

Apostrophizing the "citadels of light" once more, the recharged speaker links herself temporally and spatially to them, imagining herself there rather than at home in the starlit plane of earthly nature: "Perhaps my future home, from whence the soul / Revolving periods past, may oft look back." But this hypothetical vista is inadequate to the soul's ambitions, and Barbauld collapses the time frame from the "future" to "now" in the next phrase: "O be it lawful *now* / To tread the hallow'd circle of your courts" (emphasis added). After a deferential nod to the "seats of Gods," the speaker gives herself over to fancy's most grandiose possibilities:

> Seiz'd in thought,
> On fancy's wild and roving wing I sail,
> From the green borders of the peopled earth,
> And the pale moon, her duteous fair attendant;
> From solitary Mars; from the vast orb
> Of Jupiter, whose huge gigantic bulk
> Dances in ether like the lightest leaf;
> To the dim verge, the suburbs of the system. (61–78)

Here, as in so many other fanciful poems of the period, "wild and roving" fancy generates figures of dancing and ethereality, with both of these compressed into the merely seasonal and almost weightless wind-driven leaf. We know this is still the aesthetic of fancy rather than the sublime because Jupiter's "huge gigantic bulk" is perspectively transformed into familiar diminutives.

The strength of the feminine lyric subject's ego rises and falls in relation to space and scale. Immensity is a trope for women's public ambition and for the doubts to which ambition is prone. Barbauld's fancy could not rove without a "gigantic" cosmos. In her tour of the "system," she passes one patriarchal form after another, from "solitary Mars" to Jupiter and finally "cheerless Saturn." Having passed these depressing hulks, the contemplative soul is further exhilarated: "fearless thence / I launch into the trackless deeps of space." Among "ten thousand suns . . . / Of elder beam," she reaches the first of two crises of confidence. "Here must I stop," she thinks, then asks, "Or is there aught beyond?" To ask about "aught beyond" is already to be in the grip of its "hand unseen," already a seer. And here the soul finds itself in a version of the womblike space that had represented subjective coherence at the beginning of fancy's galactic voyage. She is impelled onward

> To solitudes of vast unpeopled space,
> The desarts of creation, wide and wild;

> Where embryo systems and unkindled suns
> Sleep in the womb of chaos

Fancy travels through its own reproductive zone, its chaotic womb, where the systems that consciousness will continue to explore take shape. Passages like this make it difficult to determine what is internal and what external, what psychological and what "public" in this poem. And it is difficult not just for the twentieth-century reader, but also for Barbauld. Confronted with its own inside as the ultimate outside, or vice versa, the soul reaches its second, and decisive, crisis of confidence: "fancy droops, / And thought astonish'd stops her bold career" (75–81, 89–98).

In fact, fancy doesn't just "droop"; it all at once abases itself. "Where shall I seek Thy presence," she queries of "thou mighty mind!" Still disoriented, she wonders how, "unblamed," she is going to "[i]nvoke thy dread perfection?" The only thing the soul can be blamed for is its vertical approach to divinity, a conclusion verified by the rapidity with which the meditative speaker now places herself below the divine:

> O look with pity down
> On erring, guilty man; not in thy names
> Of terror clad; not with those thunders armed
> That conscious Sinai felt, when fear appalled
> The scatter'd tribes;

The poem concludes rapidly in a chastened and not much comforted key. The "bold career" of fancy reaches its limits when "thought" cannot go further back than the generative "desarts of creation." Creation marks the point of transgression, and the chaotic womb is superseded by a single origin, the "mighty mind." The speaker collapses "appalled" before the deity's "names / Of terror," then reminds divinity that it possesses a "gentler" internal voice of heart-intuited "whispers." The "soul, unused to stretch her powers / In flight so daring, drops her weary wing." She plants herself firmly in "the known accustomed spot" that sheltered the figure of Contemplation at the beginning of the poem. Here she will "wait" for death and immortality, when "splendors" of the "world unknown" will come to her, rather than she to them (99–122).

Barbauld depicts this expansive, rather secular mind as alternately bullied and lured into humility by the combined voices of Old and New Testament deities. But the initial shock comes when fancy encounters deep space. It is unclear whether it is the cosmic vacuum—"solitudes of vast unpeopled space"—or the cosmic "womb" and its plenitude of "embryo systems" that "stops" fancy cold. Since the "fearless" speaker has already braved "the trackless deeps of space," emptiness does not seem to be the problem. Rather, having traveled across the whole cosmos, the speaker confronts the source of future worlds in a kind of infinite regress, systems within systems. That abstract term, "systems," marks a conceptual limit of prospective meditation experienced as panic or extreme alienation. The fertile womb of deep space is feminine and nocturnal, like the groves from which fancy departed at the beginning of the poem. But the horizon of unfolding systems calls up the patriarchal "mind" and "word" that bar further speculation: "Thus let all things be, and thus they were." The tension between masculine authority and feminine ambition is played out in the field of cosmic perspectives. The idea of the system provides an opportunity for the woman writer to expand her scope, but then turns into a conceptual frame from which she cannot escape.

Barbauld entertains the class-inflected perspective for which the elevated view is the goal of educated thought. For her, this strategy offers access to or agency within a large cultural universe. Such agency can take the form of mobile spiritual cognition in "A Summer's Evening's Meditation," but this is not the only use to which fancy may be put by sensibility. And in her 1773 essay, "An Enquiry into those kinds of Distress which excite Agreeable Sensations," Barbauld clearly expresses her opinion that sensibility should be morally useful.[17] Fancy reveals the logic of human systems and economies in the culture of sensibility. "Epistle to William Wilberforce, Esq. on the rejection of the bill for abolishing the slave trade" (1791) is a critique of sentimental portrayals of slaves as victims. That is, Barbauld criticizes the antislavery campaign mounted by many women writers, among others, in the 1780s. She argues that the rhetoric of victimization has failed and should be replaced by the systematic logic of moral economy. She declares that the conventions of abolitionist sensibility are obsolete. They persist as structural elements of Barbauld's own revisionist alternative, but with a crucial shift in tone from pity to indignation.[18] Both pathos and protest share fancy's systematic overview and rely on emotion to establish the poet's right to cultural citizenship.

The "Epistle" opens with an exasperated catalog of speakers who have used the bodily rhetoric of sensibility on British audiences to no avail:

> The Preacher, poet, Senator, in vain
> Has rattled in [Britain's] sight the Negro's chain;
>
> .   .   .   .

> Forc'd her averted eyes his stripes to scan,
> Beneath the bloody scourge laid bare the man,
> Claim'd Pity's tear, urged Conscience' strong controul
> And flash'd conviction on her shrinking soul.

Barbauld's account of abolitionist writing makes clear the link between vicarious suffering and political criticism. Indignation causes abolitionists to torment their readers with depictions of "the Negro's" tormented flesh in order to coerce identification with the victim. The "scene of distress" "forces" the reader to gaze on the beaten slave and "assails" the audience with his groans. Barbauld characterizes the rhetoric of sensibility as itself a scourge that, like the whip, "lays bare" the suffering body of the reader. Barbauld values the language of Wilberforce and his allies insofar as it amplifies the groans and tears of slaves for the resistant British public. But, while praising the attempt to make the guilty suffer, she zeroes in on the shortcomings of rhetorical flagellation. Poetry designed to make the nation know slavery proved that knowledge, however visceral, is not enough: "She knows and she persists—Still Afric bleeds, / Unchecked, the human traffic still proceeds" (3–17).

Barbauld attributes the failure of sensibility to inspire legislative action to the systematic effects of slavery itself. Wilberforce's cause is hopeless in the face of Britain's immunity to feeling guilty. "Wit, Worth, and Parts and Eloquence"—poets, writers, and rhetoricians—have rallied to Wilberforce's cause: "All, from conflicting ranks, of power possest / To rouse, to melt, or to inform the breast." But against the language of "Avarice," the "Nation's eloquence" fails: "th'unfeeling sneer / . . . turns to stone the falling tear" and "[f]ar from the sounding lash the Muses fly." Sentimental representations of pain duel with conscious cynicism and lose: "In Britain's senate, Misery's pangs give birth / To jests unseemly, and to horrid mirth." "Seek no more to break a Nation's fall," Barbauld urges Wilberforce. Just give up. Britain has accepted itself as a profit-driven society, and against this self-knowledge, "[t]h'acknowledged thirst of gain," the appeal for vicarious suffering is useless (21–33, 85, 41–42, 117–18).

Barbauld prophesies Africa's revenge on Britain through the systematic, impersonal operations of empire. This retaliatory logic is set in motion by "Heaven's impartial plan," not by the "injur'd" themselves, despite the attribution of agency to the oppressed continent:

> injur'd Afric, by herself redrest,
> Darts her own serpents at her Tyrant's breast.

Each vice, to minds depraved by bondage known,
With sure contagion fastens on his own.

The suburbs of this system poison the capitol reflexively, through the numbed emotions and degraded appetites of the slave economy. The loop of vice and disease hastens the venom's progress through the body of Great Britain. Drawing on a familiar convention, Barbauld shows how slaveholding turns women into tyrants. The mistress embodies the "monstrous fellowship" of "Scythian, and . . . Sybarite," of "indolence to fierceness join'd." [19] The East Indian trade, meanwhile, evicts the figures of "Simplicity," "Stern Independence," and "Freedom" from rural England: "By foreign wealth are British morals chang'd, / And Afric's sons, and India's, smile avenged." [20]

Barbauld replaces the conventions of sensibility, which rely on vicarious emotion to induce pity, with the threat of contagious corruption. African slaves and colonized Indians become spectators, as England's free population sinks to the condition of slaves: "Shrieks and yells disturb the balmy air, / Dumb sullen looks of woe announce despair, / And angry eyes thro' dusky features glare" (44–49, 62–66, 101–6, 82–85). This process of role reversal or poetic justice seems to abandon moral judgment to the impersonal reflexes of economic logic. The shift makes possible a change of tone from pity, directed at generic victims, to prophetic, almost Blakean, exasperation. The "angry eyes" glaring out of the sullen faces of degraded British citizens mark the extent to which sensibility could be revised in the disinhibiting aftermath of 1789. The victim's body houses rage, not the slave's "constant tear."

Barbauld's most remarkable work combines the tense connection between sensibility and system with the power of fancy. It does so, furthermore, through an explicitly transatlantic vision. "Eighteen Hundred and Eleven" joins the strengths of "A Summer Evening's Meditation" and the "Epistle to Wilberforce." In "Eighteen Hundred and Eleven," the logic of systematic moral correction again prevails in declarations that irritated some of Barbauld's original readers: "Britain, know, / Thou who has shared the guilt must share the woe." [21] The speaker surveys the empire from India to "the Apalachian [sic] hills," evoking the spread of British culture "o'er transatlantic realms." When the visionary tour speeds up and shifts into an apocalyptic tone, Fancy materializes both to suffer and to stage the show, and finally to offer commentary on it. Weeping Fancy represents the fusion of sensibility and mental voyaging. Fancy, a sentimental reader or, perhaps, theatergoer, travels through time, which takes the form of "imaged" events.

> Where wanders Fancy down the lapse of years,
> Shedding o'er imaged woes untimely tears?
> Fond, moody power! as hopes—as fears prevail,
> She longs, or dreads, to lift the awful veil,
> On visions of delight now loves to dwell,
> Now hears the shriek of woe or Freedom's knell:
> Perhaps she says, long ages past *[sic]* away,
> And set in western wave our closing day,
> Night, Gothic night, again may shade the plains
> Where Power is seated, and where Science reigns;
> England, the seat of arts, be only known
> by the gray ruin and the mouldering stone;
> That Time may tear the garland from her brow,
> And Europe sit in dust, as Asia now. (83, 111–26)

The poem begins by detailing the contemporary Napoleonic wars and their human cost abroad and to British families at home. With the accusation of Britain's guilt, Barbauld starts to prophesy the future doom of the empire, moving between tones of rebuke, bitter fantasy, and elegiac regret.[22] She no longer refuses pathos, but embraces its theatrical power. With the long passage quoted above, increasingly agitated emotions find a vehicle in Fancy. Fancy's emotional volatility transforms prophecy into a series of competing fictions. Oscillating between "fond" or "moody" feelings—depending on whether hope or fear, longing or dread, delight or woe is "imaged"—the figure of Fancy abandons the narrator's dignified tonalities and overreacts. Her "untimely" passion over unrealized events climaxes in the vision of a new dark age, a "Gothic night." The trope refers both to the gothic genre of Fancy's sentimental trepidation and to the historical return of the feudal, or gothic, past. Fancy utters a vision of the orientalization of the West, relying on the topos of the progressive westering of empire that leaves lands further east in ruins: " 'Perhaps,' she says, long ages past away," Europe may "sit in dust, as Asia now."

After speaking as passionate historian in the British present, Fancy becomes the agent of American inspiration. And the thought of America brings with it a utopian scene of harmonious racial and ethnic variety. Ages hence, fanciful young Americans will tour the ruins of empire "just as our young noblemen go to Greece."[23] With "throbbing bosoms" and "musing mind[s]" but most of all with Fancy's "mingled feelings," these "wanderers" will visit the remnants of London. Animated by the fantasies of tourists, the lost capitol will be remembered as the center of an internationally dominant but generously multiracial empire. The mixed population of the city and the mingled feelings of the travelers both exemplify Fancy's heterogeneous aesthetic:

> The mighty city, which by every road,
> In floods of people poured itself abroad
> Ungirt by walls, irregularly great,
> No jealous drawbridge, and no closing gate;
> Whose merchants (such the state that commerce brings)
> Sent forth their mandates to dependent kings;
> Streets, where the turbaned Moslem, bearded Jew,
> And woolly Afric, met the brown Hindu;
> Where through each vein spontaneous plenty flowed,
> Where Wealth enjoyed, and Charity bestowed.

As Barbauld's retrospective, then prospective, narrative continues to unfold, history appears to be the random consequence of "changeful fancy." The "Spirit" that roams the earth, "Moody and viewless as the changing wind," governs the progress of empire in its passage through Babel, Egypt, and Troy (177, 187, 157–68, 215–17, 259–65). In a fine example of how historical prospects celebrate heterogeneity, then convert it into unity, a long passage surveying the complicated mix of cultures from Syria to Scandinavia climaxes in praise of modern British refinement.

At this juncture, Barbauld's "Spirit" acts in accord with teleological westerly movement. As "the Genius soars" toward South America—executing a striking swerve away from the devotees of British culture in North America—the systematic justice of imperial decay sets in: "Arts, arms, and wealth destroy the fruits they bring. . . . With grandeur's growth the mass of misery grows." As the Genius of history "pours through feeble souls a higher life," shedding its transcendental influence on "Andes' heights," "Chimborazo's summits," and La Plata's "roar," it seems to promise both cultural multiplicity and manifest destiny. The Genius "Shouts to the mingled tribes from sea to sea / And swears—Thy world, Columbus, shall be free" (315, 320–34). What kind of resolution is effected by these paradoxical lines, and in what tone? The Genius unifies "mingled tribes" through the imperial singular ("Thy world, Columbus"), but the energetic new world mix is never wholly homogenized.

The personified spirit of historical change has multiple relationships with the poetics of fancy, then. The personification itself is invented by Barbauld's fancy. The vistas of past empire created by fancy turn the faculty itself into a spectator, and fancy crystallizes briefly as the temporally fluid and overemotional audience of projected historical scenes. Britain's cultural heirs in North America exhibit a more temperate but still fanciful connoisseurship as they re-imagine, among London's future ruins, its present flawed glories. History itself, finally, is an artist in fancy's mode, insofar as it repeatedly creates empires out of "mingled tribes." Racial heterogeneity is a sign of health and energy for Barbauld, as long as she can channel the diverse, lively origins of great cultures into a single historical meaning. "Mingled tribes" are infused with the "higher life" of cultural purpose, with its intrinsic tendencies toward self-destruction.

Barbauld, who refused to take a stand in favor of female authorship, uses the language of fancy to engage the pathos of public time.[24] This strategy characterizes authors of both sexes who mourn the violence of the systems they analyze, who cannot think systematically without pity, or mourn without analysis. Yet when women relied on the politics of fancy, criticism of their positions collapsed into attacks on their sex. Reactions to "Eighteen Hundred and Eleven" conformed to party lines. The reviewer for the *Anti-Jacobin* argued that the *Monthly Review* praised the poem only because Barbauld expressed Dissenting views. Croker's article in the *Quarterly Review* lumped Barbauld with "her renowned compatriot," William Roscoe, whose two pamphlets on parliamentary reform are critically, though affectionately, reviewed in the same issue. But while the *Anti-Jacobin* categorized the poem's genre as prophecy and dismissed it as Dissenting propaganda, the *Quarterly* called it satire and attacked it on grounds of gender: "Our old acquaintance Mrs. Barbauld turned satirist! . . . We had hoped, indeed, that the empire might have been saved without the intervention of a lady-author." And Croker goes on to deplore the "irresistible impulse of public duty—a confident sense of commanding talents" that "induced her to dash down her shagreen spectacles and her knitting needles, and to sally forth . . . in the magnanimous resolution of saving a sinking state, by the instrumentality of . . . a pamphlet in verse."[25] In order to oppose the Dissenter, Croker excoriates the woman. In order to turn a poem into a pamphlet, he shrinks fancy to polemic. And in the process, he marks off political prose as the preserve of men. Fancy becomes the emotional excess that allows Croker to claim that "Eighteen Hundred and Eleven" fails because of a mismatch of gender and genre. But whatever he had wrong, Croker had one thing absolutely right: it is precisely the "irresistible impulse of public duty" and "a confident sense of commanding talents" that fuels the hallucinatory rage of "Eighteen Hundred and Eleven."

"Mental Optics" and the "Love of Freedom"

Phillis Wheatley's *Poems on Various Subjects* was published in the same place (London) and year (1773) as Barbauld's first collection of poems. Her career predates the outpouring of sentimental abolitionist poems by women in the late 1780s and some of the differences between her work and later texts—including Barbauld's "Epistle to Wilberforce"—stem from the altered rhetoric of that decade. Nonetheless, Wheatley's poems, too, are structured by the adventures of self-conscious artistry at work in dilated arenas of space and time. Her contemporary status as emblem of slavery and commentator on tyranny charges her relation to sensibility.[26] She works with and against British and North American poetic genres that combine emotion, art, and otherness. She accepts the historical identity of slave while refusing that of victim.

In the culture of sensibility, the alternative to victimization is a grasp of the system. And so Wheatley typically refuses to read her own captivity as a tragedy and elects as her subject matter the collective pathos of the Atlantic theater. She draws on the available rhetoric of protest to characterize America as the weeping child of Britannia, the colonies' "dear mama" ("America," 13–26).[27] In the few passages that do present Wheatley's memories of her enslavement, fancy is momentarily the route to recollected pain. But fancy is also a form of ambitious address. And while the language of this ambition is derived from the culture of Wheatley's captors and owners, it uses Wheatley's own forced transatlantic exposure to achieve historical and spatial reach. Her poetry shifts between hopeful prophetic urging in its public moments and a severe view of personal sin. It altogether avoids the mood of collective imperial guilt. Or rather, Britain's "tyrannic sway" is exposed, but, because she is other to it, Wheatley does not feel corrupted by it ("To . . . Dartmouth," 31).

We see Wheatley's self-protectiveness in her evasion of the victim's position. To locate sin in the individual spirit rather than the institution of slavery may be a necessary indirection, marking the limit of the slave writer's power of complaint and accusation. Wheatley's principal tonal difference from more canonical British poets of historical fancy—such as Goldsmith (*The Deserted Village* had appeared in 1770) or the Dissenting Barbauld—and from more conspicuously anxious North American poets—such as Brackenridge and Freneau in the first version of *The Rising Glory of America* (1771) or Freneau alone in "The Power of Fancy" (1770;

1786)—lies in the optative pressure of her work. She represents her own poetry as pleasure, adventure, and moral opportunity; she experiences as pure gain the writing of poetry and the transatlantic vision it permits. Landry suggests that Wheatley's mimicry of British styles, her acquiescence to the expectations of white readers, causes her to suppress direct references to the catastrophes she herself has suffered.[28] I propose a somewhat different, though, I think, complementary reading. Refusing to testify to her own victimization makes it possible for Wheatley to address the public preoccupations of the British North Atlantic. Sentimental conventions invite her to display the history of her pain, to stage herself as sufferer. Her resistance is apparent precisely in her refusal to do so.

Fifteen years after the publication of *Poems on Various Subjects* and a few years after Wheatley's death, Hannah More made the connection between fancy and guilt explicit in her influential work, "Slavery, A Poem" (London, 1788). More views Africa by the power of "more than Fancy" here, meaning that Fancy's images have been verified or confirmed:

> Whene'er to Afric's shores I turn my eyes,
> Horrors of deepest, deadliest guilt arise;
> I see, by more than Fancy's mirror shown,
> The burning village and the blazing town:
> See the dire victim torn from social life,
> The shrieking babe, the agonizing wife!
> She, wretch forlorn! is dragg'd by hostile hands,
> To distant tyrants sold, in distant lands!
> Transmitted miseries, and successive chains,
> The sole, sad heritage her child obtains.[29]

Fancy provides More with vignettes that prove England's guilt, and the "dire victim torn from social life" is the focal point of these evidential scenes.[30] If Wheatley had represented herself as a "wretch forlorn" she would have participated in the rhetoric of liberal guilt—or, since More is no liberal, of what we might better call the rhetoric of vicarious relations. Wheatley avoids mounting such a protest, in which she would have to play the role of both victim and witness. But she does use the available conventions of fancy to link active poetic subjectivity to North Atlantic public life. Indeed, while she makes no effort to hide her slave status, she vigorously embraces the "social life" of Anglo-American culture. She downplays emotion of and for slavery's victims while exploiting the brief pleasures of fancy's upward rush and of her own entry into public address.

"On Recollection" and "On Imagination," which appear sequentially in *Poems on Various Subjects,* comprise flights of fancy similar to those narrated in Barbauld's "Summer Evening's Meditation" of the same year.[31] Both of Wheatley's poems link the mind's motion with fancy's capacity for moral critique. Wheatley's "mental optics" combine inspirational ascent with prospective authority. The poet/speaker of "On Recollection" refers to the "eighteen years" of her own life as an instance of memory's Christian power to expose and judge. Wheatley volunteers this span of time as the object of retrospective scrutiny: "In Recollection see them fresh return, / And sure 'tis mine to be asham'd, and mourn." But aside from her testimony to recollection's power to unveil forgotten things and to inspire penitence, the author's past—the narrative of her enslavement, transportation, purchase, conversion, education, and labor—is suppressed. She announces her race and place of origin when she names herself as the "vent'rous *Afric*" (31, 35–36, 2). She then goes on to describe recollection's acts of vision without telling the reader what it sees.

Recollection, fancy, and the speaker interact as closely related agents of poetic action. The poet establishes a symbiotic relation to Mneme, the muse of recollection: "Assist my strains," she prays, "while I thy glories sing." Mneme, in turn, recuperates "[t]he acts of long departed years" and sets them "in due order rang'd" before fancy, who presides over the domain of the visible: "the long-forgotten . . . sweetly plays before the *fancy's* sight." Mneme shares fancy's wandering habits and its vertical expansiveness:

> Swift from above she wings her silent flight
> Through *Phoebe's* realms, fair regent of the night;
> And, in her pomp of images display'd,
> To the high-raptur'd poet gives her aid,
> Through the unbounded regions of the mind,
> Diffusing light celestial and refin'd.

By referring to herself in the second line of the poem as the "vent'rous Afric" who undertakes a "great design," Wheatley has defined the educated slave's literary "venture" as the desire for both extension ("great") and coherence ("design"). It is hard to separate the poet from the poet's fancy, and to distinguish either from recollection. The net effect is of an overdetermined or redundant aspiration. If recollection offers the "pomp of images," the "high-raptur'd poet" seems majestic enough already. If recollection diffuses the "celestial" light that turns the mind into deep space, that mind already possesses "unbounded regions" (4–8, 11–16, 2).

Design and the view from on high go together. The chief power of recollection turns out to lie in its ability to see the simultaneous operation of different peoples from above: "The heav'nly *phantom* [Mneme] paints the actions done / By ev'ry tribe beneath the rolling sun." And here the pleasurable dilation of fancy's perspectival power changes to judgmental scrutiny that transforms the "high-raptur'd poet" into a self-tormented, if representative, sinner. Mneme combines the prospective energy of fancy and the internalized, monitory voice of Christian conscience:

> *Mneme*, enthron'd within the human breast,
> Has vice condemn'd, and ev'ry virtue blest.
>
> . . . .
>
> . . . how is Mneme dreaded by the race,
> Who scorn her warnings, and despise her grace?
> By her unveil'd each horrid crime appears,
> Her awful hand a cup of wormwood bears.
> Days, years mispent, O what a hell of woe!
> Hers the worst tortures that our souls can know. (17–30)

When the poet's delighted imagination is forced to land, its prospective advantage is converted to discipline. The references to "ev'ry tribe beneath the . . . sun" and to "the race" that ignores its own memories of "crime" suggest that Wheatley has aimed recollection's judgmental force against the internal violence of the culture of slavery. But at precisely this juncture Wheatley offers herself as an example of the mourning induced by "follies . . . / Unnotic'd, but . . . writ in brass!" (33–34). Just when we think the poet/speaker is forcing upon the white "race" its own repressed memory of the violence done to herself and her "tribe," she refuses this option and turns the force of recollection religiously against herself.

Seeming to veer away from political implication, the poem concludes with a prayer for virtue's revisionary effects: "O Virtue," Wheatley prays, "Do thou exert thy pow'r, and change the scene." Virtue becomes the recollective "pow'r enthron'd / In ev'ry breast" and directs "the vengeance of the skies" to the wicked while sheltering the good from heavenly "wrath" (37–50). Is this a self-wounding swerve away from the collective memory of slavery performed on behalf of Christian rationalization, which might hold that the converted (and hence penitent) slave is better off than the free African? Is it a variant of the collapse experienced by Barbauld's fancy, the feminine imagination traumatized by its own "vent'rous" dilations? Or is it a shift away from the historical circumstances that separate Wheatley from her white reading audience by virtue of their transgressions and her victimization, and toward the Christian community of "our souls," of all sinners? Wheatley's performances of the risks and payoffs of fanciful prospects suggest that she will only articulate resistance or negativity from a perspective of inclusion.

In the next poem in the 1773 volume, "On Imagination," Wheatley gives imagination an empire. She empowers the poet through the aerial adventures of fancy and subjects the speaker, finally, to poetry's antithesis, the inhibition of the wintry north. Wheatley addresses imagination as a faintly orientalized "imperial queen," the queen of prospects, whose "forms" and "acts in beauteous order stand." Fancy enters both as the means of transport through imagination's empire and as the drama of falling in love with the aesthetic "object":

> Now here, now there, the roving *Fancy* flies,
> Till some lov'd object strikes her wand'ring eyes,
> Whose silken fetters all the senses bind,
> And soft captivity involves the mind. (1–3, 9–12)

Imagination, like Barbauld's "self-collected soul," seeks and finds celestial perspectives. Unintimidated by the "thund'ring God" who serves as an ostensible destination, the poet and her inspirational faculties take charge of space ("surpass," "Measure," "range," "grasp"):

> Soaring through air to find the bright abode,
> Th' empyreal palace of the thund'ring God,
> We on thy pinions can surpass the wind,
> And leave the rolling universe behind:
> From star to star the mental optics rove,
> Measure the skies, and range the realms above.
> There in one view we grasp the mighty whole,
> Or with new worlds amaze th' unbounded soul. (15–22)

Imagination is tantamount to the relationship between vertical motion, organizing vision or "mental optics," and the variegated plane of "the mighty whole" thus perceived. Poetry emerges from the momentary revelation of an ordered strangeness, "new worlds."

Wheatley claims elsewhere that "an intrinsic ardor prompts to write" ("To the University of Cambridge, in New-England," 1). In "On Imagination," Fancy and Imagination divide up emotional labor in ways that suggest some tension between affection and power as the two aspects of "ardor." The fond gaze of Fancy bestows spring on the landscape, creating the "gay scenes" that captivate it. Fancy, the lover, is subordinate to the more glamorous Imagination. Imagination wields "the sceptre o'er the realms" of emotion: "Before thy throne the subject-passions bow, / Of subject-passions sov'reign ruler Thou." When Imagination commands, "joy rushes on the heart" and spirits hurry "through the glowing veins." The "passions" are Imagination's slaves, and Wheatley seems to glory in the rush from feeling to writing. But the Imagination is subject to austerity's weather. Immediately after these lines, Wheatley shifts into the subjunctive: "*Fancy* might . . . her silken pinions try"; Aurora "might . . . rise"; "I"—the poet/speaker—"might behold" the sun, "monarch of the day." The subjunctive mood bodes ill for "th' unbounded soul." Winter pulls the speaker down and away from Imagination's peaks. In the competition between a hot queen and a cold climate, the queen loses:

> But I reluctant leave the pleasing views,
> Which *Fancy* dresses to delight the *Muse;*
> *Winter* austere forbids me to aspire,
> And northern tempests damp the rising fire;
> They chill the tides of Fancy's flowing sea,
> Cease then, my song, cease the unequal lay. (24, 36 – 46, 48 – 53)

If winter is a trope for the North Atlantic zone of Wheatley's adult life, then the locale of her slavery "forbids" the tropical imagination "to aspire." But since New England is also the site of authorship, its chilly dampness may induce warm aspiration, as well as discourage it. Wheatley, unlike Barbauld in "A Summer Evening's Meditation," attributes the "inequality" of her song to its earthly circumstances, not to fancy's anxiety attack in the face of a patriarchal heaven. Winter, if clearly masculine and frowning, snags the poet from below instead of bullying her from above. And a seasonal cause of poetry's cessation is both more temporary and less transcendent than a celestial one. She concedes much less. Power is less absolute, in Wheatley's poetry, and aspiration is less self-wounding.

In the genre of political panegyric, Wheatley identifies the northern zone with Liberty's kindling effects. In the public sector, Wheatley is finally free to refer to herself. Wheatley's poem, "To the Right Honourable WILLIAM, Earl of Dartmouth, His Majesty's Principal Secretary of State for North American, &c.," recalls a collective experience of colonial mourning. New England's "race no longer mourns," because the presumably sympathetic Dartmouth, a friend of the Countess of Huntingdon, has been appointed secretary of state for the American colonies and president of the Board of Trade and Foreign Plantations (287 n.). But

Wheatley's contrast between the present rejoicing of the "northern clime" and its previous lamentations sustains those complaints as a reminder to Dartmouth of the need for revised policies:

> No more, *America*, in mournful strain
> Of wrongs, and grievance unredress'd complain,
> No longer shall thou dread the iron chain,
> Which wanton *Tyranny* with lawless hand
> Had made, and with it meant t'enslave the land. (5, 15–19)

In this verse paragraph, which had been edited for the *Poems on Various Subjects* and for the volume's English audience, Wheatley retains the by-now generic connection between tyranny, slavery, mourning, and the rhetoric of complaint. In an earlier 1772 draft, Wheatley used this passage to vent colonial impatience in the name of Liberty:

> No more, of Grievance unredress'd complain,
> Or injur'd Rights, or groan beneath the Chain,
> Which wanton Tyranny, with lawless Hand,
> Made to enslave, O *Liberty!*, thy Land.—
> My Soul rekindles, at thy glorious Name,
> Thy Beams, essential to the vital Flame.—
> The Patriot's Breast, what Heavenly Virtue warms,
> And adds new Lustre to his mental Charms!
> While in thy Speech, the Graces all combine,
> Apollo's too, with Sons of Thunder join.
> Then shall the Race of injur'd Freedom bless,
> The Sire, the Friend, and Messenger of Peace.[32] (12–24)

Dartmouth is assimilated, through the ambiguous repetition of "thy," to the allegorical figure of Liberty. This strategy binds him rhetorically to a program of justice for the colonies. Wheatley is less flattering here, hedging her bet on Dartmouth's commitment to New England's interests.

In both versions of "To . . . Dartmouth," however, New England's memories of its own "enslavement," its identity as "the Race of injur'd Freedom," leads directly and quite unexpectedly to Wheatley's personal testimony to the link between suffering, slavery, and the poetry of freedom. In the collective experience of enslavement, tyranny, and mourning, she finds a public purpose for her own traumatic past. She dramatizes herself as writer and Dartmouth as reader of this poem. Having led him to question the origins of her "love of Freedom"—"Should you, my lord, while you peruse my song, / Wonder from whence my love of *Freedom* sprung"—she restates that question in less individual terms: "Whence flow these wishes for the common good, / by feeling hearts alone best understood?" The love of freedom manifests itself in the community brought about by sensibility, the "common good" of "feeling hearts" that Dartmouth is invited to share. Wheatley creates an audience for her own suffering in the projected understanding of the sensitive reader. She presents the story of her own enslavement as the motive for her literary participation in the sentimental community. And she justifies her use of the personal by giving it public value. The same "feeling hearts" in New England that lamented their subjection to Britain's tyranny, along with Dartmouth himself, will be sympathetic readers of her own experience of "tyrannic sway" (20–23, 31).

The poetic representation of enslavement is split by the conflict between Wheatley's need to depict her own authentic suffering (and thus to justify her empathy with New England's cause), and her desire to acknowledge the fortunate teleology of her enslavement and conversion, the conditions for her public voice:

> I, young in life, by seeming cruel fate
> Was snatch d from *Afric's* fancy'd happy seat:
> What pangs excruciating must molest,
> What sorrows labour in my parent's breast?
> Steel'd was that soul and by no misery mov'd
> That from a father seiz'd his babe belov'd:
> Such, such my case. And can I then but pray
> Others may never feel tyrannic sway? (24–31)

The key phrases, "seeming cruel fate" and "fancy'd happy seat," introduce Wheatley's reading of slavery both as familial catastrophe and as historical reality subject to recuperation. Imputing "pangs," "sorrows," and "misery" to her father, she constructs him as the suffering subject whose pain is sympathetically but vicariously experienced by Wheatley. The violence of the verb "snatch'd" exceeds that of the ambiguous phrase, "seeming cruel." Still, this swerve away from personal sensation, just when we have been led to expect confessional evidence, seems to confirm Landry's opinion of Wheatley's inability to remember. But there are other possible significances.

Instead of remembering her own pains, she speculates about her father's: "What pangs . . . What sorrows?" Not unlike the abolitionist poets, the Man of Feeling, or even Adam Smith, she becomes the artist of long-distance sympathy who has to imagine the pain that others feel. At the same time, however, this is her father, or, as she puts it, "my case," with the claim of personal immediacy. From whose point of view, then, is her fate "cruel"? From whose perspective was Africa "happy"? Clearly from her father's. His experience is one of a stark difference between before (his daughter's presence) and after (her subsequent captivity). The Christian apologist, however, could understand "seeming" and "fancy'd" as code words meaning "not really." He or she might read Africa's happiness as illusory and enslavement as a not-entirely cruel means to the sacred end of conversion. But here the speaker, while validating both the familial and the apologetic interpretations, also insists on her representative status as one of many victims of "tyrannic sway." She treats her own capture as part of a larger narrative by which the victim protests but also recuperates her suffering by authoring the poetry of Anglo-American public life.

In looking at Barbauld and Wheatley together, I have stressed what they have in common. First, sensibility, the language that turns politics into psychodrama and makes fancy a legitimate vehicle of cultural criticism. Second, the celebration of fancy as an allegory of women's literary ambition. For both Barbauld and Wheatley, the fanciful subject is powerful, mobile, and self-pleasing, if often only briefly so. The feminist effect of fancy is shaped by the politics of imperial sensibility. Slavery, revolution, and economic stratification became matters of public dispute through sentimental politics—that is, through the claim to suffering. Sensibility's appeal to women writers is not through sentiment per se, since pathos is also a hallmark of a wide variety of masculine reactions in this period. Rather, sensibility offers women historical and geographical scope. Otherness—in the form of racial difference, class separations, primitivistic contrasts—brings with it representations of distance and perspective that invite the adventures of fancy. The subject of slavery, in particular, calls forth large-scale scenes of warning, hope, and prophecy.

Sensibility had a powerful homogenizing tendency on eighteenth- and nineteenth-century verse, but we need to resist this effect even as we investigate it. Neither Barbauld nor Wheatley had a simple or consistent relation to the conventions of sensibility, and they certainly do not have a simple or consistent resemblance to each other. No writer, in fact, was unambivalent concerning the vicarious suffering that forms the core of sensibility. Sensibility knew itself to be alienated and guilty from the start, or conducive to guilt in others.

CHAPTER FIVE

Vagrant Races

Vanishing Americans and Early National Prospects
Sarah Wentworth Morton (1759–1846), Ann Eliza Bleecker (1752–
1783), and Philip Freneau (1752–1832)—poets of the American Revolution and the early Republic—composed emotional treatments of Native Americans in ambitious fancy-driven works that marked their entry
into authorship. Key works by all three poets are organized by sensibility
that apprehends the continent, or even the hemisphere, through tropes
of mobility rather than settlement. And the muse of mobile affect is the
Native American. "As melancholy figures [Native Americans] reminded
white Americans of the passage of time and of the march of empires,"
observes Warner Sollers.[1] The figure of the literary Indian is a symptom
of the "imperialist nostalgia" that gives rise to the "vanishing American"
syndrome: "When the so-called civilizing process destabilizes forms of
life, the agents of change experience transformations of other cultures as
if they were personal losses."[2] Dana Nelson rightly argues that sympathetic portrayals of Native Americans and African Americans were a
good career move, allowing white writers "to gain authorial advantage in
Anglo-American culture."[3] The specific benefit to these poets was the
engagement of global histories and spaces. Sensibility is the practice of
mobile connection. Properly applied, it enables the fusion of historically
informed civic commitments with geographical heights, depths, and expanses. Morton, Bleecker, and Freneau create transatlantic and transcontinental vistas where once and future nations pass in parade. These
vistas, in turn, become the correlative of citizenship as understood by the
public-spirited intellectual.

Morton's *Ouabi* (1790) is a long narrative poem that sustains a vision
of racial harmony made possible by imaginary premodern masculinity.
Bleecker's poems of combative motherhood similarly derive their emotional energy from the figure of the Indian, but in her case dread and
anger impel the speaker to position herself amid historical forces and imposing landscapes. Philip Freneau's 1786 version of *The Rising Glory of
America* features young intellectual men who don't really know how they
feel. Through their debates, Freneau rewrites colonialism for the national

era. The one thing that is clear about his speakers is that they are determined to think big and be taken seriously. They perform a full repertoire of historical, political, and ethnographic speculation—the entire Princeton curriculum provoked by one question about Native American origins.

Emotional writing marks the onset of national cultural participation. National stature, however, is earned through supranational perspectives, in addition to or instead of through territorial attachment. In chapter 4, I emphasized how crucial fancy is to the meanings of late eighteenth-century sensibility. Fancy is one strategy for modulating between inward-looking subjectivity and the prospects of historical time and space. Melancholy is another. The literature of sensibility relies on sorrow, as well as fancy, to navigate a racial world—sorrow in its gendered particulars.[4] For Bleecker, maternal grief intensifies scenes of racial violence. She relives the American Revolution as the terrifying masculine predation of Indian, not British, fighters. For the liberal, urban Morton, sympathy toward the racial other is mediated by the European man lost in North America. His story makes public the idealistic scope of the white woman poet. Like Freneau, Morton is close to the tradition of Whig sentimentalism and its scenes of male bonding. She attributes to masculine friendship a depth of interpersonal transparency not present in heterosexual encounters. Finally, Philip Freneau seems absorbed by associative speculations concerning the origins of humanity, nationality, and poetry. He stages a same-sex conversation about the morality of European settlement in the Americas. More than either Bleecker or Morton, Freneau, a journalist and coastal trader along the Atlantic rim, depicts the nation as curiously unbound.

I will first continue the discussion of female authorship begun in the previous chapter by comparing Bleecker and Morton to each other. I then turn to Freneau, who researches the troubling ethics of territorial occupation. Freneau's masculine difference does not lie in his ambivalent sympathy for Indians or in his fanciful tour through dynasties and continents—nor, for that matter, in the effect of the ungrounded mind. All these qualities are present in the work of Bleecker and Morton. His distinction can be found, rather, in the clubbish voices of his conversationalists and in their jostling competition for cultural authority, quite unlike the somewhat lonelier heroics of the ambitious women poets who take the Atlantic theater as their imaginative domain.

"Down Rush'd the Tawny Natives from the Hill"

*T*he poems of both Bleecker and Morton exhibit the defining qualities of North American sensibility, including its preoccupation with race. Although stories of interracial encounter leading to affective crises are common to both, their attitudes about race are markedly dissimilar. Writing as the Revolutionary War churned through her upstate New York neighborhood and amid complex interactions among the Five Nations of the Iroquois, British regulars, Loyalists, and assorted rebel units, Bleecker dreads the Native Americans that would appeal to Morton a decade later.[5] After the death of her daughter from illness during the family's retreat before the advance of Burgoyne in 1777, Bleecker laments that she has been doomed to a life of mourning by the assaults of the Iroquois. The strength of feminine rage and grief, which constitutes the most impressive feature of her poetry, is motivated by the chaotic violence of the racial other. She draws heavily on the conventions of captivity narratives, a genre revived during the French and Indian War and again during the Revolution. In Bleecker's work, the captivity narrative reveals its investment in powerful feminine sadness that often takes the form of an attachment to place. She juxtaposes the racial terror and feminine sanctuaries of the captivity narrative in ways that accentuate women's risk. She also situates her family home in national and international perspectives, however. Bleecker's poems reread the Bible, the *Aeneid*, and English landscape poetry in terms that elevate women's indignant mourning to literary and public significance.

Though Morton, too, would write poems of motherly mourning, her first major publication distributes high-minded pathos among the three members of a love triangle comprising one European and two Native American protagonists.[6] In her long narrative poem, *Ouabi*, the virtuous European's assimilation into the life of the Illinois tribe leads to the Illinois sachem's convenient death after the white man proves himself worthy to be his successor. Sensibility's Roman ethos persists in the suggestion that warriors of different races may be sentimentally bound to one another in an archaic revenge culture that views them as peers. For in this vision of racial concord, masculine friendship depends on a primitive social frame.

Morton's celebration of the link between melancholia and virtue transforms the Indian death song into narrative romance. Morton had considerable access to and sympathy for the idealizations of liberal ethnography. Along with Mercy Otis Warren and Judith Sargent Murray, she was prominent in the literary renaissance among liberal privileged women in revolutionary and early national Boston. She is certainly a more sentimental writer than either Warren or Murray, and, not surprisingly, more absorbed in "writing race," a "committed abolitionist as well as a defender of Native American culture."[7] By contrast, Bleecker represents the subordination of her family's black servants unquestioningly if sometimes sentimentally. She is troubled by race only insofar as she wishes to "give . . . some idea of savage cruelty" in order to "justify our fears" of Native Americans.[8] The comparison between Morton and Bleecker thus suggests that the affinity between melancholia and racial difference prevails regardless of whether the racial other is heroicized or detested.

Bleecker is characterized by her daughter as having always been prone to fluctuations between delight and suffering. Margaretta Faugeres, herself a poet and editor of Bleecker's works, writes that her mother periodically turned against her own verse in the grip of mood swings that catapulted her from "flights of fancy" to "dejection":

> she was frequently very lively, and would then give way to the flights of her fertile fancy, and write songs, satires, and burlesque: but, as drawing a cord too tight will make it break, thus she would no sooner cease to be *merry*, than the heaviest *dejection* would succeed, and then all the pieces which were not as melancholy as herself, she destroyed. (xv)

With the onset of war, fear intervened between fancy and melancholia. History's intrusion shattered the self-delighting inventiveness of the retired family. This is the tale of loss told by the poet as suffering subject.

Though Bleecker was a precocious writer as a girl growing up in a comfortable Manhattan merchant family, her career as a serious author began with her marriage in 1769, at age seventeen. She and her husband, John Bleecker, a wealthy lawyer from New Rochelle, settled after a year in a new estate on inherited land at Tomhanick, twelve miles north of Albany. John Bleecker encouraged her to preserve her poems. The move to Tomhanick eventually exposed Bleecker to the traumas that would become the subject of her verse. And retirement—the rural life of a large landowner's family—affected the choice of poetic genres that she henceforth favored.

The Bleeckers' privileged rural domesticity was committed to and at risk from the politics of independence. This predicament is reflected in Bleecker's use of the conventions of the poetry of prospect. The Tomhanick estate is the central figure in Bleecker's poetry. Or rather, it is the place from which figuration flows. John Barrell has described the prospect in the English poetry of sensibility as a class-inflected view of the landscape, an aestheticized vista that signifies leisure.[9] The prospect also permits a view, beyond the temporal horizon, of the progress or ruin of empires and nations. Furthermore, the prospect requires a malleable subjectivity or intersubjectivity. The speaker links poetry to history by offering a play-by-play account of the mind's faculties and moods—fancy, imagination, dejection, ambition, prophecy—and their various itineraries at home and abroad; then, now, and in future time.

Bleecker's prospective poetry is altered from its British precedents by the fact that war, racial conflict, and national destiny do not observe their habitual remoteness on the poet's horizon. Rather, they break through the frame of leisured sensibility and require different kinds of representation. Bleecker's writing darkens into elegy, indignant complaint, and anxious topographical surveys after the assaults of Iroquois and British forces around Tomhanick in 1777. With her two children and "a young mulatto girl" (almost certainly a slave), she joined the precipitous retreat from "the infatuated Burgoyne" and his "savages." First her daughter, Abella, and shortly afterwards her mother and sister died of sickness (v). Under these pressures, the poetry of prospect absorbs the captivity narrative.

Bleecker's *History of Maria Kittle,* written in 1779, contains the alternately visceral and refined language of the captivity genre. In this prose work,

> "Ceres" presides over fields through which screaming Indians run, killing and tearing off scalps. The tomahawking of the pregnant Comelia, with details of her cleft white forehead, the dead staring of her "fine azure eyes," and the ripping out of her fetus and dashing it to pieces are unusually concrete, if grim, visualizations. Purple passages describe Maria's sorrows as her abductors drag her to their allies in Montreal.[10]

Though set during the French and Indian War (1754–63), *The History of Maria Kittle* conveys Bleecker's sense of the alien terror unleashed upon Anglo-American women in 1777. Her treatment of Native Americans as instigators of violence against mothers suggests that the popularity of captivity narratives during and immediately after the Revolution was motivated by the need to express the cultural value, physical exposure, and political entanglements of white women.[11] Bleecker does not use the Indians to demonize their British allies, whom she regards as still capable of politeness. Rather, she locates the whole terror of war in the Iroquois. Bleecker views Native Americans as a mobile strike force, as embodied panic, and as a de-domesticating energy that frightens families out of their homes, then makes them fall ill.

Faugeres' memoir tells the story of Ann Bleecker's escape from Tom-hanick in terms derived from Bleecker's own accounts. The "perfect tranquillity" of an extended family in the "green valley" with "fair prospects . . . opening on every side" had already been disturbed by the danger of Burgoyne's attack. While her husband was in Albany looking for another place to live, Bleecker "received intelligence that the enemy were within two miles of the village, burning and murdering all before them." From this moment on, maternal action and maternal anguish pervade the account:

> Terrified beyond description she rose from the table and taking her Abella on her arm, and her other daughter (about four years old) by the hand she set off on foot with a young mulatto girl, leaving the house and furniture to the mercy of the approaching savages. The roads were crowded with carriages loaded with women and children, but none could afford her assistance—distress was depictured on every countenance, and tears of heartfelt anguish moistened every cheek. (iv–vi)

During this phase of the retreat, Bleecker repeatedly sought help—a ride, a room—but was turned away. Finally reunited with her husband in Albany, they joined a group traveling downstream on the Hudson until Abella became too ill to travel and died shortly thereafter.

In 1781, four years after Abella's death, a raiding party of Tories, British regulars, and Hessians seized John Bleecker; an elderly slave or servant, Merkee; and an unnamed "white servant" while they were harvesting the Bleeckers' crops. Although this was not an Indian attack, the terror of the event confirms Bleecker's sense of the racial horror of the haunted woods.[12] Her revulsion persists despite her appreciation of British sensibility as it manifested itself during John Bleecker's week of captivity. Merkee invoked her feminine anguish at the very moment of capture, speaking on behalf of her feelings while testifying to his own emotional negligibility. "I am an old Negro—no matter for me," Merkee is reported to have said, but "my dear mistress will break her heart" (135–36). Distinguishing one race from another, contrasting Merkee's knowledge of her sensibility to enemy savagery, Bleecker goes on to admire the Anglo-American male bonding made possible by the image of her suffering articulated by the empathetic slave. As the raiding party and its captives traveled through the woods, sensibility transcended politics. Merkee is not mentioned again, but "the British were humane, and wept whenever my sad spouse deplored the mournful fate of his wife and child" (136). John Bleecker was unexpectedly liberated by Connecticut troops six days later. But, as in 1777, the consequence of familial trauma and dislocation was maternal loss. "Soon after I fell into premature labour, and was delivered of a dead child," Ann Bleecker tells her correspondent. "Since that I have been declining" (178).

Bleecker's poetry was thus shaped by the sudden change from domestic idyll to domestic tragedy in 1777 and again in 1781. Whether she represents herself thereafter as the victim of violent assaults, a mourner whose grief and anger react to a shattered New World pastoral, or a commentator who locates her personal calamities in a narrative overview of the war, Bleecker treats Abella's death in 1777 as pain cherished in proportion to the horror of its shockingly alien cause. Bleecker regards Abella as the direct victim of the "cruel savage," of "conflagration in the blooming wild" (221).

Bleecker's poems center, then, on the "Abella topos," the loss that structures the speaker's relation to all other events and texts. In addition to the many lyrics that respond directly to the child's death, two other kinds of writing reveal the scope of this trauma. Interweaving characterizations of the Tomhanick estate before and during the fighting, Bleecker describes the war from the point of view of the domestic female of the landed merchant or professional class.[13] Her spouse, politically engaged and a member of the militia, is mostly absent, and during the war she feels her home to be surrounded by aliens. From this perspective, the fighting becomes a contest over who rules the "shade," the "woods" and the "groves." The forces of darkness take over the woods and issue forth in a rush that becomes Bleecker's figure for the temporality of shock: "Down rush'd the tawny natives from the hill" ("A Pastoral Dialogue" 258). Abella dies because the family is driven from its home.

The pastoral-cum-war poem becomes a figure for the state of poetry itself, whose cultivated genres are incongruously called upon to describe terror. Prospects or moments of geographical survey modulate into personal chronicles of the war. Such writing narrates progress toward American independence in terms of the alternation between violence and tranquillity. The rural sanctuary has already been constructed, by Bleecker herself and by poetic convention, as a venue that is neither urban nor savage. In these texts, North American captivity narratives by and about women intersect the British poetry of meditative retirement. The poet speaks as the victim, aesthetician, and caretaker of an exposed estate. Remembering Abella means memorializing and renovating the Bleeckers' groves through the poet's own patriotic elegies.

Bleecker's "Written in the Retreat" declares itself throughout to be written after the retreat, after Abella's death, and in defiance of "relief." The speaker demands to know: *Was it for this?* The question that Wordsworth will later ask about Nature's intent in the first book of the *Prelude* here proclaims the mother's tragic investment in the daughter:

> Was it for this, with thee a pleasing load,
> I sadly wander'd thro' the hostile wood;
> When I thought fortune's spite could do no more,
> To see thee perish on a foreign shore?

The rhetorical question, or protest, is interrupted by the first of several bursts of apostrophe:

> Oh my lov'd babe! my treasures left behind
> Ne'er sunk a cloud of grief upon my mind;
> Rich in my children—on my arms I bore
> My living treasures from the scalper's pow'r:
> When I sat down to rest beneath some shade,
> On the soft grass how innocent she play'd.
>
> .   .   .   .
>
> Unconscious of her danger, laughing roves,
> Nor dreads the painted savage in the groves.

The journey defers but does not evade the threat of the "hostile wood." The maternal power to carry children bodily out of danger—a feminine strength that depends on the catalyzing presence of an embowered enemy—proves temporary, though its force will revive in Bleecker's obstinate grief.

When "fallacies" of maternal rescue collapse, the speaker is at first silent before Abella's corpse ("sorrow chain'd my tongue"). She finds her voice in a defense of mourning that proclaims, "I lov'd my grief." The poet becomes brilliantly articulate when she finds an antagonist in the banalities of consolation, which she parodies. She furiously relegates false comforters to the hostile wood where death dwells in the shape of the savage. Grief frees her from conventional pious submission and permits a newly resistant poetic authority: "Comfort I wish'd not for." She rewrites Scripture to defend Christ as a man of feeling and dismisses Stoics.

In the process, she links the partisan maternity of the white frontier poet with its cultural ally, tenderhearted manhood:

> "Go!" cried I raging, "stoick bosoms go!
> "Whose hearts vibrate not to the sound of woe;
> "Go from the sweet society of men,
> "Seek some unfeeling tyger's savage den,
> "There calm—alone—of resignation preach,
> "My Christ's examples better precepts teach."
> Where the cold limbs of gentle *Laz'rus* lay
> I find him weeping o'er the humid clay;
> His spirit groan'd, while the beholders said
> (With gushing eyes) "see how he lov'd the dead!"
> And when his thoughts on great *Jerus'lem* turn'd!
> And sad *Gethsemene's* nocturnal shade
> The anguish of my weeping Lord survey'd:
> Yes, 'tis my boast to harbour in my breast
> The sensibilities by God exprest.

"*Gethsemene's* nocturnal shade" redeems the hostile wood of the Hudson River Valley. The only fit company for the grieving poet is the savior with his godly "Sensibilities." "Society" comprises the small circle of the dead, the principle mourner, and the "beholders," whose "gushing eyes" confirm their understanding of Bleecker's love. In a December 1777 letter, she moves similarly from exasperation to the demand for sympathy: "Curst be the heart that is callous to the feelings of humanity, and which, concentered in itself, regards not the wailings of affliction!" Although she apologizes for her "enthusiasm," or anger, her curse validates her loss. She was "concentered" in Abella, and human community should form itself to her lamentation:

> I have supported every shock with tolerable fortitude, except the death of my Abella—She indeed had wound herself round every fibre of my heart—I loved, I idolized her. . . . I could . . . have beheld with less anguish the dissolution of Nature than the last gasp of my infant. (viii–x)

Relying on the catalyst of the racial other, Bleecker can move from the testimony of personal suffering to active political assertion and back. Necessary, though less obvious, in this early American version of "the female complaint" is the shadowy "good" otherness of the sympathetic slave or servant (Merkee and the "mulatto girl").[14]

Bleecker's complaint authorizes her to revise the classics as she does the New Testament. In "On Reading Dryden's Virgil," she is audacious in her willingness to plant herself squarely in Virgilian narrative. She writes herself succinctly into epic loss, retold as the cyclical fate of sensibility. Bleecker's formulaic "scenes of horror"—the fiery vista surveyed from a distance, the yelling savage who represents terror close at hand— establish the connection between the history of the war and the history of the family:

> Now cease these tears, lay gentle *Vigil* [Virgil] by,
> Let recent sorrows dim the pausing eye:
> Shall *Aeneas* for lost *Creusa* mourn,
> And tears be wanting on *Abella's* urn?
> Like him I lost my fair one in my flight
> From cruel foes—and in the dead of night.
> Shall he lament the fall of *Illion's tow'rs,*
> And we not mourn the sudden ruin of *our's?*
> See *York* on fire—while borne by winds each flame
> Projects its glowing sheet o'er half the main:
> Th'affrighted savage, yelling with amaze,
> From *Allegany* sees the rolling blaze.
> Far from these scenes of horror, in the shade,
> I saw my *aged parent* safe convey'd;
> Then sadly follow'd to the friendly land,
> With my *surviving infant* by the hand.
> No cumb'rous houshold gods had I indeed
> To load my shoulders, and my flight impede;
> The hero's idols sav'd by *him* remain;
> My gods took care of me—not *I* of *them!*
> The Trojan saw *Anchises* breathe his last,
> When all domestic dangers he had pass'd:
> So my lov'd *parent,* after she had fled,
> Lamented, perish'd on a stranger's bed.
> —*He* held his way o'er the Cerulian Main,
> But *I* return'd to hostile fields again. (pp. 230–31)

Bleecker focuses on the moment in Book II of the *Aeneid* when Aeneas, having led his small son, his father, and his wife, Creusa, out of the fires of Troy, realizes that Creusa is lost. Distraught and disoriented, he returns to Troy to look for her. The ghost of Creusa appears to him and accepts her role as a sacrifice to the Roman future—a consolation available to but disregarded by Bleecker, who chooses not to think of her daughter as an avatar of the new nation. Instead, Bleecker sympathizes with the hero who returns home for his wife, as she identified with the weeping Christ. But she measures her difference from Aeneas by going home and staying there, where "home" and "hostile fields" are synonymous.[15]

Bleecker's dialogues, pastorals in a time of war, show clearly how her sufferings during the Revolutionary War connect local and national perspectives. In "To Miss Ten Eyck," one of two poems addressed in an epistolary vein to her half-sister, Bleecker imagines her distant correspondent in an idealized pastoral of feminine pleasure replete with "sylvan bow'rs," "salubrious flow'rs," and moonlit reflections: "[You] view your blushes mant'ling in the stream, / When Luna gilds it with her amber beam." If "Kitty" blushes in New Jersey, the poet blanches in New York: "The brazen voice of war awakes our fears, / Impearling every damask cheek with tears." She retells the story of an Indian massacre that closely resembles *The History of Maria Kittle,* even down to the scene of the mutilated baby. The indirectness of Abella's death—from disease, not wounds—is suppressed:

> The savage, rushing down the echoing vales,
> Frights the poor hind with ill portending yells;
>
> . . . .
>
> She drops her blooming infant from her breast;
> She tries to fly, but quick recoiling sees
> The painted Indian issuing from the trees. . . .
> Oh horrid sight! her partner is no more;
> Pale is his corse, or only ting'd with gore.
> Her playful babe is dash'd against the stones,
> Its scalp torn off, and fractur'd all its bones.
> Where are the dimpling smiles it lately wore?
> Ghastly in agony it smiles no more! (231–32)

When Bleecker celebrates the end of the war in "Peace," she focuses on exorcising the woods, whose natural shade erases memories of racial otherness and terror. Bleecker uses patriotic resistance to Britain to fuel demonic representations of Native Americans so that race and nationality are conflated in the figure of the enemy of rural mothers. "The groves we now safely explore, / Where murd'ring banditti, the dark sons of treason, / Were shelter'd and aw'd," she exults, restoring "the aspect of the land" to its proper serenity. The "swain with his oxen" gives thanks in a mood of combative pastoral "that *Britain's* black ally / Is chas'd to *Canadia's* deep woods." With the Indians relegated to someone else's forest, Bleecker reappropriates the trees for the purposes of republican panegyric:

> *Echo* no longer is plaintively mourning,
> But laughs and is jocund as we;
> And the turtle ey'd nymphs, to their cots all returning,
> Carve "WASHINGTON," on every tree. (252)

The recurring scene of the Indian issuing from "his dark recess / With fell intent" reappears in Bleecker's most overtly political poem on the war, "A Pastoral Dialogue." Pastoral dialogue, a genre designating the conversational ethic of women, describes attacks on, precisely, the pastoral. The pastoral, however, has the last word. Because it is capable, finally, of telling the story of the Revolution from the point of view of the winners, the genre narrates its own victory. The allegorized history of political events leading up to the Revolution, in which the protagonists are "Columbia," "George," "Virtue," "Oppression," and "Freedom," alternates with a more sensuous, descriptive account of the Hudson River Valley as the figure of "Desolation" storms through it.

Bleecker's dialogue (between "Susanna" and "Eliza") begins with the dilemma of its own composition at the point when an American victory was likely but not yet achieved: "these hostile shades refuse / Admission to the lute or peaceful Muse." The "awkward swain" carries a musket, not a crook, and the poet protests that, under the circumstances, she is not up to the pastoral genre: "From undissembled grief my numbers flow, / And few the graces that attend on woe." Urged to "sing" despite (or because of) her melancholy frame of mind, Eliza summarizes the history of European settlement in North America, recites the causes of the war, and recounts British onslaughts on American abundance. The settlers "with incessant toil" created a landscape of cottages, "golden harvests," and "harbours open'd wide" to "wealthy ships." Then Bleecker's middle-class utopia of industrious citizens encountered the "ambitious homicide," George III, egged on by "the hydra Envy" to restrict American freedoms and successes. The colonies are conventionally portrayed as an emotional suppliant or victim: "*Columbia* weeps, she kneels before the throne, / But plaints, and tears, and sighs, avail her none" (254–56). Mourning is inseparable from resistance for Bleecker, however, and weeping Columbia rallies and fights.

When the figure of the Iroquois, *"Britannia's ally,"* enters "from his dark recess," the "scene" shifts away from a general history of the colonies to Bleecker's own position. "Look from this point," the speaker directs her companion, "where op'ning glades reveal" the prospect that is about to be assaulted: "The glassy *Hudson* shining 'twixt the hills; / There many a structure dress'd the sleepy shore, / And all beyond were daily rising more." After a lengthy passage lauding cultivated and natural abundance, terror strikes: "Down rush'd the *tawny natives* from the hill." The difference between white women and the combined forces of the "dark sons of Treason" (Tories) and their "black" allies (Indians) becomes the difference between peace and war. "Every place" is filled "with fire and murder" distributed by Indians "Arm'd with the hatchet and a flaming brand." The consequence is topographical. The attackers

> reverse the aspect of the land:
> Observe, *Susanna*, not a bird is there,
> The tall burnt trees rise mournful in the air,
> Nor man nor beast the smoking ruins explores,
> And *Hudson* flows more solemn by these shores. (257–58)

If mourning leads Bleecker in some poems to resist false comforters and in others to revise the masculine epics of imperial history, here Susanna's "silent anguish" provokes partisan noise. The poet, who referred to her own mourning earlier, now sees the effects of her poem on her friend, Susanna: "ah! I see thee turn away and mourn, / Thy feeling heart with silent anguish torn." But pathos again leads to defiance and melancholia to martial vigor. "Cheer up," says Eliza, and shifts from lament over a lost pastoral to fervent personifications who insist that paradise can be regained. She points to divine intervention ("His obvious arm how lately interpos'd, / To render Britain's *northern phalanx* vain") and then to the invincible team of Freedom and Conquest ("For *Conquest* loves to be on *Freedom's* side"). The poem ends abruptly with a vision of Britain's "disappointed navy" in retreat and with the racket of victory: "acclamations fill the region round, / And from their hollow ships loud shouts rebound" (259).

"A Pastoral Dialogue" links American ground to the fluctuating voice of the female poet. It develops a topography that accommodates suffering and aggression. Both moods, terror leading to melancholia and melancholia leading to indignation, depend on the figure of the Indian for their affective charge. Sadness is transformed into energy once it finds an enemy. Bleecker's vision of winning means both coming home ("all hail my well-known trees!") and thinking nationally ("I told them I could not see how they dared break through the confederacy while they were sensible all America's happiness depended upon the union") (260, 153). Her version of sensibility leads, not to an ideology of republican motherhood, but to one of resistant republican mourning. The nation appears where the child once was. The nation is the best revenge.

"Guilty Anguish" and Cross-Racial Friendship

*U*nder her pen name, "Philenia," Sarah Wentworth Morton published three long narrative poems in the genres of sentimental politics: *Ouabi, Or the Virtues of Nature, An Indian Tale in Four Cantos* (1790); *Beacon Hill, a Local Poem, Historic and Descriptive,* which moves from topographical prospects to the history of the war, to end with a "Prophetic Apostrophe to the Progress of Freedom" (1797); and *The Virtues of Society: A Tale Founded on Fact* (1799), the story of an Englishwoman's pursuit of her captured husband through American lines.

Ouabi marks the self-conscious beginning of a female career. Prior to this first publication, however, Morton had arrived on the American literary scene through an ordeal of embarrassment. As a consequence of her husband's attraction for her younger sister, who later committed suicide, Morton saw herself written into "The Story of Ophelia," the "incestuous" subplot of William Hill Brown's *The Power of Sympathy* (1789). Cathy N. Davidson has pointed out the way in which *The Power of Sympathy* conflated "truth" and exposé, a strategy most evident in Isaiah Thomas's marketing strategy for the novel, which foregrounded the link to the scandal.[16] A year after the publication of *The Power of Sympathy,* Morton dedicated *Ouabi* to James Bowdoin. The former governor of Massachusetts and a family friend, Bowdoin had helped conduct the official investigation of Fanny's suicide. Morton's personal response to the scandal combined dignified public loyalty to her husband with significant personal estrangement.[17] Her literary response was indirect but pointed.

Ouabi defines the "virtues of nature" as the qualities that make possible the honorable negotiation of extramarital love. Celario, "Europe's fairest boast," rescues the radiantly innocent Illinois woman, Azâkia, from rape at the hands of a Huron enemy. A triangular dilemma ensues. Celario lusts after Azâkia from the moment he sees her, while also bonding passionately with Ouabi, her spouse. Ouabi, the Illinois sachem, is tender to his friends but perpetually and vengefully at war with the Hurons. Azâkia is powerfully attracted to Celario, but unambivalently loyal to Ouabi. Ouabi generously understands the dynamics between the two of them and finally permits Celario to earn Azâkia through heroic demonstrations of loyalty to himself on the field of battle. The terms of Native American "marriage," as described by Morton, are flexible enough to permit the satisfaction of both desire and honor. Thus *Ouabi* is in some ways the pointed antithesis of the novel of seduction. But its affective commitments—to high-minded eroticism that crosses the boundaries of cultural difference, to tormented male friendship, to female fantasy, and to the ever-present option of suicide—clearly belong to the discourse of seduction in the early Republic.[18] They show how closely related sentimental seduction plots and narratives of race relations could be, and how, together, these elements provided a way for female authors to explore the psychology of power.

Morton's introduction and footnotes contain the poem's most self-conscious rhetoric, in both senses of the word "self-conscious": at once embarrassed and sophisticated. The volume opens with the dedication to Bowdoin of Morton's "wholly American" production, signed "Philenia." This is followed by a constipated letter from Bowdoin thanking Morton for the dedication and chiding her on her pseudonym: "In room of Philenia, he thinks it would be best the real name of the fair author should be substituted."

In this context, anthropology is a masculine discipline that women study. Morton's own "Introduction" is really a set of acknowledgments in which she enumerates her sources, especially Major General Benjamin Lincoln, whose "obliging communications" on "local rites and customs" constitute the "best information" available, and William Penn, who attests to the Indians' "comely, European-like faces" and their capacity for friendship, self-control, and self-government. She introduces anecdotal proof that "an amiable and polished European" can become an assimilated Native American under the influence of love.[19] She took the story of *Ouabi*, she says, from a prose tale in "Mr. Carey's entertaining and instructing Museum" *(The American Museum)*, which she does not hesitate to criticize and improve. Relying on anthropological "authorities" allows her to tell a tale of wife-switching and sentimental friendship between men of different races in terms of Native American rituals. Indian lore sanctioned by male experts is "a subject wholly American." Respect for the racial other is assimilated to national loyalty, a shift that legitimates the female poet's cultural authority.[20]

Celario, having fled Europe after a duel or other accidental murder, has wandered into the North American interior where, "[i]n hopeless exile," he "mourn[s] the tedious day" (10). One wonders whether Celario catches the habit of auto-elegiac reflection from the Native Americans he encounters, or whether he transmits sadness to them from the Old World. Having come to America afflicted with guilt and disenchantment, Celario seems to bring melancholia to the Illinois. But Ouabi, the singer of the

"Death Song" who concedes Azâkia to Celario and then expires, makes virtuous suicide look more indigenous than imported. And Azâkia, driven by folkloric authority to interpret her dreams literally, is only restrained from killing herself by the strength of her promise to Celario to postpone such drastic action. All three take turns offering to die for one another, showing repeatedly that suicide is proof of natural virtue, as well as providing an ostensibly nonaggressive way for the white male to win.

Ouabi is about men's sentimental homosocial dilemmas. Morton celebrates the bond between a European fleeing a duel gone wrong and a Native American sachem dedicated to a culture of hand-to-hand combat and personal revenge (19). This masculine primitivism is an implied criticism of the behavior of contemporary Anglo-American men, with their adulterous insincerity and antiheroic attention to business. It also lets Morton favor a blend of sentiment and aggression in a way quite different from the connection between mourning and resistance in Bleecker's poems. In *Ouabi,* masculine sensibility leads to action, and masculine suffering is catalytic. The passionate terrain reflects the emotional velocity of its inhabitants, and even their death songs react passionately to "the flames":

> Where MISSISSIPPI rolls his *parent flood*
> With slope impetuous to the surgy main,
> The desert's painted chiefs explore the wood,
> Or with the thund'ring *war-whoop* shake the plain.
>
> There the fierce *sachems* raise the battle's din,
> Or in the stream their active bodies lave,
> Or midst the flames their fearless songs begin—
> PAIN HAS NO TERRORS TO THE TRULY BRAVE. (10)

By contrast, the feminine melancholia that afflicts Azâkia produces the mental hyperactivity of suffering that has no outlet in action. In the opening episode of the poem, Celario draws "the deathful tube" (thereby introducing firearms into mid-America) and saves Azâkia from rape at the hands of a Huron brave. Her stance as a "soft captive" who "sickens with alarms" positions her as the one who suffers vicariously with and on behalf of male protagonists. Her suicidal desires when she is later convinced that Ouabi has died stem from dreams and fantasies that are shown to be erroneous (34, 41). Azâkia, whose experience is imaginative and figurative, dramatizes the connection between stasis, suffering, and poetry. Only through negotiations between the two men can her desire for Celario be fulfilled. Her feelings have the same transparent integrity as theirs and her psychological life is far richer, but she is never instrumental.

Celario's Italianate masculinity is marked by a similar proneness to mental torments. The poem implies that he has been unfairly punished, "banish'd" from his "native shore" after an honorable fight. Though he is disgusted now by Europe's "perfidious vice" and "the glare of wealth" (15), he is still looking for a place where he can fight unimpeded. He explains: "Far beyond the orient main, / By my rage a youth was slain; / He this daring arm defied, / By this arm the ruffian died" (12). Celario is delighted to discover that the North American interior is dominated by feuds between the Illinois and the Hurons and governed by an enthusiastic ethic of revenge. Indeed, the Hurons, as "bad Indians," are not much different than Bleecker's "scalpers." "Revenge," Morton specifies in one of her many ethnographic footnotes, is cultivated by the Indians as "one of their first virtues," but one taught "rather [as] a deliberate sentiment of the mind, than a rash ebullition of passion" (15, 29).

Given to choleric and sexual passions, Celario suffers from guilty feelings that do not afflict the Native Americans for whom revenge is a system, not a mood. Celario's guilt—especially the guilt that follows his erotic stares at Azâkia—is a sign of the European decadence that Ouabi heals. When Ouabi enters while he is trying unsuccessfully to seduce Azâkia, Celario stands "with averted mien, / Struck to the soul, by secret guilt oppress'd" (26). Ouabi proves his wisdom by entrusting his tribe, and particularly Azâkia, to the wounded Celario's care while he goes off to war. Overcome by Ouabi's generous trust, Celario launches into a rhapsodic hymn to masculine sensibility and homosocial friendship:

> Native reason's piercing eye,
> Melting pity's tender sigh,
> Changeless virtue's living flame,
> Meek contentment, free from blame,
> Open friendship's gen'rous care,
> EV'RY BOON OF LIFE IS HERE! (27)

In response to Ouabi's earlier questions about what ails Europeans, Celario itemizes the "traitors of the mind": terror, guilt, envy, fear, suspicion, affectation, passion, and more (p. 17). Ouabi treats guilt, not desire, as Celario's problem, a diagnosis with which Celario concurs much later, confessing his "guilty flame" and "perfidious art" (pp. 43–44):

> Thus great *Ouabi* sooths with gentle care
> The guilty anguish of *Celario's* breast,
> Dissuades his purpose from the coming war,
> And calms his stormy passions into rest. (28)

The relationship between cross-racial guilt and homosocial bonding is very strong here, as it is throughout the literature of sensibility. Moral as well as power differentials frequently organize scenes of masculine affection. One man becomes emotionally transparent to another when his guilt is perceived and forgiven. Morton's focus on masculine love is pertinent both to her defense of Native Americans and to her concern with how men treat women. Ouabi dramatizes the moral rescue of European manhood by means of Indian friendship. And Celario's ability to restrain his impulses toward seduction, with Ouabi's help, advances him toward a noncoercive marriage with Azâkia.

After Celario and Ouabi have been saved by each other, the two friends are briefly poised in moral equality. But Ouabi quickly removes himself from competition with Celario, bowing out not once, but several times over. He renounces his "marriage" to Azâkia so that she and Celario can finally become the couple they were always meant to be. Ouabi vows to pursue a career of revenge against the Hurons and quickly selects another woman in a spirit of sexual pragmatism and formal symmetry: now there can be a double wedding. Finally, during the celebratory dance, he keels over and dies (47). Morton gives Ouabi two death scenes, therefore: the earlier one in which he actually sings a "Death Song" while being tortured by the Hurons, and his actual last words delivered near the end of the poem. In this final speech, Ouabi interprets the meaning of his demise and completes Celario's assimilation into the tribe by sending him off to war in his stead: "*Celario!* thou my place sustain, / The chiefs expect thee on the plain" (48).

Ouabi's exit conforms to the plot of the "Vanishing American" syndrome in texts by white writers, according to which Indians die bravely at each other's hands or sing themselves to death alone in the forest.[21] The structural convenience of this device, of course, lies in the way North America depopulates itself to make room for white settlement. Morton downplays the pathos of belatedness that pervades some versions of the Indian death song. Ouabi is not unhappy in love, but drawn to war. His proleptic death song looks beyond stoicism toward defiance: "*Rear'd midst the war-empurpled plain, / What Illinois submits to pain!*"[22] Ouabi's song ends by confronting the problem of succession: "*Think not with me my tribe decays,*

/ *More glorious chiefs the hatchet raise;* / *Not unreveng'd their sachem dies*" (37). The new sachem is Celario. Having thought he was about to enjoy "pleasure, wealth, and fame" with Azâkia (47), Celario finds himself slated to reenact the energizing but endlessly repetitive contest between the Illinois and the Hurons.

Ouabi ends with a double coda. The first, within the frame of the Indian tale, focuses on the "spot" where Ouabi is buried, transformed into a monument where his "NATIVE VIRTUES shine." The three stanzas dedicated to the "sacred pile" honored by "each lonely *Illinois*" are heavily glossed. One footnote comments on Native Americans' visitations to the "sepulchres . . . of their chiefs" and to "rites and ceremonies" performed there, rites "not precisely known to the Anglo-Americans." Another note describes the physical appearance of the burial pile and likens it to ancient structures of England and Wales (50), a comparison that prepares the way for the parallels between Anglo-Saxon and Native American virtue claimed in the poem's concluding lines. A typographical ornament isolates the last two stanzas of the book. Here Morton addresses the republic:

> Let not the CRITIC, with disdainful eye,
> In the weak verse condemn *the novel plan;*
> But own, that VIRTUE beams in *ev'ry sky,*
> Tho wayward frailty is the lot of man.
>
> Dear as ourselves to hold each faithful friend,
> To treat the path, which INNATE LIGHT inspires,
> To guard our country's *rites,* her soil defend,
> Is all that NATURE, all that HEAV'N requires. (50–51)

In juxtaposing these two concluding passages, Morton implies that "our country's *rites*" are analogous to Native American practices of piety and war. By eliding the difference between the "rites" of Anglo-American and Indian cultures, Morton uses ethnography to suppress the knowledge of violent colonization. Both the Illinois nation and the United States, these stanzas suggest, must honor their dead, bring marriage in line with desire, and defend their territories. This parallelism works only as long as the Americans are thought of as defending their lands against the British, not against the Illinois. For once Native and European Americans want to defend the same soil against each other, therapeutic parallels break down. Morton, sensing this, lets Ouabi withdraw before he is beaten.

Morton, like Bleecker, relies on the connection between emotion and history. In the poems of both writers, racial issues are experienced as collective, national, or public realities. Race is inseparable from the politics of war, whether war occurs in the context of the Iroquois alliance that haunts Bleecker or the Huron-Illinois rivalry that structures Morton's *Ouabi*. At the same time, emotion takes the form of longing, and melancholia becomes a figure for subjectivity itself. If race is a historical theme and if melancholy is inseparable from subjectivity, then the Age of Sensibility can be defined by its focus on the moments when consciousness dilates to historical horizons and when history is compressed into consciousness. The "rites" of grief—Bleecker's mourning for Abella, inseparable from her Indian-hating commitment to national unity, and Morton's admiration for both Native American and Anglo-American memorials, inseparable from her liberal urban patriotism—are central to the careers of both.

Race and "Rising Glory"

*P*hilip Freneau's nationalist poem, *The Rising Glory of America*—begun before the Revolution and rewritten after it—is organized by the geography of sensibility. Geographical and emotional mobility have an exceptional affinity for one another in Freneau's work. His career was shaped jointly by a print culture fervently engaged in promoting a republican America and by the trade routes of the British Atlantic. Freneau was intermittently a sea captain engaged in the coastal trade and trade with the West Indies, Bermuda, and the Canary Islands. He missed most of the first three years of the American Revolution because he had shipped to St. Croix (Santa Cruz) and other West Indian islands. He voyaged to Teneriffe in 1779 and was captured and interned for three months on a British prison ship while heading for St. Croix again in 1780. Later in life, for several long stretches, he captained vessels owned by others or owned jointly with his brother. In between these seafaring periods, he managed and wrote for anti-Federalist, eventually Jeffersonian, publications.

A collaborative production by Freneau and Hugh Henry Brackenridge, the first version of *The Rising Glory of America* was read at the Princeton commencement exercises of September 1771. Freneau was the eldest son of an educated Huguenot merchant and landowning family of Manhattan and, later, New Jersey. Brackenridge, from western Pennsylvania, went on to a career in law; he published a magazine, poems, plays, memoirs, legal commentary, and the picaresque novel, *Modern*

Chivalry. Brackenridge and Freneau, along with James Madison and William Bradford, son of a Philadelphia printer and later printer for the first Continental Congress, formed the American Whig Society at Princeton in opposition to the Tory Cliosophic Society. Princeton gave all four men access to a newly activist homosocial politics. They instigated voluntary associations crafted for experimental debates over the culture and politics of the British Atlantic—debates over diversifying ideologies.[23]

The Rising Glory of America was at first an ambitious, complimentary overview of Britain's colonial expansion in North America. The 1771 version was published in pamphlet form the next year. Freneau reprinted the poem in the first edition of his collected poems, which appeared in 1786. He cut several long sections either because they were Brackenridge's contributions or because they exalted Britain as the carrier of ethical empire. He replaced them with attacks on the British in the name of liberty and by new visions of a Pax Americana. Despite the reversal of the moral status of Britain between the first and second versions of *The Rising Glory of America*, though, the poem's repertoire of thematic, narrative, and perspectival devices remains largely the same.

Emerging from collegiate collaboration, subtitled "part of a Dialogue pronounced on a public occasion," *The Rising Glory* takes the form of a "conversation" among three young Americans with the unlikely names of Acasto, Eugenio, and Leander. The moods of the three male voices— their itinerary through melancholia, ambition, anxiety, and exaltation are fully part of the plot. We may be used to thinking of the relationship between gender and allegory in this period in connection with feminine personifications of Fancy, Liberty, Nature, and Evening. But the practice (loosely grounded in classical reference) of attaching masculine voices to allegorical talking heads with exotic or abstract names was equally conventional. This is a habit reinforced by the Augustan tradition of Horatian satire and verse epistles, by Shaftesbury's *The Moralists*, by the Roman signatures attached to political pamphlets and letters to the editor ("Brutus," "Cato," "Democritus," "Jurisperitus"), and by the personas of periodical essayists ("the Spectator"). The net effect of such naming strategies is to dignify opinion by disembodying it. Put more charitably, thinking aloud is shown to be identical to the work of the imagination.

The three *Rising Glory* discussants argue about colonization and racial origins. They take up the relative guilt and innocence of Spanish and English settlement, or, in the 1786 version, the morality of the expansion of the new republic. Fundamental to this theme is their attention to the comparative degrees of violence inflicted *on* native peoples and then—particularly in the 1786 text—*by* them.[24] The connection between thinking, imagination, and racial consciousness is played out in an international arena. Finally, the preoccupation with imperial ethics expresses a highly literate masculine melancholia. Indeed, the question of race seems to arise in order to induce the fantastically enlarged subjectivity of the melancholy individual.

Fancy is the device that carries sensibility into the public history of the world. In its double character as poetic agency and as historical film-maker, fancy demonstrates the compatibility of private and public fantasy. One sees the same combination in Freneau's "Power of Fancy," written at Princeton in 1770. Here fancy is the spirit who walks at night—in a wonderful phrase—"On the surface of the brain." Fancy leads the poet on an accelerated tour of the moon, hell, Arcadia, the Hebrides, and Bermuda. Then we swoop over the "chalky cliff" of "Britain's fertile land," shifting to temporal movement. At Dover, we "Look back and view, thro' many a year / Caesar, Julius Caesar, there." In a little over 150 lines, fancy leads us eastward past Greece, Troy, Rome, the Ganges, California, and finally, "returning home," to a melancholy site, "Belinda's tomb."[25] Freneau's early poem on the subject thus sums up fancy's power as the muse of the liberal arts curriculum. We found the same structural affinity between imagination and historical survey in Wheatley's "On Imagination" and "To . . . Dartmouth," and in Barbauld's "Summer Evening's Meditation" and "Eighteen Hundred and Eleven." The connection between public culture and fancy also offers a precedent for poems like Coleridge's "Destiny of Nations" of 1794–96, and even to Blake's phantasmagoric responses to the American and French revolutions. The link between history and fancy lasts longer and structures a larger body of poetry than it is given credit for.

The prospect is the topographical correlative of fancy from Denham's *Cooper's Hill* (1642) to Pope's *Windsor Forest* (1712) and Thomson's *The Seasons*. This tradition operates powerfully in Timothy Dwight's long poem on Connecticut. *Greenfield Hill* (1794) has sections titled "The Destruction of the Pequods" (a reference to the Pequot War of 1637 that led to the tribe's dispersal); then, "Prospect of the Country between Greenfield Hill and the Sound," and finally, "The Vision, a Prospect of the Future Happiness of America." Dwight makes the codependence of the poetry of prospect and the history of conquest fully explicit.[26]

The most telling difference between the two versions of *The Rising Glory of America* is that, by 1786, Indians had become the subject of speculations about origins that are inseparable from speculations about the epistemology of racial explanation. The displacement of British heroes by American ones and of Britain's empire by American expansion produces more complicated emotions about Native Americans. The speakers take race as their subject, acknowledge and bemoan the violence of territorial conquest inflicted on native peoples, and express active hostility to Native Americans, all at once.[27]

The first speaker, Acasto, begins the 1786 version of *The Rising Glory of America* by trying to deflect the tragic results of Spanish conquest: "But why, to prompt your tears, should we resume, / The tale of Cortez," he asks: "Better [that] these northern realms demand our song"—realms not built on mining fortunes (1.49–51). Eugenio, however, is not ready to dispense with myths of origins. For Eugenio, the history of American native folk everywhere is a knotty intellectual problem: "But whence arose / That vagrant race who love the shady vale. . . . / For long has this perplext the sages' skill / . . . Tradition lends no aid / To unveil this secret to the human eye, / When first these various nations, north and south, / Possesst these shores, or from what countries came" (1.51). The possibilities are several. Did they spring "from some primaeval head / In their own lands" (1.52)? What would have happened in the Andes when, according to Biblical history, "the general deluge drowned the world"(1.52)? But other "philosophers" hold that it was the flood that created mountains in the first place (1.52). "Perhaps," Eugenio continues, imagining land links in the Arctic, "the hardy tribes / Of banished Jews, Siberians, Tartars wild / Came over icy mountains, or on floats, / First reached these coasts" (1.53). This is not satisfying either, and he offers "yet another argument more strange, / Reserved for men of deeper thought, and late" (1.54). Maybe there was a continent "which once sustain'd / Nations and tribes, of vanished memory" as they passed through the Atlantic Ocean, "Where navies now explore their briny way" (1.55).

Leander chides the "roving mind" that "thinks his knowledge far beyond all limit" (1.55). In place of the "flimsy cobwebs of a sophist's brain," the rational Leander provides "the voice of history"—which turns out to be the record of "venturous seamen" who left Africa for the Canary Islands, the West Indies, and the coast of Brazil (1.55–56). The descendants of the Carthaginians built the "huge cities" of Peru and Mexico (1.58). But Leander is sure such cultural rivals never made it up as far as the "northern dark domain"(1.59). They founded "No towns . . . No arts" among the "tribes unskill'd" (1.59). This proves, he concludes, that North American Indians "were a different race; / From whom descended, 'tis not ours to say" (1.59). Leander becomes helplessly mystical in turn in order to make it all right to displace native peoples in North America: "That power, no doubt, who furnish'd trees, and plants, / And animals to this vast continent / Spoke into being man among the rest" (1.59). Neither European nor Carthaginian, the racial identity of American Indians takes the form of an epistemological dilemma that men bond over. The problem of race makes the club part of national culture.

Finally, we arrive at the Euro-American line of descent: "what a change is here!—what arts arise! / What towns and capitals!" Acasto prompts "learned Eugenio" to explain "the cause" of European settlement. Eugenio starts with religious freedom, clearly the central motive for Freneau's Huguenot forebears: "By persecution wronged / And sacerdotal rage, our fathers came" (1.61). They encountered Native Americans and their own capacity for massacre: "what streams / Of blood were shed! what Indian hosts were slain" (1.62–63). Leander, sounding much like Bleecker, seizes on this point, emphasizing not the Indian dead but "fierce Indian tribes" moved by "vengeful malice" and egged on "by Gallia's hostile sons" (1.63). As part of the nervous legitimation of the spreading U.S. population, George Washington comes on stage, a young man riding out of the "distant wilds" of Virginia to fend off "bold invaders" (1.65–66). Freneau's Washington uses the Anglo-American "we": "we boast no feats / Of cruelty like Europe's murdering breed." Once we've won, we're content to stop, displaying the clemency of the sensitive republican: "each American, true hearted, learns / To conquer and to spare," instead of seeking revenge "on a vanquished foe." Eugenio and Leander proceed to an American pastoral that quickly becomes an American georgic, while Acasto praises "commerce," "the wished exchange" that gratifies "the varying mind of man." Trade—as "adventurous" as fancy itself—is the cure for the lurking guilt of Euro-American settlement.

At this point the poem shifts from a retrospective to a futuristic orientation. Leander looks ahead to the next stages of the progress of empire "when we shall spread / Dominion." Acasto, "warmed" to the point of tears, prophesies the subsequent fame of the "rising" American "empires." Eugenio contributes a snarling diatribe against British kings, Leander shudders at the memory of the revolution, and Acasto glimpses on the horizon "A new Jerusalem. . . . Millennium. Paradise Anew" (1.82). The millennium pulls together the speakers' different idioms into a shared nationalist agenda—even if the verse persists in sounding like an anthology of rhetorical styles.

The Rising Glory demonstrates how from the very start of its national poetry, the United States was situated in a speculative topography that was mobile, miscellaneous, and highly disjunctive or episodic. The same, of course, is true of Britain's national poetry. The nation is not fixed in place or time, according to this aesthetic, but is deterritorialized and constructed as a series of nonconsecutive vignettes. The nation becomes stylistically available through spatial or temporal fluidity, an unceasing tour with several talkative guides.[28]

Eighteenth-century serial prospect poems like *The Rising Glory* are vehicles for the citizen-subject who draws other cultures within the scope of his or her attention. Its vistas convey the perspective of intellectual, comparative experiment and dramatize long-distance sympathy. Or they can signify the commercial analogue of the overlooking eye, the unifying back-and-forth of trade. The prospect can be the device of protest against oppressive global systems such as slavery. The prospective aesthetic bears all these meanings. But it does so through scenic transformation in a way that is singularly, even disturbingly, nonpossessive—even as possession is a major theme. Those of us engaged in cross-cultural, interdisciplinary, multivariate scholarship may think that mobile, serial forms are postmodern. However, the talking heads of eighteenth-century poems who string prospective vignettes together remind us that the master narratives of nation, race, and manhood, of liberty and sympathy, did not require either stable images of the nation or images of the nation as itself stable in place or time. Sensibility is orchestrated by flights of fancy as well as by the desire for local ground.[29] What does persist throughout the practice of fancy in the works of Bleecker, Morton, and Freneau is the embarrassed, guilty sense of being implicated in imperial or national violence. In most instances, fancy comes close enough to depicting the real politics of colonialism to wish, ambivalently, that it were actually possible to conquer *and* to spare.

CHAPTER SIX

Walkers, Stalkers, Captives, Slaves

Sensitive Veterans

*H*umanists and artists of every stripe are rediscovering the civic gratification of the link between culture and place.[1] Scholars interested in cultural geography and its impact on the perturbations of citizenship are
particularly engaged by the question of what happens when space is defined by mobility instead of by habitation. Patsy Yaeger asks, "Why has
the spatial world . . . become such an indispensable category of social and
cultural analysis? Why space now?"[2] My response to this question is to
wonder, why space then? We are witnessing the revival of this question,
not its invention. Speculative operations in late eighteenth-century texts
are geographically configured. Actively vacant spaces and human circu-
lation through them do not have the same cultural meaning today as they
did two hundred years ago. They are amenable, however, then and now
to description through spatial vocabularies.

In the decades of the American early national period and the Napoleonic wars, Anglo-American literary works were heavily populated with
sensitive veterans. Embodying both virtue and obsolescence, such figures
appear to be lost in movements across oceans and nations dictated by
obscure but potent forces. Disoriented veterans and characters like them
are seeking both new professions and recovered influence. They exhibit
a postwar vocationlessness that is markedly prone to conspiratorial or,
conversely, paranoid feelings. The title character of Charles Brockden
Brown's *Edgar Huntly or, Memoirs of a Sleep-Walker* (1799), who is not a veteran but simply a bewildered member of the postrevolutionary generation, is plagued by this condition from beginning to end. Dr. Updike
Underhill, the protagonist of Royall Tyler's fictional narrative of North
African captivity, *The Algerine Captive* (1797), successfully negotiates—by
way of slavery—the transition from underemployed veteran to physician.

The Algerine Captive is part of a substantial body of writing inspired by
the imminence of the new republic's first foreign war. War against the
Barbary States broke out officially in 1801 and again in 1815, but conflict
simmered throughout the 1790s, too. In the literature of the Barbary conflicts, the civic place of forward-looking national masculinity is secured

by racial role-reversal, a moral test administered in an international setting. The white man from the United States, where captive Africans are held as slaves, finds himself in Africa in chains, owned by Algerians.[3]

Edgar Huntly and *The Algerine Captive* utilize perspectives that we can find in British works of the same period, despite the fact that critics have read these works as being solely about America. Brown and Tyler show that even the discourse of American exceptionalism at work in the fiction of the early republic relies on a more broadly shared transatlantic idiom. These novels have in common views of the nation which can be found in works by Wordsworth, Edgeworth, or Byron. Their protagonists experience the nation—and sometimes the world—as a spatial field in which men wander around, afflicted by disorientation and hypermobility. Theirs is the geography of masculine sensibility.

Despite the porous spaces in which the novel is set, Edgar Huntly never has enough mental room for the intersubjective transactions of sensibility. Such relationships, after all, require a perceptible distance between self and other. Huntly has enjoyed and lost sympathetic male friendship, and that is why he is so invested in understanding the death of his intimate friend, Waldegrave. Edgar Huntly is a character who keeps failing at sensibility. When other characters migrate from Ireland to Pennsylvania, he finds that the masculine homosocial bonds surrounding him multiply and close in on him. These bonds are felt as epistemological crisis, obsessive curiosity, and mourning. The transatlantic and Mediterranean arena, by contrast, makes sympathy possible for Tyler's Underhill. Only international space allows the protagonist of *The Algerine Captive* to discover his national feelings, his views on American slavery, and his capacity to be at once the subject and the object of masculine pathos. At the heart of each novel is an experience of captivity that brings about temporary racial role-reversal. Edgar Huntly falls into an imprisoning and ensavaging cave. When he finds his way out into the campsite of Native American warriors who have seized a white woman, he returns to a world of more conventional captivity. Underhill is himself enslaved, and becomes fully American by becoming more sentimental.[4]

James Grantham Turner once remarked that if the phrase "secret ministry" had appeared in a Restoration text instead of in Coleridge's "Frost at Midnight," it would have referred not to the weather but to political conspiracy. The relationship in Anglo-American culture between conspiracy and the passionate male subject remains close in this period. Gordon Wood begins his 1982 essay with the unbeatable line, "Were the American Revolutionaries mentally disturbed?"

Seventeenth-century England was filled with talk and fears of conspiracies of all kinds. . . . Yet by this period many of the conspiracies had become very different from those depicted . . . earlier. . . . The term . . . became used more vaguely and broadly to refer to any combination of persons . . . united for a presumed common end. The word acquired a more general and indeterminate meaning in political discourse. Its usage suggested confusion rather than certainty. . . . Accounts of plots by court or government were no longer descriptions of actual events but interpretations of otherwise puzzling concatenations of events. By the eighteenth century conspiracy was not simply a means of explaining how rulers were deposed; it had become a common means [especially by those removed from the sphere of direct political agency] of explaining how rulers and others directing political events really operated.[5]

Modern masculine affection emerged under the aegis of political conspiracy long before Charles Brockden Brown turned a murder mystery into a thicket of homosocial loyalties on the American frontier. By Brown's time, conspiracy had become less of a political movement and more of a masculine world view. Wood quite rightly attributes conspiracy theories to political conditions specific to the 1790s. The pervasiveness of masculine conspiracy stories before and after this decade, however, bolsters the argument that the *emotions* of conspiracy account for the persistent literary adaptability of such theories.

Compared with Gordon Wood, Eve Sedgwick, starting from literary instead of constitutional history, provides us with a different time line for the evolution of "the paranoid Gothic." This genre, she suggests, is defined in later eighteenth-century British texts by "a male hero . . . in a close, usually murderous relation to another male figure, in some respects his 'double,' to whom he seems to be mentally transparent."[6] The plots of such novels zero in on an intimate, mutually suspicious dyad or triad of would-be conspirators. Sedgwick reads gothic fiction in terms of male panic with a material social origin in homophobia, "a structural residue of terrorist potential, of blackmailability." How do we relate an argument like Wood's, which stresses the shifting political meanings of conspiracy, to Sedgwick's view that the late eighteenth-century gothic was a cultural formation based on the continuum of homosocial-homosexual desire?

Late seventeenth- and early eighteenth-century texts and plays dealing with conspiracy are about masculinity. These works foreground the overheated emotional atmosphere of the conspiratorial group, where passionate male friendship and deadly mutual suspicion often reside together in the imploded oedipal model that Sedgwick describes. This is how I would start to read Sedgwick into Wood. Likewise, a reading of Wood into Sedgwick interprets the masculine conspiratorial bond as being quite directly about politics and about the emotional labor required for political opposition. Actual or suspected political conspiracies from the Restoration through the early eighteenth century and the repeated treatments of conspiratorial emotions in drama and fiction are as much about establishing legitimate male political subjectivity in a parliamentary era as about extremist fantasies of overthrow or assassination. As I proposed in earlier chapters, constituting a group of men as a political interest or party was inseparable from the conspiracy model, because political parties were initially viewed as transgressive or dangerous. The paternal and brotherly cathexes of conspiracy narratives carry over into gothic tales in verse and prose, which regularly connect political identities to transgressive or marginal forms of masculine subjectivity and intersubjectivity.

In Barbary captivity narratives, which connect "otherness" within the nation to "otherness" without, veterans represented the quest for meaningful postrevolutionary manhood. The aftermath of the War of Independence overlaps with America's first foreign conflicts. This is why *Edgar Huntly* and *The Algerine Captive,* written within two years of each other, share a strong thematic resemblance despite the obvious differences between them. Masculine melancholia of the kind we see in *Edgar Huntly* carries over into the international trauma of North African captivity. These works feature vocational coming-of-age narratives in which the central characters are solitaries who nonetheless desire the company of other men. Both protagonists experience interracial trauma (absorption, attack, or enslavement) and the fluctuations of sensibility within a clearly transatlantic culture.

In the literature of the North African conflicts, Tyler's picaro moves between different kinds of masculine communities. His vocational itinerary includes the passage through an archaic orientalist state of tyranny and immobility. The centrality of slavery to the future of the United States must be collectively and individually reconciled with the memory of the struggle for independence. A sense of white male citizenship is inseparable from vocational definition through property in one's own free labor. The converse is also true, so that worries about white men's roles in the republic give rise to a market for tales of unfree white labor at the mercy of Africans.

The ideological outcome of these tales is complex. Racial "others" are depicted as savage, but chattel slavery in the United States is deplored. Free white labor (the rationale for race-based retaliation against Native Americans) and the self-critical subjectivity of the masculine citizen form a single intricate agenda. White men are veterans, victims, and sympathizers for victims. Policies of national militancy and international aggression provide the context for antislavery positions. The bond between free labor and the construction of white masculinity operates powerfully—but also ironically, for white manhood also requires, quite often, cosmopolitan empathy.

"Why Should I Proceed Like a Plotter?"

Charles Brockden Brown's *Edgar Huntly; or, Memoirs of a Sleepwalker* is a novel of perpetual motion.[7] The action is set in two countries, the United States and Ireland, and deals with settled Euro-Americans, new immigrants, and Native Americans in Pennsylvania. We expect its dramas of speculation and misunderstanding, enacted by characters following one another through a porous semiwilderness, to configure an idea of the nation or the national subject through comparative devices: the new world compared to the old, good intentions compared to bad faith. But our expectation is substantially foiled. National difference dissipates or fails to emerge in the facile though deeply upsetting flow of masculine homosocial ties from Ireland to Pennsylvania. The novel turns on the possibility that old-world relationships may be restaged in North America. Delusional doubles cross the Atlantic essentially intact in order to continue their mystifying career in a different historical geography. *Edgar Huntly* subordinates the difference between Britain and America to the seemingly more profound disorientations of their resemblance. Even the crucial substrate of racial difference—the apparent operation of Native American conspiracy—mirrors rather than opposes the intimate confusion of the white male characters.

Edgar Huntly seems to be distinguished by its lack of investment in national territory or national character. How can we consider the role of history, as well as the meaning of place, in the peripatetic action of *Edgar Huntly?* The main event is a man walking constantly through half-familiar settlements and wilderness, followed by another man who tries to catch him, or to catch up with him. Does walking signify the lack of place in *Edgar Huntly,* or is place constituted, if not possessed, by the act of walking through temporal and topographical hollows? In a narrative where so many principles of causal connection are strategically repressed, the bonds of homosocial masculinity constitute relationships that are periodically comforting but disastrous in their final outcome. Conspiratorial men play out the consequences of cheating Indians out of their lands in thoroughly muddled states of mind.

Brown's novel falls squarely in the tradition of male stalking stories. As Sidney Krause notes, later variants range from Poe's "William Wilson" and Wilde's *The Picture of Dorian Gray* to "The Secret Sharer" and *Invisible Man*.[8] I would add *Frankenstein* and Melville's *Pierre* to this list, as well as *The Scarlet Letter* and *Moby-Dick*. In its immediate context, *Edgar Huntly* is closest to the English Jacobin type of masculine mysteries. Its generic cousins include Godwin's *Caleb Williams* (1794) and Bage's *Hermsprong or Man As He Is Not* (1796), in which the protagonist is the son of an Englishman mysteriously hounded into the wilderness.[9]

By the time Brown's work was published in the late 1790s, as Wood notes, conspiracy "suggested confusion rather than certainty," and accounts of plots consist of lengthy speculations regarding causality. Conspiracy narratives become "interpretations" rather than statements of events believed to have actually taken place. Here is where the category of space comes in. By the 1790s, the genre of male stalking stories represents just one of many kinds of narratives structured by imaginative and geographical mobility, by fancy and wandering, by hyperbolic prospects and inexhaustible protagonists who seem never to stay put. If this is not the rhetoric of deterritorialization in Appadurai's sense of a severed link between identity and place, it is a rhetoric in which both place and identity are constituted through mobility.[10]

Conspiracy and paranoia induce a particular geography, a subset of the literature of wandering. Mobility takes the form not only of transatlantic displacement and the appropriation of native lands on the frontier, but also of repetitive, obsessive pacing back and forth over the same ground. "America" emerges, in *Edgar Huntly,* as the place where white men end up walking in circles, obsessively focused on one another, feeling all the emotions of conspirators but having entirely repressed the knowledge that land ownership is a political act. This conspiracy ends up being about the conspirators' feelings for one another.

The book begins as a murder mystery. The precipitating action of *Edgar Huntly* is the murder of Huntly's close friend, Waldegrave, near Huntly's uncle's farm in Pennsylvania. Huntly's proclaimed desire throughout is to catch the killer. At the end of the book, he learns, through no agency of his own, that Waldegrave was murdered by a "sanguinary and audacious" Indian determined to have "some gratification of his vengeance" for land seizures.[11] The mystery, ultimately, *is* a race-based conspiracy in the tradition of the legendary Indian plotter, Pontiac.

For almost three hundred pages, however, the murder mystery keeps Huntly obsessing about Clithero, an Irish immigrant laborer who resides on a nearby farm. Two of Brown's three protagonists are sleepwalkers, mysteries to one another and to themselves. They are periodically swallowed up by hollow spaces in the permeable Pennsylvania ground. All three are builders of ingenious boxes, drawers, and cabinets in which risky documents are concealed but not safely contained by systems of hidden mechanisms. An older man, Sarsefield, who has been entangled in the earlier lives of both Clithero and Huntly, constitutes the third member of the novel's organizing masculine triangle. When Sarsefield arrives on the scene, he applies a Sherlock Holmes–type logic that helps clarify some of the action, but it is precisely this clarity that Huntly rejects in favor of the inexplicable behavior of Clithero.

Clithero tells his life story in response to Huntly's interrogation. Because of Clithero's melancholy aspect and secretive nocturnal wanderings, Huntly suspects Clithero of murdering Waldegrave. A good deal of the peripatetic quality of the novel comes from following Huntly's endless treks on the trail of Clithero through unpredictable wilderness terrain. Clithero, of course, is a sleepwalker, but Huntly is, too. He does not realize that he himself has taken his treasured collection of Waldegrave's theologically daring letters out of the secret cabinet he himself has built under the fatherly tutelage of Sarsefield and hidden them "between the rafters and shingles" of the house (250).

Carroll Smith-Rosenberg offers the best treatment of *Edgar Huntly*, one fully attuned to the transatlantic structure of the story.[12] I agree with Smith-Rosenberg that *Edgar Huntly* takes place on profoundly colonized terrain: "the novel moves from a former site of British imperialism, Pennsylvania, to an ongoing site of British imperialism, Ireland—and back again—from the struggle of a landless Pennsylvania youth to find a secure niche in the middle classes to the struggle of a landless native Irish boy to find the same security." Smith-Rosenberg illuminates the dynamics of class at work in the intricacies of land ownership and inheritance. She foregrounds the dynamics of gender, particularly the places in the novel where white women inflect relationships between men. Her account highlights the embedded conventions of Indian captivity narratives that govern Huntly's realization that Native Americans have taken a white woman captive. And she emphasizes the important fact that

Pennsylvania had paid its militia after the War of Independence in two-hundred-acre pieces of Indian land.

I differ from Smith-Rosenberg in my conclusion about the meaning of the relationships between geography and subjectivity, motion and masculinity in *Edgar Huntly*. She proposes that in the world of this novel, property constitutes both the social and the psychological stability of the middle-class subject. Conversely, to be dispossessed of land is to be regarded as subjectively fragmented. That is, *Edgar Huntly* is about America insofar as it shows how property acquisition through the appropriation of Indian lands enables middle-class selfhood.

But I argue that the incoherence or madness of the old and new worlds *includes* the landowning classes, and that subjective instability, therefore, is not so easily linked to the lack of real property. Paranoia, irrational violence, and a demonic twin brother plague Mrs. Lorimer, the Irish landowning lady, as well as Clithero, the psychopathic steward whom she has raised from his peasant origins. Both of them end up miserable in Pennsylvania. One of the key points in Smith-Rosenberg's argument is that the figure of the white woman—marginal to or absent from the narrative action—provides a recuperative possibility for the Euro-American male subject. The white woman provides him with a socially appropriate "other" and enables him to "eliminate his confused, colonized double." "Is gender a more telling fetish of difference," Smith-Rosenberg asks, "and hence of stability, than race?" Her answer is yes. I disagree. In a novel where the landowning Irish widow cares passionately for unpredictable men who care passionately for one another, white womanhood does not seem to me to offer a domesticating defense. Heterosexual relationships are decidedly in thrall to male homosocial ones.

Land has a spatial dimension other than possession or property in this book and in other texts where the topographical gothic is a prominent feature. While the ontological fluidity of the land is certainly linked to masculine paranoia, landownership by married couples does not seem to offer any normalizing solution. Some of the characters seem to be upwardly mobile, some permanently dispossessed, but there is no stabilization of these tendencies, even at the conclusion of the novel.

Patsy Yaeger's suggestion that "folds and pockets" in the landscape can both signify and hide histories of racial violence works well for *Edgar Huntly*. The cave into which Huntly falls provides the setting for an encounter with the repressed terror of racial difference. As Smith-Rosenberg argues, the cave ritually transforms Huntly into one of the "savages" whose land his family claimed and whose vengeance was visited upon his parents. The consequence of his fall is redoubled violence, of which he is the agent. But the unstable ontology of space in *Edgar Huntly* includes more than the cave to which Huntly, while awake, tracks Clithero and into which Huntly, while sleepwalking, later drops. All topographies, household spaces, and containers in the novel are plagued by a tendency to open in unexpected ways. What categories or histories are incorporated into and spring out of these other spaces?

Yaeger invites us to think about "geography as ghost story" in order "to invent a lexicon or dictionary of the strange effects of space." For "what is unrepresentable about space" includes "the . . . pressure of what is hidden, encrypted, repressed, or unspoken in global and local histories." The categorical or foundational struggles to which Yaeger refers are located in depths that are simultaneously close to the surface:

> Although space seems to work horizontally . . . , it also possesses a history: not as a vertical dimension but as a series of folds and pockets, as the dimensional incorporation and exhalation of time. We could argue that, just as time enfolds and produces space, space also enfolds and tries to consume time.[13]

As Yaeger implies, finding these "folds and pockets" brings us into contact not with recovered historical memory but with the haunted atmosphere that provokes historical investigation itself.

In *Edgar Huntly* cavernous spaces are figures of an explanation pathology. Suddenly empty receptacles or houses and suddenly hollow ground precipitate lengthy meditations on knowledge, analysis, and perception. The reasonings dramatized throughout the book focus not on comparison—not on questions of resemblance and difference that could support the discourse of cause and effect—but on motives, which seem much less manageable. Some mysteries are never solved, such as the subplot involving the illogic of Waldegrave's finances. The ones that are solved, such as Huntly's own behavior while sleepwalking, bring no cessation of questioning. And once the murder mystery ends with the suspiciously ad hoc news (near the close of the twenty-seventh and last chapter) that a Delaware Indian killed Waldegrave, the dilemma of whether Clithero is Sarsefield's victim or his tormentor sustains the reader and Huntly in a condition of uncertainty through the concluding "letters" until the end of the story. The lack of causal relations drives Huntly and Brown to keep asking questions about termination, while it is precisely the absence of causal explanation that makes the narrative so repetitive

or interminable. The absence of causality and the absence of work-
able cultural comparison in this transatlantic novel are two sides of the
same coin.

Edgar Huntly interweaves speculation and topography. A particularly
striking aspect of the intellectual walks that constitute *Edgar Huntly* is the
relationship between an immense curiosity and the utter lack of categorical difference or causal understanding available to gratify that curiosity.
When Edgar Huntly, seeking the murderer of his friend, begins to suspect
the Irish immigrant, Clithero, his questions are narratively reiterated as
perambulation. The interrogative pressure in chapters 2 and 3 is remarkable. Huntly asks himself twenty-three questions in approximately ten
pages, and typically the questions are posed in consecutive spurts of three,
four, or five. Wandering gives rise to speculation, and speculation repeats
itself as wandering.

> The more I revolved the pensive and reserved deportment of this
> man, the ignorance in which we were placed respecting his for-
> mer situation, his possible motives for abandoning his country
> and chusing a station so much below the standard of his intellec-
> tual attainment, the stronger my suspicions became. . . .
>
> But how were these doubts to be changed into absolute cer-
> tainty? Henceforth this man was to become the subject of my
> scrutiny. I was to gain all the knowledge, respecting him, which
> those with whom he lived, and were the perpetual witnesses of
> his actions, could impart. For this end I was to make minute in-
> quiries, and to put seasonable interrogatories. From this conduct
> I promised myself an ultimate solution of my doubts. . . .
>
> But it suddenly occurred to me—For what purpose shall I
> prosecute this search? What benefit am I to reap . . . ? How shall
> I demean myself when the criminal is detected? I was not in-
> sensible . . . of the impulses of vengeance. . . . Yet I was fearful of
> the effects of my hasty rage. . . .
>
> But why, said I, should it be impossible to arm myself with
> firmness? If forbearance be the dictate of wisdom, cannot it be so
> deeply engraven on my mind as to defy all temptation, and be
> proof against the most abrupt surprise? . . .
>
> No caution indeed can hinder the experiment from being
> hazardous. Is it wise to undertake experiments by which nothing
> can be gained, and much may be lost? (14–16)

After all this second-guessing, Edgar Huntly returns home late: "[I] . . . explored the way to my chamber without molesting the repose of the family" because "our doors are always unfastened, and are accessible at all hours of the night"—another example of the way in which domestic and natural space gapes wide open for no apparent reason in this novel (16). The next night he goes to a hilltop in order to plan his investigation of Clithero. Here, however, he is stricken by "insupportable disquiet" and further self-questioning:

> Why should I proceed like a plotter? Do I intend the injury of this person? A generous purpose will surely excuse me from descending to artifices. There are two modes of drawing forth the secret of another, by open and direct means and by circuitous and indirect. Why scruple to adopt the former mode? Why not demand a conference . . . ? (17)

Huntly finds Clithero at the foot of a portentous elm tree and pursues him across the countryside. This trek occasions further speculations, doubts, decisions, and memories, with motion as the as the geographical correlative of ratiocination. Clithero is transformed into his itinerary. The "guide" who is "perpetually changing his direction" merges into the disorienting and "dreary vale" (18–19). The curious Huntly remembers that, as a youth, his curiosity had taken him through these parts before, reiterating the status of the landscape as a map of mental questioning:

> The way that he had selected, was always difficult. . . . I thought I might proceed, without fear, through breaks and dells, which my guide was able to penetrate. He was perpetually changing his direction. I could form no just opinion as to my situation or distance from the place at which we had set out.
>
> . . . A suspicion . . . suggested itself to my mind, whether my guide did not perceive that he was followed, and thus prolonged his journey in order to fatigue or elude his pursuer. . . .
>
> . . . The desert tract called Norfolk . . . my curiosity had formerly induced me to traverse in various directions. . . . This vale . . . suggested the belief that I had visited before. Such an one I knew belonged to this uncultivated region. If this opinion were true, we were at no inconsiderable distance. . . . Where, said I, is this singular career to terminate? (18–19)

At this point, Clithero disappears into a cavern, precipitating another spate of paranoid questions: "Was this person an assassin . . . who would take advantage of the dark . . . or was he maniac, or walker in his sleep?" (19) Is Clithero, in other words, motivated (as an assassin) or unmotivated (as a maniac or sleepwalker)? Despite further surveillance throughout the night, Huntly returns home at dawn still mystified, and the whole process repeats itself, with variations: "What could be the inducements of this person to betake himself to subterranean retreats?" (22)

The motive and meaning of subterranean retreat leads us back to Yaeger's suggestion about the rifts and pockets of repressed historical categories. The thought of the cavern into which Clithero formerly vanished brings about a shift into the register of memory for Huntly. But what does memory reveal? His memories themselves consist of resonance and echo—he recalls romantic air pockets that once signified to his younger self an enlarged or more glamorous imaginative capacity:

> The basis for all this region is limestone; a substance that eminently abounds in rifts and cavities. These, by the gradual decay of their cementing parts, frequently make their appearance in spots where they might have been least expected. My attention has often been excited by the hollow sound which was produced by my casual footsteps, and which shewed me that I trod upon the roof of caverns. A mountain-cave and the rumbling of an unseen torrent, are appendages of this scene, dear to my youthful imagination. Many of romantic structure were found within the precincts of Norwalk. (22)

The resonant landscape cyclically returns us to earlier relations between Edgar Huntly and Sarsefield. The landscape is distinctively part of the field of white masculine connection. Several chapters later, we learn that Huntly's first guide to this landscape of "rifts and cavities" was Sarsefield himself, the man who had been Mrs. Lorimer's lover, Clithero's mentor, Waldegrave's spiritual adviser, and finally Huntly's own surrogate father.[14] In addition to being Huntly's guide to the pocked landscape of Norwalk, Sarsefield had also taught him how to make ingenious cabinets. Reinforcing their twinship as Sarsefield's pupils, both Clithero and Huntly have constructed for themselves artful wooden boxes in which to hide secret papers (109–11). Huntly breaks into Clithero's and thinks Clithero has broken into his, although it turns out that he has riddled his own safe while sleepwalking.

Huntly's discovery that the packet of letters is missing sets off another crisis of inquiry (127–28). Waldegrave had written the letters during a period of radical skepticism: "His earliest creeds, tended . . . to destroy the popular distinctions between soul and body, and to dissolve the supposed connections between the moral condition of man, anterior and subsequent to death" (125). Not surprisingly, it was Sarsefield who created a "sphere of religious influence" that led Waldegrave to return to the world of stable moral and ontological distinctions (126).

What exactly, one wonders, are the "synthetical reasonings" spoken by Sarsefield and recalled by Huntly, and are they different from Huntly's own thought processes? We can conclude that these "reasonings" recalled by Huntly from Sarsefield's earlier teachings are explanations, because Sarsefield is the only character in the book who can successfully operate in the mode of causality. Huntly has no way of correlating the episodes of finding himself in a cave, killing and eating a panther, fighting with Native Americans, entering empty houses, and being pursued by members of his own village. When he finally encounters Sarsefield, he falls apart completely. Living through a captivity narrative that has been disassembled into unmotivated bits, Huntly lacks macropolitical cognition.[15] Emotional breakdown casts Huntly, the man of sensibility, on the apparently protective male breast of his stoic mentor: "My deportment . . . was that of a maniac. . . . I held him in my arms; I wept upon his bosom, I sobbed with emotion" (232–33). Sarsefield then pieces together the cause-and-effect dimension that Huntly cannot grasp for himself. Sarsefield diagnoses Huntly's sleepwalking problem as "a freak of Noctambulation." Sleep itself functions as a cave or cabinet in the book's topography, a region entered without apparent cause, a hollow in the temporality of explanation. In this claustrophobic universe, sensibility is incapable of thinking about itself, and stoicism takes control by virtue of its ability to reason.

The most interesting thing about the closing chapters of the book is the way in which Huntly rejects Sarsefield, whose power of comprehension he has greeted with desperate relief. Forced to choose between myopic sensibility and critical stoicism, Huntly prefers the fraternal relation to Clithero to the paternal analysis of Sarsefield. The affective bond between Huntly and Clithero has been articulated throughout. "I can feel for you," Huntly says to the Irishman early in the tale when he still thinks that Clithero killed Waldegrave: "I once imagined, that he who killed Waldegrave inflicted the greatest possible injury on me. That was an error, which reflection has cured. Were futurity laid open to my view, and events, with their consequences unfolded, I might see reason to embrace the assassin as my best friend. Be comforted" (31). At this point, Huntly is still promising friendship in exchange for explanation. But, while he does receive evidence that Clithero has killed someone other than Waldegrave, Huntly finally commits his loyalties to Clithero for no reason at all. Indeed, he chooses Clithero as *unreason,* acting against Sarsefield as the avatar of logic. Having a friend is more important than having an explanation.

The true counterconspiracy in the book—the one that does have a conscious motive—is led by the Indian woman that Huntly calls Queen Mab. She encourages a band of Delaware braves to attack the settlement that has displaced them. Edgar Huntly, when he is made savage by killing and eating a panther and then by killing Indians, participates in the logic of their conspiracy without ever getting the point. White masculine friendship blocks the will to think about the politics of property. And the blocking agent is mobility. "To walk is to lack a place," argues de Certeau.[16] This is not quite the case in *Edgar Huntly.* Walking creates places in this novel, but also renders them inexplicable. This is a different kind of mobility than the fancy considered in earlier chapters. Here, the citizen of active imagination becomes the vagrant postrevolutionary for whom motion never offers a clarifying view of the system from an elevated perspective. In North African captivity narratives written by white Americans, transatlantic overviews are once again possible though never easily achieved.

"Columbia's Son to Market Bro't"

*F*or the first three decades of its existence, the United States had to cope with the fact that it had inherited from Great Britain an entanglement with the Barbary States, the North African principalities of Morocco, Algiers, Tunis, and Tripoli. From 1783 until 1815, the new republic found itself in the same messy but predictable choreography of trade, state piracy, captivity, ransom, bribery, treaties, and periodic warfare that had enmeshed large and small European maritime powers for centuries. Two phases of military conflict, the Barbary Wars of 1801–5 and the Tripolitan War of 1815, were embedded in a much longer period of low-level crisis punctuated by flurries of diplomatic activity.

The Barbary captivity narrative as a genre had preceded British settlement in North America by a century or more. The practices of capture and ransom in North Africa, originating in the Crusades, decisively took shape after the expulsion of the Moors from Granada in 1492. It is important to appreciate the systematic quality of Mediterranean piracy, captivity, and ransom from 1198 until 1815. Its institutional participants included churches, states, and joint-stock companies. Ransoming North African captives generated some of the first large-scale charities in England and thus became part of the social history of pity. Organized fundraising for ransom in the Barbary States started in 1567. First-person accounts by individuals captured by North African corsairs and later ransomed were composed in England as early as 1577 and published in Hakluyt's compilations. These works helped to create a taste for subsequent captivity narratives.[17] In the British colonies themselves, the reverse is true. Indian conversion-captivity narratives began with Mary Rowlandson's *Sovereignty and Goodness of God, Together with the Faithfulness of His Promises Displayed* (1682) and were followed by the publication of North African captivity narratives.[18] The first British North American ships captured by Barbary pirates demanding ransoms were seized as the Jamestown colony was being founded in Virginia in 1625.

The texts associated with the Barbary conflicts are preoccupied with personal and collective solvency, with the price of the individual and the humiliations of exchange. And they are tied to the staging of gender identities, as the imaginary East had always been. Some Barbary captivity narratives claim that the North African enslavement of white Americans and the North American enslavement of black Africans are morally parallel.[19] This assertion, the central ethical result of the North African wars, emerges from the connection between masculine stoicism and masculine sentimentality in stories of cross-racial encounters.

Although the crises that encouraged the publication of Barbary captivity narratives arose during the years when Addison's *Cato* and other Republican plays would have still been widely known, the history of the Roman presence in North Africa was not explicitly related to the predicaments of the new nation. This is consistent with the long-standing repression, in Britain and the United States, of the notion that African stage characters had any historical referentiality whatsoever. We do find significant indirect references to Roman North Africa through strategies of contiguity or association, however. In 1804, *The Port folio*, a conservative Federalist magazine published in Philadelphia by Joseph Dennie, carried a long, appreciative commentary on a heroic couplet translation of the siege of Saguntum in "the Punicks," along with substantial extracts from the poem. The quoted passages feature the Carthaginians, "Afric's sons whose garments flow, unbound, / A motley race for breach of faith renown'd." They also showcase a "Lybian Amazon" fond of "sports of labour, and more manly joys"; much heroic single combat; and a debate carried on by the Roman legates at Carthage over whether to pursue peace or war.

A few weeks later, *The Port folio* printed a six-line item in the column titled "Miscellaneous Paragraphs" that refers to Algiers sardonically as a "fellow republic." Subsequently, the magazine printed a selection of four "Moorish Songs" of love offered by one "Ithacus," who writes, "Several years ago I resided on the coast of Barbary and in my leisure hours amused myself in collecting specimens of the poetry of the country." It is hard to imagine a more idealized detachment from the miserable plight of most Americans who had recently "resided on the coast of Barbary" or a mood more compatible with genteel philology as practiced by romantics everywhere.

Also in 1804, during the Barbary War, Dennie's *Port folio* included the latest article in a series devoted to Cicero's oratorical works, dealing with the orations against Verres. These orations berate the miserable Roman praetor of Sicily charged with raising public monies in order to fight "the pirates [that] infested the seas." His job was to "maintain the navy, which the republic had armed to fight them, and [to] defend her commerce." Verres neglected his duty and lost to the pirates, who "burned the forsaken vessels in the sight of Syracuse, and entered even into the port." To add insult to injury, Verres accused the innocent Sicilian commanders of treason and put them to death.[20] Dennie sympathizes with Roman regimes struggling to keep order in the republic's empire, although he had published no news of the Barbary conflicts. This reference to the war with Tripoli is indirect but pointed, given the topicality of matters involving Mediterranean pirates and an American republic interested in defending its commerce.[21]

The captivity narratives of the Barbary and Tripolitan Wars foreground the figure of the impoverished veteran of the War of Independence. In the anonymous *American in Algiers, or the Patriot of Seventy-Six in Captivity: a poem in two cantos* (1797); in William Ray's genuine captivity narrative, *Horrors of Slavery; or the American Tars in Tripoli* (1808); and in Royall Tyler's picaresque novel, *The Algerine Captive* (1797), economic desperation drives the American protagonist to sea, where he is removed from national or personal ground and exposed to capture. At that juncture, he intuits the centrality of slavery in the American future.

In 1808, William Ray published *Horrors of Slavery*, a fast-paced miscellany of poetry and prose with appended diplomatic correspondence. *Horrors of Slavery* joins the quest for a career to the story of the protagonist's exposure to racial violence. Ray was one of the American naval vessel *Philadelphia*'s captives, who spent from 1803 until 1805 in Tripolitan prisons. Born in 1771, he was too young to have been a veteran of the Revolution, but his vocational crisis takes him to the nation's founding capital in a reprise of *The Autobiography of Benjamin Franklin:*

> At the time of my entering the service, no person could have been in more distressing circumstances. I had been sick among strangers until I had expended the last solitary cent I was commander of, and not yet restored to health; but was in a debilitated state of convalescence. I tried every mean, and exerted every faculty in my power to obtain employment, but in vain. . . . I now found myself in the . . . flourishing city of Philadelphia, without a shilling—without a friend or acquaintance—unable to labour, and too proud to become a mendicant.

Ray contemplates suicide on the banks of the Delaware, but instead signs up as a United States marine and boards the *Philadelphia* "to take a luckless voyage."[22] Like Wordsworth's misfortune-plagued men, who turn to the army when their farms fail and are thenceforth exposed to disease and capture, Ray's North African captivity results from his marginal status in his own land. His citizenship is confirmed by his melancholia.

The anonymous poet of *The American in Algiers, or the Patriot of Seventy-Six in Captivity* is a veteran. This positions him as a patriot and gives him access to the rhetoric of sensibility. He devotes one of the poem's two sections to Barbary captivity and the other to a critique of American slavery. *The American in Algiers* works hard to inspire the reader's moral, historical, and emotional understanding of the connections between North African and North American slavery, and between African-American and Euro-American slaves. The discourse of sensitive manhood provides the medium for transatlantic commentary, and the transatlantic perspective supports a direct critique of the United States.

"I claim the gen'rous sympathetic tear," the speaker announces at the start of canto 1, "Trembling I bend beneath a tyrants rod." His military service, in which he suffered wounds for the cause of freedom, is both the analogue and the antithesis of his current torments in North African captivity: "I serv'd my country eight long years / To end my days in slavery in Algiers." After the war he had gone home, married, and had a child. His "Misfortunes" were economic in nature: "dread poverty drew on apace, / And stern misfortune star'd me in the face." His father's property had been stolen in his absence; his military wages of "[t]heir real

value scarce one tenth would yield." Bitter at the prosperity of "the sun-
shine patriot," he pawns his household furniture, takes out a loan, and
embarks for Genoa with an investment in the ship's cargo, which is successfully traded. [23] The ship is captured by Algerian corsairs on the return
voyage.

Having passed from self-reliant American liberty, through what felt
like a postrevolutionary recession that discriminated against veterans,
and into slavery, the protagonist is now thoroughly commodified. The
transformation of the patriot into property began at home and is fulfilled
at the slave auction in Algiers:

> Follow'd by crouds, on change I next appear'd,
> Where boys huzza'd, and men and women jeer'd.
> And as hogs, sheep, or oxen oft' are sold
> To him who pays the weightiest mass of gold,
> So was Columbia's son to market bro't,
> And by a Moor at public auction bought;
> In whose dark bosom all the vices reign,
> The vilest despot and the worst of men. (15)

Economic and racial inversion go together in this scene, where "Columbia's son" is publicly sacrificed to the "market." The speaker both displays
and despises his own pathos. Masculine citizenship, for this American,
requires a racist war on slavery. The United States is to blame, he implies,
for allowing the impoverishment of veterans in the first place, and for
forgetting the principles they stood for. Canto 1 of *The American in Algiers*
is not a plea for ransom, but a call to a war that will not only liberate the
captives but also give American patriots property in the nation once
again. Sensibility expresses the connection between downward mobility
and masculine feeling. Instead of discrete stoic and sentimental positions,
the single figure of the impoverished veteran embodies both bravery and
pathos. In this context, war will cure the humiliations of slavery that
prove the betrayal of the revolutionary generation. Racial disgust, civic
disfranchisement, and poverty must be cured by the "vivifying air" of
armed decisiveness. Canto 1 closes with the white captive's prayer:

> "Rouse! rouse! my country, from thy torpid dream.
> "Unsheath thy sword, let vengeance by [be] thy theme;
> "Thy long triumphant flag once more unfurl,
> "And on piratic fleets thy thunders hurl;
> "Then steer the hostile prow to Barb'ry's shores,
> "Release thy sons, and humble Afric's pow'rs." (16)

The speaker abruptly changes his persona in canto 2 of *The American in Algiers,* however. He composes "The African's Complaint," a genre derived from English antislavery verse and conventionally centered on a representative deep-feeling slave. He now ventriloquizes "a sable bard" whose "undaunted" pen takes on a "world of critics" in defense of "his helpless race":

> On yon wide plains, toward the rising sun,
> (Lords of creation and the world their own)
> Free as wild nature's self with guiltless souls,
> Near where the Gambia's mighty current rolls,
> My ancestors from immemorial time,
> Had liv'd contented in old Afric's clime. (27–28)

Cross-racial identification with the African slave in America is clearly compatible with international aggression against North Africa. The white captive of canto 1 is a solitary figure, surrounded by other prisoners, imagining his wife and child at home, but mostly dwelling in exasperated suspense, waiting to be ransomed but hoping to be avenged. The African speaker of canto 2 describes how he was captured on his wedding day. The author's emotions, suffused with heterosexual romance, extend sympathetically to his fellow sufferer: "Stoicism itself, must shudder" (21n). The African setting is pastoral, accentuating the degree of violation inflicted by the slave trade. The story of capture starts to induce the sensitive testaments demanded by most antislavery poetry of the period. But then the speaker, in the voice of the African slave, resorts to blunt opposition: "I crave no sympathetic tears from you." The African slave stands in judgment on George Washington, an apostate from the cause of liberty: "If you whose sword still reeks with despots blood, / Have drench'd your fields with Afric's purple flood; / Sure some malicious fiend to blot your fame, / Has sanction'd usurpation with your name" (25).

The African slave confronts Revolutionary War veterans with a view of human rights depicted through the image of symmetrical but morally opposite battlefields, one marked by the blood of "despots," one by "purple" or African blood. Crisp syllogisms juxtapose the rhetoric of the revolutionary generation to subsequent racist practices justified by color differences:

> If love of liberty impell'd the fight,
> Why now deprive another of his right? . . .
> . . . .
> You say all men were first created free,

Whence then the right t'usurp their liberty?
Hath not the African as good a right,
Deriv'd from nature to enslave the white? . . .
Do we not see where'er we turn our view,
Throughout all nature's children different hues?
And do white hogs the unjust priv'lege claim,
To make the black ones root the ground for them? (26)

Here, the speaker's anti-essentialist irony denies both North Africans and North Americans any "right, / Deriv'd from nature to enslave" each other. This strategy would seem retroactively to undercut the attribution of racial depravity to the "Moor" of canto 1, "In whose dark bosom all the vices reign, / The vilest despot and the worst of men." In language consistent with British antislavery writings as well as with the Philadelphia-based abolitionist movement of the 1790s, the speaker attacks North American slavery as a "system" possessed of a "Theory." Whereas the Arab North African could be despised as a conflation of darkness and vice, white North American slave owners could not be condemned on the basis of their whiteness. Rather they were attacked as participants in an immoral economic structure—attacked, that is, on the basis of function and position, rather than race. At the end, the African speaker sardonically addresses the question of property in these terms: "'Tis a vast crime to steal man's worthless pelf, / But virtue rare to steal the man himself. / Such is your system which all good men curse, / The Theory is bad, the practice worse" (27).

"Misery in a Strange Land"

*R*oyall Tyler's *Algerine Captive* begins as satire and moves toward sensibility under the influence of the topic of slavery.[24] It is only when the narrator, Underhill, feels implicated in slavery that the discourse of sympathy comes to the fore. The picaresque hero generates a sophisticated itinerary that achieves inclusive breadth. But the picaresque narrative does not create the standpoint of the prospect, the view from on high, from which the whole system is visible. Tyler's "and then . . . and then" narration ultimately does concoct a political teleology, as his peroration in favor of resolute federal coherence demonstrates. But mostly *The Algerine Captive* is driven by what we might call the vocational picaresque. Even the long period of Underhill's captivity is far from being static, given his fluctuating social and occupational career as a slave. This narrative logic is fundamental to the book's representation of masculinity. The search for work drives Underhill from classical language study to school teaching to medicine, from New England to the South. Disgusted with Southern slavery and Southern manhood, he also suffers from "the embarrassments of debt" by the time he accepts a job as ship's surgeon.[25] As in most Barbary captivity narratives, poverty sends the narrator to sea and, ultimately, into captivity.

Underhill, Tyler's protagonist, is born in New Hampshire in 1762 and heads off to college in 1780. One of the oddest aspects of the book is its elision of the Revolutionary War, reminiscent of Brown's *Edgar Huntly*. Aside from one passing mention of George Washington and close encounters with Franklin and Paine, the American Revolution might as well not have happened. The historical connection between Barbary slavery, U.S. slavery, and Indian captivity is established symbolically in *The Algerine Captive* by relating what Underhill's mother dreamed shortly before his birth. In her nightmare, "the house was beset by Indians" who seized Underhill from the cradle. His mother looked out the window to see "a number of young tawny savages playing at foot-ball with my head." In interpreting this dream as a prophecy of his future slavery, Underhill jokes that the Algerians are even worse than "the monsters of our woods" (1:26). Tyler chronologically places the Indian captivity narratives before either the Revolution or the Barbary Wars: the nightmare occurs prior to both the narrator's and the nation's birth. This "early" quality, however, is complicated by the ontology of the dream, which is both foundational and fantastic. The dream mocks the marketing of terror in narratives of Indian captivity. It takes on the air of a parodied cliché designed to show that the discourse of prophecy is irrelevant and that the protagonist will find his way into North African slavery through the demands of other kinds of historical symmetry.

Book 1 of *The Algerine Captive* is insistently satirical in its account of the protagonist's alienation. When he is enslaved in North Africa, however, in book 2, the radical change of position introduces the conventions of sympathy, friendship, and filiopiety. The pattern is identical to *The American in Algiers*.[26] Underhill sails to England, then to Africa, aboard the aptly named ship *Sympathy* and is exposed to capture while caring for ailing slaves on shore. This establishes in no uncertain terms the connection between antislavery politics and the performance of sensibility. Tyler dramatizes the moment of shock when he first encounters the workings of the slave trade and realizes that he "had a principal . . . part in this inhuman transaction" (1:165–66, 168). The horror of being implicated propels him into an uncharacteristic flight of fancy. The passage shows the rapidity with which this text, like many others, can oscillate between racist contempt and cross-racial sympathy:

> The day after our arrival at Cacongo, several Portuguese and negro merchants, hardly distinguishable however by their manners, employments, or complexions, came to confer with the captain about the purchase of our cargo of slaves. They contracted to deliver him two hundred and fifty head of slaves in fifteen days' time. To hear these men converse upon the purchase of human beings, with the same indifference, and nearly in the same language, as if they were contracting for so many head of cattle or swine, shocked me exceedingly.

This reaction inspires his imagination. Aesthetic capacity and the ethics of sensibility act together to tell the story of violence against African pastoral life. We have encountered similar assaults on the pastoral in the poetry of Phillis Wheatley, the autobiography of the Gambian speaker in *The American in Algiers,* as well as in Underhill's mother's dream of a Native American attack on the family home. Underhill now strips that nightmare of its irony and with the help of fancy translates it into a more probable, though still literary, Africa:

> . . . when I suffered my imagination to rove to the habitation of these victims to this infamous cruel commerce, and fancied that I saw the peaceful husbandman dragged from his native farm, the fond husband torn from the embraces of his beloved wife, the mother from her babes, the tender child from the arms of its parent, and all the tender endearing ties of natural and social affection rended by the hand of avaricious violence, my heart sunk within me. I execrated myself for even the involuntary part I bore in this execrable traffic: I thought of my native land, and I blushed. (1 : 165 – 66)

Once he is consciously guilty and capable of sensibility's civic blush, once he is knowingly in the grip of the slave system or "traffic," Underhill is prepared to internalize the connection between slavery in the United States and his own captivity in Algiers. If his capacity for liberal guilt takes hold at the moment when he sees himself systematically implicated in the slave trade, Underhill's most visceral critique of slavery arises from his subsequent discovery of a true slave mentality in himself. "I now found that I was indeed a slave," he confesses:

the terrour of the late execution, with the unabating fatigue of my
body, had so depressed my fortitude, that I trembled at the look
of the overseer, and was meanly anxious to conciliate his favour,
by . . . personal exertions beyond my ability. The trite story of the
insurgent army of the slaves of ancient Rome, being routed by
the mere menaces and whips of their masters, which I ever scept-
ically received, I now credit. (2 : 79).

Underhill's sympathy both for his fellow slaves in Algeria and for the
African slaves he helped transport is inseparable from his growing investment in male bonding. "If [a man is desirous] to know how he loves his
countrymen, let him be with them in misery in a strange land," he observes. His fondness for other men is expressed through feelings of kind-
ness for his fellow captives in Algiers and through a longing for citizenly,
even linguistic, community. "Among the slaves of my new master, I was
received with pity, and treated with tenderness, bordering upon fraternal
affection," he recalls. "The religion of my country was all I had left of the
many blessings, I once enjoyed, in common with my fellow citizens." His
homesickness, focusing on the image of the "cold spring" on his father's
farm, overwhelms him with heartbroken filiopiety: "When I ate of the
bread of my father's house, and drank of his refreshing spring, no grateful
return was made to him." When Underhill returns home, "Being presented with a tumbler filled from this spring . . . in a large circle of
friends . . . I could not drink the water, but had the weakness to melt into
tears" (2 : 186, 27, 82, 38).

Underhill's recuperated manliness transforms the tears of the prodigal
son into a clarion call to Federalism at the very end of the book, where
he exhorts his "fellow citizens" to join together for reasons of international self-respect: "If they peruse these pages with attention they will
perceive the necessity of uniting our federal strength to enforce a due
respect among other nations" (2 : 241). This occurs at the moment of the
narrator's emancipation from the international society of slaves held by
North African principalities. The exposure of white American men to the
economy of the Atlantic slave trade fosters patriotism, for sentiment arises
from a world of racial difference. The conflict between the United States
and the North African states is a case study in the problem of styling the
precise balance of aggression and guilt desirable for manly nations.

CONCLUSION

Liberal Guilt and Libertarian Revival

I   "Who Knows How Best to Think about Victims?"
*I*n the New York City mayoral elections of 1993, David N. Dinkins, the African-American Democratic incumbent, lost to Rudolf W. Giuliani, an Italian-American Republican running on an anticrime platform. That fall, an editorial cartoon appeared in *The New York Observer* and was then reprinted in the "Week in Review" section of the *Sunday Times* (figure). It features a man on a psychiatrist's couch, wearing a sweatshirt under his rumpled suit jacket that reads, "I voted for Rudy." His female psychiatrist reacts by dropping her notes and pencil in astonishment, accompanied by the following caption: "You what?!" The cartoon's title describes the scene as "Neo White Liberal Guilt." The office windows reveal the shop across the street: Zabar's, the upscale West Side apotheosis of the Jewish deli. The cartoon refers to New York City Jews who voted for the law-and-order white candidate, Giuliani, instead of the liberal black one, Dinkins. The cartoon also alludes to the ongoing conflict between the Hasidic and African-American communities in the Crown Heights neighborhood of Brooklyn: The 1991 Crown Heights riots had been provoked by the murder of a Hasid and the trial of a young black man, who was acquitted of the crime in 1992. And, finally, the female psychiatrist with her hair in a bun suggests the guilt induced—and hence personified—by Jewish mothers or by mothers in general. Here therapy is a mutually sadomasochistic relationship. The patient's admission torments the therapist-qua-mother, who is an old-style liberal. At the same time, her presence forces the man on the couch to panic and confess.

In this cartoon, liberal guilt refers specifically to white male guilt in the context of modern racial politics. Liberal guilt is about race, and it always was. "White guilt" and "liberal guilt" emerged as synonymous terms during the Civil Rights movement.[1] The term designates a position of wishful insufficiency relative to the genuinely radical. The New York liberal is guilty because he is no longer behaving liberally; he has voted Republican out of fear of racial violence. Guilt no longer motivates him to support those more radical than himself. Rather it is the mark of the apostate liberal who has cast his vote with the conservatives. In the cartoon, sensations of sympathy and identification cause the ex-liberal male

'You *what*?!'

© R. J. Matson, *The New York Observer* 1993

to feel guilty, for he imagines the suffering of others that a conservative victory will cost—and this drives him into therapy.

Liberal guilt is an embarrassed position no one wants to occupy. It is persistently denied or ignored by writers who defend liberalism or its recent, grimmer sequel, neoliberalism.[2] "The racial project of neoliberalism," Michael Omi and Howard Winant write, "seeks to rearticulate the neoconservative and new right racial projects of the Reagan-Bush years in a centrist framework of moderate redistribution and cultural universalism." The language of neoliberalism, Omi and Winant posit, avoids the subject of race altogether, relegating racial issues to the domain of euphemism or code: "Neoliberals argue that addressing social policy or political discourse overtly to matters of race simply serves to distract, or even hinder, the kinds of reforms which could most directly benefit racially defined minorities. To focus too much attention on race tends to fuel demagogy and separatism. . . . To speak of race is to enter a terrain where racism is hard to avoid." The authors conclude their book with a pithy imperative aimed at the perception of race as an unspeakable subject: "To Oppose Racism One Must Notice Race."[3] While liberal guilt does not necessarily oppose racism, it does make race noticeable. The man on the couch is silent; his T-shirt has to speak for him. Liberalism, the cartoon implies, operates as a repressed youthful cathexis that requires psychiatric help to understand. "I was liberal once," the patient might eventually say, able to name his malaise after several sessions of the talking cure. "Now I suffer from neo–white liberal guilt."

Insofar as "neo" marks a historical recurrence of memories of the most recent era of liberal and radical initiative, both terms relate to Lauren Berlant's reading of "'68, or something." "What does it mean to be accused of being '68 in the 1990s?" she asks, with '68 representing "the risk of political embarrassment" associated with utopian tactics. Berlant's essay pursues embarrassments other than liberal guilt, though with strong affinities to it. She focuses on academic adaptations to conservative success and sets against them "a left/feminism that refuses to lose its impulse toward a revolutionary utopian historicity."[4] I share Berlant's fascination with the way embarrassment and utopian language coincide. Because liberal guilt can thrive even—or especially—when people are convinced that utopian projects are failing, my account of the political malleability of liberal guilt and earlier forms of cross-racial sympathy is a study in comparative embarrassments. The discourse of liberal guilt can "notice race" from a critical, oppositional, or "minor" position. Or, as in the *Observer* cartoon, it can admit the charge of political apostasy even as it confirms the pragmatic value of a shift from idealism to fear. Although the point of this concluding chapter is not to recuperate liberal guilt for the left, one of my intentions certainly is to show how the historical residue of sensibility can be enfolded by effective antiracist positions.

The dilemmas of liberal guilt have been exposed and described by practitioners of subaltern studies, critical legal theory, and feminism. These commentators have zeroed in on the most significant political change in the culture of vicarious sympathy, or liberal guilt: the moment when "the other" becomes the author. The adaptability of liberal guilt, translated by gender and racial differences, shows how serviceable the nerve-wracking moods of sympathy can be. But liberal guilt has become interesting to academically situated cultural critics partly because they simultaneously agree with and object to its doom in the national political arena. In Washington, liberalism in its current abject mode and liberal guilt in particular signify sentimental indecisiveness over political identity, a failure of tough-mindedness. As my invocation here of a conventionally gendered vocabulary ("sentimental," "tough-mindedness") suggests, liberalism and its attendant anxieties involve ongoing crises of masculinity. Since I firmly believe that second-wave feminist politics and the increased economic visibility of women over the last thirty years have had a significant impact on the politics of emotion in the nineties, it may seem paradoxical to insist on the constitutive role of masculine sensibility in the present formations of liberal guilt. But while liberal guilt is not and has not historically been assigned a masculine gender, it is a form of discomfort that has mattered most politically when it afflicts men.

It is not hard to scorn the marketing of sympathetic men. The popularity of advertisements in which shirtless men with washboard abs get off the Soloflex machine to bathe their infants has coincided with the equally popular notion that liberalism is effeminate because it involves impulse buying at the federal level. Disciplining the federal deficit became the test of manliness for the neoliberal. Bill Clinton found himself in the peculiarly embarrassing position of demonstrating masculine sensibility while having to disavow the policies of sympathy. The sensitive male has continued to be marketable even in the lengthening wake of the congressional elections of November 1995, which shifted the majority from the Democrats to the Republicans. The pressure on Democrats to cultivate a stance of combative rigor in the political theater has perturbed, but not stopped, the commodification of male sensibility ("this vast national wash of masculine self-pity") that marked the late eighties and early nineties.[5] In making these observations, I am deliberately echoing the binary constructions that inform Susan Jefford's argument that the politics of the 1980s made allies of Nixon, Reagan, and Robert Bly and pitted "hard bodies" against national effeminacy in Hollywood movies. Jeffords starts with the contest between hard and soft manhood, and argues that the difference between the two became more ambivalent over time. By the early nineties, she concludes, violence needed to be bound to sensitivity. Hollywood had decided that "if there is to be a future for humanity at all, it lies in the hearts of white men."[6] Jeffords' premise is oversimplified: The political viability of the hard body has depended on either having a heart or bonding with those who do for three hundred years. And the discourse of sensitivity has long since been wrested from an exclusive association with powerful white men.

In the throes of liberal guilt, action risks becoming gesture, expressive of a desire to effect change or offer help that is never sufficient to the scale of the problem. Actions are carried out in sorrow. One is sorry in advance for the social consequences of one's acts.[7] Because, as Omi and Winant note, we live in an era when not just liberal guilt but the whole topic of race relations is generally regarded as embarrassing, it is not surprising that antiracist strategies often involve a commitment to performance. President Clinton did the same thing when he formed a national commission charged not just with studying the problem of race in America but with talking about it in public.

For the persons who experience them, crises of liberalism can easily take the form of identity crises, because sympathy—the relationship of "identifying with" others—makes the identity of the person who extends that vicarious support tentative or uncertain, and, hence, nonviolent. Liberals are generally believed to feel particularly malleable, always in danger of having their too-ready sympathy absorbed by someone else's agenda, or at least are thought to worry more about this potential than other people. Liberal guilt, then, is inseparable from the feeling of being implicated in systems of domination and the subsequent awareness of emotional instability produced by this ambivalent position.[8] Experiences of liberal guilt, one might think, would be inevitable for middle-class persons in industrialized societies: We are involved in systems like global markets from which we consciously benefit; we know that distant populations suffer from the consequences of those very systems; we put a high priority on personal states of feeling; we reward the public performance of care or of a diffuse but quintessentially American niceness.

Or perhaps what I am describing is not quintessentially American. For a book that claims to be about Anglo-American culture, my introductory and concluding chapters create an unfortunate asymmetry. In both places, I have wanted to call attention to the specific cultural setting that gave rise to this study, and that setting, of course, is the United States. I am convinced, nonetheless, that the predicaments I describe concern cultural and political situations in the whole Anglo-American sphere. In spite of Britain's flourishing history of sentimental culture, the relationship between emotion and politics in the twentieth century has been significantly different in the United Kingdom than in the United States. The British difference comprises at least three elements: a more deeply felt national self-image as empire and a stronger sense of racial "others" as foreign; a more overt political acceptance of socialism, which works against cross-class pathos; and an embrace of British stoicism in the face of catastrophe as an important element of national character, particularly during and after World War II. The traditional discipline of feeling in the United Kingdom is changing, though. In 1997 Prime Minister Tony Blair succeeded overwhelmingly at the polls, cast as a sensitive pragmatist of the Bill Clinton kind. Immediately afterward, Blair's open acceptance of the sentimental popular response to the death of Princess Diana seemed to forecast a new prestige for civic sensibility in Great Britain— as long, that is, as it is combined with fiscal restraint.

The liberal aspect of liberal guilt concerns not only its epistemological structure but also its performative qualities, real or imagined. Shelby Steele, who despises white guilt, understands it in terms of moral episte-mology. It springs, he suggests, "from a knowledge of ill-gotten advan-tage": "[G]uilt must always involve knowledge. White Americans know that their historical advantage comes from the subjugation of an entire people." Steele describes the shift from black deference in the fifties to black power in the sixties in terms of the rearrangement of guilt. White individuals who confronted him with segregationist policies once made him feel guilty: "If there was guilt, it was mine. . . . I can remember feeling a certain sympathy for such people, as if I was victimizing them by draw-ing them out of an innocent anonymity into the unasked for role of racial policemen." A decade later, "this huge vulnerability had opened up in whites and, as a black you had the power to step right into it."[9]

This perception that guilty feelings involve a sensation of transferring "moral power" is challenged by the many episodes in the long history of liberal sensibility that are devoid of any rearrangement of authority. Nonetheless it matters that Steele's disgust for the economy of guilt arises from the sense of being one who inflicts, rather than suffers, liberal guilt. Steele experiences guilt to the second power: he feels guilty about his epistemologically sophisticated participation in guilt inducement. The crucial scene of his corrupt assent to using the theater of liberal guilt against white people is associated with a betrayal of black fatherhood. The emotional core of Steele's narrative is his hatred for the knowingly theatrical quality of the whole dynamic.

Steele's account of white guilt focuses on his observation of a perfor-mance, or confidence trick, involving an educated black man, a successful white businessman, and the figure of a hotel restroom attendant. The manipulative black man in this tale, a friend of Steele's whose "race ex-periments" embarrassed him, relies on two spectacles that are insidiously linked: the restroom attendant treated as a representative figure of a ra-cial past and the story of his own father. The attendant was a frail, elderly, and very dark man in a starched white smock that made the skin on his neck and face look as leathery as a turtle's. He sat listlessly, pathetically, on a straight-backed chair next to a small table on which sat a stack of hand towels and a silver plate for tips. (500)

Steele's friend eventually convinces the white businessman to leave a tip of twenty dollars instead of one dollar. The friend's success depends not only on an emotional or "sentimental" interpretation of the attendant but also on autobiographical revelation that stages African-American fatherhood with maximum pathos. He tells the story of his father's life, says Steele, in a way that entails "using—against all that was honorable in him—his own profound racial pain to extract a flash of guilt from a white man he didn't even know" (500).

The ludic coerciveness of this "race experiment," its purposeful insincerity, distinguishes it from other tales in the genre of liberal guilt stories. But it is more typical than not, both in its choreography of fraught male homosocial relationships and in its preoccupation with spectacle. Liberal guilt, which from the very beginning is bound up with self-conscious racial difference, is repeatedly staged through stories of cross-racial spectatorship. It relies on visual practices of seeing pain and being seen to be afflicted by it. Liberal guilt thus has certain affinities with surveillance, which is one reason conservatives love to hate it. Insofar as the state became identified as the force that "legitimated group rights, established affirmative action mandates, and spent money on a range of social programs" that required diligent "bean counting," these programs have been opposed by the desire to eliminate "record-keeping," the desire not to know.[10] Steele wants to end affirmative action programs but criminalize civil rights violations.[11] Legislating sympathy insults him, but punitive antiracism, consistent with masculine aggressiveness, does not. There is no inherent reason, of course, why social welfare and forceful judicial approaches to racism could not be pursued simultaneously, as they have been in the past—no reason other than the narrative logic of performed masculinity. According to Steele's drama, discipline cures embarrassment and applying anticrime rhetoric to racism saves us from the intimate visual contests of guilt.

Unlike conservatives, recent liberal philosophers hardly ever talk about liberal guilt. In the most self-avowedly liberal philosophical discussions, the emotions of liberal guilt are firmly suppressed, despite the conceptual centrality of pain. Judith Shklar puts forward her definition of liberalism as "putting cruelty first." Liberalism is the set of values produced by the fear and loathing of cruelty. In Shklar's hands, this "liberalism of fear" becomes an ordeal of temperate manliness exemplified by Montaigne. Shklar defines the liberal as reacting against the sight of the victim, but doing so in a manner that is tough-minded, unhopeful, without illusion, and certainly not guilty. The "we" to which she refers when she talks about "our ordinary vices" is liberal society imagined as an idealized graduate seminar. This dialogue is created by those Shklar characterizes as "people who are familiar with the political practices of the United States and who show their adherence to them by discussing them critically, indeed relentlessly," sharing a common "fund of historical and literary memories on which we can draw as we contemplate ruling and being ruled." [12]

Shklar is nervous about the particular experience of those in pain. This reinforces her sense of liberalism as revulsion in the face of cruelty. "Who knows how best to think about victims?" she asks rhetorically. The question implies that it is impossible to contemplate victimization without embarrassment and therefore that such sentimental relationships are to be avoided: "Victimhood may have become an inescapable category of political thought, but it remains an intractable notion. . . . we do not know how to think about victimhood. Almost everything one might say would be unfair, self-serving, undignified, untrue, self-deluding, contradictory, or dangerous." Precisely, I say. Speaking about "victimhood" when one stands in a vicarious relation to it is embarrassing—and interesting— precisely because it does not produce reflection and dialogue. Liberal guilt signifies a loss of control. Increasingly, too, it signifies a loss of money, as though the donor individual or class cannot afford to give anything away without impoverishing itself. Shklar labors to separate liberalism from sentiment, therefore. The most powerful mood in Shklar's political universe is fear, "the underlying psychological and moral medium that makes vice all but unavoidable." Against fear—a "medium" rather than an emotion—one utilizes strategies of limitation. Liberalism is for Shklar a defense against, not a structure of, feeling. [13]

Richard Rorty is the exception to the evasion of liberal guilt by philosophers of liberalism. He crafts a "utopia" populated by intellectuals who conceal their deconstructive insights while publicly expressing liberal hope. In this fashion, he finds a place for the malaises of liberal guilt. For Rorty the value of descriptive discourses like literary criticism and ethnography lies in their power to increase the liberal ironist's sensitivity toward sufferers. Fiction, for instance, gives us "details about kinds of suffering being endured by people to whom we had previously not attended." Crucial to Rorty's ironic community is the feeling of moral uncertainty, which he defines as a temperate embarrassment closely related to liberal guilt: "the self-doubt which has gradually, over the last few centuries, been inculcated into inhabitants of the democratic states—doubt about their own sensitivity to the pain and humiliation of others, doubt that present institutional arrangements are adequate to deal with this pain and humiliation." Doubts about "institutional arrangements" fade from his discussion, but self-doubt becomes "the characteristic mark" of first-world ethics. Rorty is one of the few writers in any century who positively delights in the experience of the liberal ironist who doubts both the emotional and pragmatic efficacy of his or her knowledge of pain. But he detaches a public commitment to liberalism from the private theoretical speculation of the ironist, with the result that, as Nancy Fraser observes, his theory proceeds on one level and his politics on another.[14]

"Needs talk" is central to the politics of welfare state societies, argues Fraser, parting ways with Rorty, who privatizes ambivalence or defines it through geopolitical sequestration. Fraser conceives a model of social discourse that "foregrounds the . . . contested character of needs talk." Fraser never talks about emotion. But she does establish a theoretical framework for the political meanings of complaint, ambivalence, guilt, and confession—space for noticing complex articulations of degrees of discomfort. She accomplishes this by asking the following questions:

> What are the vocabularies available for interpreting and communicating one's needs? . . . How are conflicts over the interpretation of needs resolved? . . . [What are the operative] modes of subjectification; the ways in which various discourses position the people to whom they are addressed as specific sorts of subjects endowed with specific sorts of capacities for action: for example, as "normal" or "deviant," as causally conditioned or freely self-determining, as victims or as potential activists, as unique individuals or as members of social groups?

Fraser accentuates the way needs talk can break out of its previous classifications as "domestic" or "economic" to become a political problem. She introduces the notion of "leaky" or "runaway" needs, "needs that have broken out of the family or the market." "Now, where do runaway needs run to when they break out of these enclaves?" she asks. They go into "the social," the arena in which "politicized runaway needs get translated into claims for government provision," where "unequally endowed groups compete to shape the formal policy agenda." [15] Sensibility is historically affiliated with social welfare, as the records of eighteenth-century debates over poor law reform, the abolition of the slave trade, missionary activity, and philanthropy demonstrate. Fraser points out that as welfare became feminized—making women its clients and workers—some of its aspects were uneasily removed from what we understand as politics. Needs now tend to re-intrude on the political sphere through the genres of the personal or the bodily. The practices of recent congressional hearings point to the interdependency of personal stories and political representation, for example. The citizen's tears matter to the state, and media coverage takes personal stories told in government buildings to the viewing public. Then, in the end, there are no legislative results—no health care program, for example.

We can situate the experience of liberal guilt in Fraser's social region, where needs have shifty identities as figures that recently led a private life but now engage in political contests, or vice versa. This is precisely the venue of liberal guilt. At this point, we can relate Shklar's cruelty to Fraser's needs talk. Needs talk defines the social realm, where conflicts and negotiations occur over what counts as cruelty and how public policy should respond to it. Cruelty, too, is discursive. It materializes socially through spoken or pictured pain, resentment, and accusation. Liberal guilt, therefore, grounded in the perception of cruelty, is connected to "needs talk," including the literature of sympathy and its attention to the figures and voices of sufferers.

Narrated scenes of pain and liberal guilt dwell in symbiotic intimacy. And it is in the microanalysis of such events, as Homi Bhabha argues, that "the social theory of pain and suffering" begins. Bhabha's treatment of guilt and melancholia is a biting response to Rorty's territorial barriers, which divide the "reflective acumen" of the west from the "raw courage" needed elsewhere. "From the limits of liberalism emerges the subaltern perspective," Bhabha declares. He is right, but only because he and others show that liberalism is absorbed by, not alienated from, oppositional or minor writing. Bhabha is exasperated by the "figure of the 'white body in pain' . . . at the bleeding heart of [Rorty's] . . . languages of solidarity and community." He concludes bitterly: "We must force [Rorty] to dialogue in order to teach him the social theory of pain and suffering." Fundamental to this perspective is a shift from the visual construction of liberal guilt as a spectacle to a more dramatic one that draws on the emotive qualities of language to resist "symbols of social order." Once again, agency and performance enter the discussion together, as they have in my own argument. Bhabha finds agency in performance, in an "exorbitant" marginality where the "ambiguities of rebel politics" find utterance in affective or "bodily" writing as opposed to static scenes of the body observed. This position is enacted in a literary version of Fraser's social realm where needs have no "proper" place.

Intellectuals currently moving back and forth on the "left-liberal spectrum" are obsessed with the subject of emotional implication.[16] The current revival of feeling in our political and popular cultures as well as in academic fields followed the legitimation of the first-person voice. Performances of the self in twelve-step programs, in confessional poetry, and in psychotherapy publicized emotion while maintaining its intensely personal character. Now, through a widely shared reorientation to the social importance of feeling, emotion is more public than ever. This marks a complementary—perhaps compensatory—reversal, on the level of affect, of Reagan-Bush economic policies of privatization. The public performance of individual pain characterizes not only the boom in afternoon talk shows, but also appears in efforts to change public or judicial policy—of which the judicial movement for "victims' rights" is one example. These civic therapies claim to serve the suffering individual and the spectator-nation. But the substitution of whites for blacks and of men for women as objects of pity indicates that antiliberalism mimetically inverts the very choreographies of liberal guilt.

The conventions of liberal guilt, if we think of it as a genre, are structured by the visualized or performed economy of inequality. When those who suffer gaze back at those who do not, guilt is the consequence. In the dynamics of guilt, Bernard Williams argues, "I . . . feel that victims have a claim on me and that their anger and suffering looks towards me." [17] Guilt is forced to constitute the subject, the object, and the moral importance of their relation.[18] Liberal guilt, viewed this way, is a highly politicized version of subjectivity per se, an application of the philosophical idea of being-in-the-world to racist societies. As such, liberal guilt is tied to the notion of vicarious experience. The word "vicarious" has shifted from its earlier dignity as a sign of authority (in the religious sense of "vicar" or the political sense of "regent") to a description of the emotional equivalent of secondhand smoke—experiences felt imaginatively through another person or agency. The more recent psychological and performative meanings of vicariousness emphasize the taking on of guilt, pain, or pleasure ("vicarious gratification") through identification with another person. These last meanings signal a culture not of identity but of identifying with.[19] For Sartre, objectivity—and hence shame—is a derived or vicarious relation. The other's objective presence confers a second-order, humiliated objectivity on the gazer. Likewise, the embarrassments of liberal guilt arise from pain greater than their own discovered by white intellectuals in the gaze of the racial other.

Embarrassment is intrinsic to the critical potential of antiracist cultural studies. Patricia Williams shares with Homi Bhabha and Gayatri Spivak a sense of being both the subject and the object of liberal guilt. This understanding lets her criticize but not escape the culture of first-world implication. Seeking to prove the discursive productivity of liberal guilt—the way it emerges as digression, anecdote, and scene—Williams describes a series of guilt-related ordeals in a chapter titled "Gilded Lilies and Liberal Guilt." The encapsulated narratives constitute a series of episodes in which she is forced to hear the confessions and denials of others' guilt or else suffers the pathos of remote sympathy herself. Twining through Williams's memoir is a gradually elaborated argument about the historical relationship of contract law to slavery, to the economic construction of the individual, and to the ways in which public life is sacrificed to notions of personal privacy as these reflect assumptions about private property. For Williams, liberal guilt arises from our embarrassments in public relative to one another's neediness. She explores why the private character of wealth results in publicly staged but highly personalized dramas of sympathy and cruelty.

The conversations that Williams narrates zero in on distinctions between animal and human, on accusation and the claims of kinship. The stockbroker with whom she talks in an Amtrak dining car tells her, "'I never give money when people beg from me. . . . I tell them I have nothing. But I always stop to chat. . . . Finding out a little about who they are,' he explains, 'helps me remember that they're not just animals.'" A little later on, she tells the story of a student who interrupts her class preparation in a rage because "She has been made to feel guilty . . . that her uncle is, as she describes him, 'a slumlord.'" Williams answers back sarcastically, then broods over the way the rich are assumed to be entitled to privacy while the "have-nots must be out in the open—scrutinized."[20]

To critique the practices of scrutiny, Williams repeats the stories she tells in her classes of encounters she has observed or participated in. Her motive is publicity, the exposure of the "commonplaces of our economically rationalized notions of humanity." One vignette features the "pretty little girl of about six" who exclaims, "Oh, Daddy, there's someone who needs our help," when she sees "an old beggar woman huddled against a pillar": "The child was . . . led . . . by her . . . father who patiently explained that giving money to the woman directly was 'not the way we do things.' Then he launched into a lecture on the United Way."[21] This anecdote supports Nancy Fraser's account of needs discourse in which institutional responses compete with personal sentimental ones. Confronting the relationship between property and sympathy, Williams values the direct expression of tragic emotion and the unmediated offer of personal help in excess of the legal, economic, and social reforms she promotes. She verges on Charles Lamb's dictum in his essay, "A Complaint of the Decay of Beggars in the Metropolis," which closes by acknowledging the possibility that the beggar is a phony—or, in essence, an actor—and then insists that theatricality and poverty are compatible: "give, and ask no questions."[22]

The next episode, not part of the summary of her class lectures but a personal account, makes Williams the agent of the cruelty of the pitying gaze. She feels herself returned to the scene of beggary taken up aesthetically in the eighteenth century, though she herself does not put it in these terms. She sees a homeless man lying on a bench with his eyes fixed half-open: "They were the eyes, I thought, of a dead man. Then I rationalized, no, he couldn't be." Williams herself is afflicted by a classic case of liberal guilt:

> Then I looked at the face of another man who had seen what I saw, both of us still walking, never stopping. . . . I tried to flash worry at him. But he was seeking reassurance, which he took from my face despite myself. I could see him rationalize his concern away, in the flicker of an eye. We walked behind each other upstairs and three blocks down Broadway before I lost him and the conspiracy of our solidarity. Thus the man on the subway bench died twice: in body and in the spirit I had murdered.

Not surprisingly, after this narrative of eyes—living eyes, dead eyes, and eye contact—the next paragraph begins, "Deep inside, I am made insecure by the wandering gazes of my students." Williams positions herself in the vicarious society of eye contact outside of which no one is permitted to reside. Her admonitions ring true as the voice of the liberal superego that treats the gaze as violent, and demands direct action beyond the visual encounter. But can she mean the overwrought bit about soul murder? This moment of excess is a confession but also a complaint.

The complaint, mentioned often in these pages, is "a performative plea," "an aesthetic 'witnessing' of injury," as Lauren Berlant defines it. The complaint is a form of opposition that does not pose a "threat to the reigning order." How does the complaint work? In the case of feminist discourse, the "witnessing mechanism," Berlant argues, "gradually incorporat[es] an ever-widening range of 'feminist' issues into the sentimental-critical gaze" in order "to construct some leverage for the speaking woman." The co-optive power of the complaint, therefore, lies in its self-limiting drama of identification across material differences in position.[23] Williams's soul murder story treats the gaze, in a state of hyperbolic connection, as violent. The multiple identifications here—with the dead man, with the man "who had seen what I saw"—defend, accuse, and confess simultaneously. This is precisely the source of embarrassment in the complaint: there is no position outside of it, and, in the end, nothing changes.

Williams's accusatory confession shows how identification works in two directions. She identifies with the victim and with the mirror image of her own detachment, the man whose eyes she meets. She concurs with those who argue that liberal guilt is an appropriate response to specific acts of wrongdoing and who defend shame as a response to unrealized ideals.[24] Williams dramatizes the sensations produced by understanding the spectacles of need historically. She defends the value of acquiring sufficient understanding to experience implicated feelings. She admits to an embarrassed intersubjectivity that fails to act. A historical understanding of racism as a systematic phenomenon is a morally inclusive strategy that puts the burden of awareness squarely on the analyst herself.

Liberal guilt is one of sentimentality's affiliated terms, not least because of the theatrical quality of vicarious cultures. Eve Sedgwick concludes that describing cultural relationships as "sentimental" sentimentalizes the critic in turn.[25] In other words, to call something sentimental is to place oneself in the chain of sentimental relations. What happens, then, to the scholar "interested" in the politics of emotion? What is the epistemology of liberal guilt for the "emotion critic" of the nineties? By writing this, am I defending myself against the dynamics of liberal guilt or perpetuating them? Or both? Or neither?

The present alliance between the cultural history of racism and the study of social emotion makes for an experimental relationship, in the university, between theory and embarrassment. When Gayatri Spivak addresses the laborious economy of cross-racial guilt, she, like Williams, focuses on the classroom. She discriminates, as Williams does, between the guilt produced by too little knowledge and the guilt that results from too much. Spivak proposes that knowledge arises from hard work. She engages two versions of liberal guilt, that of her white, middle-class students relative to herself as a postcolonial subject, and her own unease relative to subaltern women in India who form no part of her audience. For her students, she emphasizes the necessary attainment of knowledge; for herself, its necessary forgetting. She recommends work as a way of transforming her students' liberal embarrassment, a "benevolent" or wishful position, into something more efficacious. "The holders of hegemonic discourse should . . . themselves learn how to occupy the subject position of the other," she advises, "rather than simply say, 'O.K., sorry, we are just very good white people, therefore we do not speak for the blacks.'"[26] Subject positions can be learned.

But then Spivak is asked by an interviewer about her own subject position: "How is it possible to avoid a politics of representation, speaking for or on behalf of other women, retaining their specificity, their difference, while not giving up our own?" Spivak is not so naive as to believe that "a politics of representation" can be avoided. Rather, she proposes an endless process of self-delegitimation. "My project," she replies, "is . . . un-learning our privilege as our loss, unlearning one's privileged discourse so that . . . one can be heard by people who are not within the academy." Work matters because it carries out the double task of unlearning one's own dominance by acquiring specific knowledge about others, and then, using this knowledge, of continuously undoing generalizations about the other. "Unlearning," therefore, is what her students' hard work entails, also. There is something surprisingly simple about this commitment to educational agency.[27] To herself, to other feminists, and to her students in American universities, she assigns the intellectual labor of learning the "immense heterogeneity" of persons "elsewhere," stressing its effortfulness. You must "[do] your homework" so that you will have earned, through your intellectual work, the right to talk about oppressed persons:

> I will have in an undergraduate class, let's say, a young, white male student, politically-correct, who will say, "I am only a bourgeois white male, I can't speak." . . . I say to them: "Why not develop a certain degree of rage against the history that has written such an abject script for you that you are silenced?" Then you begin to investigate what it is that silences you, rather than take this very deterministic position—since my skin colour is this, since my sex is this, I cannot speak.[28]

Spivak puts her students in the paradoxical situation of having to choose between liberal guilt and curative labor. A little knowledge of the world produces guilt, but a great deal of knowledge leads to the process of unlearning or translation that results in a changed subject position. Spivak uses her own pangs of liberal guilt as spurs to historical study and theoretical revision, the laborious entry fee that the privileged intellectual pays in order to perform antiracist feminist work.[29]

The Return of Cato

*R*ichard Brookhiser's cover story in the January 1996 issue of *Atlantic Monthly,* "A Man on Horseback," is "An essay on character" in general and on George Washington in particular. This article shows that conservative libertarians are asking some of the same questions addressed by feminist academics: How is masculinity dramatized in the political arena? How does the performance of emotion affect our understanding of political positions? How do historical examples enter into debates over citizenship? The article ends by citing Addison's *Cato:*

> The result of Washington's lifelong concern with courtesy and reputation was that he was able to put the strenuous morals of the noble Romans in a social context, and make *Cato's* best lines real. "'Tis not in mortals to command success, / But *we'll* do more, Sempronius, *we'll* deserve it" [emphasis added]. How could deserving Romans justify the plural "we"? On Addison's own showing, the most deserving Roman of them all affected nothing outside his little band, and died by his own hand. Courtesy and reputation made it possible for a would-be Roman in the North American Boondocks to say to his countrymen "we," and to command a response.[30]

Brookhiser's essay on Washington ignores three-quarters of the content of Addison's play, just like almost all eighteenth-century responses. It ignores specifically the romance between the African prince, Juba, and Cato's daughter, Marcia, and the mutually legitimizing relation between Cato's stoicism and Juba's sensibility. But this is less interesting than the fact that he is interested in Addison's *Cato* at all.

Who is Richard Brookhiser and why is he drawn to Washington's performance of "courtesy and reputation"? And what does this have to do with the relationship between politics and emotion? Brookhiser describes decorum—including the impact of Washington's physique—as "the medium and the stimulus" of Washington's power to "operate on and through other people." Another essay by Brookhiser appeared in the August 1995 *Reader's Digest,* titled "What Happened to Civility: The Example of George Washington."[31] A lot of people in academic settings are interested in the same question: what happened to civility?

Brookhiser is a senior editor of the conservative *National Review*. His other writings include *The Way of the WASP: How it made America, and How It Can Save It*. He also wrote a 1991 *Time* article called "Why Not Bring Back the Czars? Restoring the Romanovs to Reign, Not Rule." This piece affirms Brookhiser's point in the *Atlantic* essay: that the public performance of manly authority is both culturally constructed and highly desirable. Leaders offer the nation "a mythic dimension" and satisfy "people's psychological needs" by providing "continuity and emotional security," Brookhiser suggests in his piece on the Romanovs. Surviving Romanovs "could audition" for the part, he proposes dryly.[32]

As a conservative intellectual, Brookhiser participates in a flourishing parallel universe of eighteenth-century studies. A recent surge of serious interest in Trenchard and Gordon's *Cato's Letters* has arisen in a different quarter than that occupied by academics investigating the history of sensibility and sentimentality. The publications sponsored by the conservative libertarian Cato Institute in Washington, D.C., suggest why Cato discourse has revived after a long dormancy.

When I phoned the Cato Institute in Washington to request their publications, explaining that I was working on "eighteenth-century Cato discourse," the man to whom I spoke took care to point out that it was specifically Trenchard and Gordon's *Cato's Letters* that had given the institute its name. The brochure promoting the Cato Institute is titled "The Cato Institute: Advancing Civil Society." The institute defines civil society as "the voluntary interaction of individuals and associations" as opposed to "political society, based . . . on rigid rules and mandated relationships." The 1978 mission statement reads as follows: "The Cato Institute is named for the libertarian pamphlets, *Cato's Letters*, which were inspired by the Roman stoic, Cato the Younger, who committed suicide when it was clear that Julius Caesar was going to defeat his last-ditch attempt at an outpost in North Africa to preserve the Roman republic." The Cato Institute, founded in San Francisco in 1977, moved to Washington in order to maximize the impact of conservative intellectuals on public policy. In this, it has been formidably successful. It inhabits a new building on Massachusetts Avenue (built strictly with private contributions); regularly briefs members of Congress, Washington staffers, and judges; has an active publishing agenda; sponsors conferences; funds resident fellows; and supports a richly furnished Web site.

The most often acknowledged intellectual father of the Cato Institute is the Austrian-born free-market economist, F. A. Hayek. This is the case despite the fact that students of contemporary political philosophy regard Robert Nozick, whose work also appears in and is invoked by the *Cato Journal*, as a more credible representative of the libertarian perspective.[33] The indebtedness to Hayek, reiterated throughout the publications of the Cato Institute, suggests that libertarian continuity with the eighteenth-century is a constructed origin, an invented past. Eighteenth-century writings seem like window dressing in view of the institute's specifically late-capitalist mode of libertarianism.

Despite the wishes of the people at the Cato Institute to establish a genealogical link to eighteenth-century Cato discourse, the text with which they identify, Trenchard and Gordon's *Cato's Letters,* was provoked by a loathing of stockbrokers that is hard to reconcile with the institute's enthusiasm for the booming investment economy of the 1990s. *Cato's Letters* responded directly to the collapse of the South Sea Bubble of 1720. The South Sea Company was created through an alliance of London financiers and the National Treasury. The company assumed a "chunk of the national debt" in exchange for what was expected to be "large profits from the sale of shares and its monopoly over all British-Spanish American trade." The scheme produced "a craze of stock-buying, a soaring of share prices," and then a bust in which "thousands were ruined." Walpole was able to shield many important members of the government from investigation and prosecution. This successful evasion—briskly summarized here by Kathleen Wilson—precipitated a barrage of attacks on the corrupt relationship between government and finance.[34] The Cato Institute, therefore, is partly correct to invoke *Cato's Letters* as an exemplary early modern critique of big government and big government debt.

But *Cato's Letters* is more than an attack on the corruption of free trade by politics. It is a celebration of the atmosphere of self-determination that free trade signified when it worked. Despite their loathing for "stock-jobbers," Trenchard and Gordon support the flow of wealth across national boundaries in search of the least restrictive conditions for mercantile entrepreneurship—and this perhaps does provide a basis for the libertarian revival in our present age of global economies. Trade, they write in palpably gendered terms, is a "coy and humorous Dame, who . . . always flies Force and Power; she is not confined to Nations, Sects, or Climates, but travels and wanders about the Earth, till she fixes her Residence where she finds the best Welcome and kindest Reception." In sum, "all Men are animated by the Passion of acquiring and defending Property, because Property is the best Support of that Independency, so passionately desired by all Men. . . . And as Happiness is the Effect of Independency, and Independency the Effect of Property, so certain property is the Effect of liberty alone." [35]

This suggests a possible ideology of libertarianism, but how does emotion fit in? *Cato's Letters* are exasperated and vehement. Trenchard and Gordon signify political virtue through rage rather than the manly friendship of other Whig subcultures more committed to the project of parliamentary gentility. But the distance between the sensitive Addison and the sardonic Brookhiser is less than we might think. Brookhiser is interested in George Washington's ability to fascinate the men who surrounded him. It is not such a big leap from his appreciation of Washington's charismatic presence to the codependent tension between stoic and weeping men in Addison's play. The Cato Institute represents a stoical opposition to liberal sensibility, an exhilarating adamancy that, as we know by now, is historically inseparable from sympathy.

The institute's public intellectuals are "less is more" or "tough love" stoics. They are opposed to supporters of national social programs whom they typecast as sentimentalists. The libertarianism of the Cato Institute is not so much characterized by overt forms of the "angry white male" syndrome—though there is plenty of anger, whiteness, and maleness to go around—as by a claim to be the rational, nonemotional corrective to sentimentality expressed through the "welfare state." But rationality is a very emotional thing. Rationality has an affect. My favorite expression of the claim to rationality by libertarian tough love is a chapter title in a Cato Institute book: "Overcoming Failure with Hard-Hearted Compassion." [36]

Why is this association between liberty, property, and impatient manliness flourishing now? From where does conservative libertarianism derive its recent legitimacy? In resisting the widely disseminated image of the sensitive man, which is often nervously connected to the image of the powerful woman, post–cold war secular conservatives with no taste for the religious right find the moral equivalent of war in the role of the stoic citizen. The rhetorical aggression of the right targets government as the embodiment of false sensibility. Liberalism—not the libertarians' "market liberalism," but the so-called welfare state—is viewed by the right as a sentimental state conspiracy. According to the logic of libertarian accusations, pity generates ever-more complex domains of subsidies, agencies, and rules. Libertarians therefore oppose government spending, which they resist both in itself and as a metaphor for the expenditure of feeling. Conversely, they see sympathy as a risky emotion because it can lead to expensive new government programs. Libertarian tough love, therefore, the stoicism of the nineties, is obsessed with its other, sensibility. It construes sensibility as at once a perpetually indebted or embarrassed condition and as an imperial one, capable of fulfilling an active desire for government's transformational energy.

Libertarians believe in two causal agents: the self-owned individual and the market. Libertarian theorists insist that they have a sophisticated understanding of social relationships and that they are not cathected to a naive notion of the isolated individual. Tom Palmer, in an essay titled "Myths of Individualism," resists the charge that "libertarians actually think that 'individual agents are fully formed . . . prior to and outside of any society.'" Palmer does subscribe to the belief that "Each person has the right to be free, and free persons can produce order spontaneously without a commanding power over them." At the same time he understands that the individual is a social construct, while holding that social constructs are almost the same thing as abstract rules: "because . . . cooperation takes place among countless individuals unknown to each other, the rules governing that interaction are abstract in nature. Abstract rules, which establish in advance what we may expect of one another, make cooperation possible on a wide scale."[37] Group identities such as those of race, ethnicity, and gender are erased through the machinery of libertarian "abstraction" into judicial essences whose unequal social and economic histories are constitutionally irrelevant. Clearly it is not abstract thinking per se that I oppose, but the link here between masculinity, rationality operating in the service of the individual who wants to "produce order," and that individual's resentment of losing control to government institutions that might "command" him.

A lot of magical thinking is involved in the idea that "free persons" can "produce order spontaneously." While celebrating market determinism, libertarian thought denies that the individual is subject to the market's command. Libertarianism is a deft psychological maneuver in the world of multinational corporations, therefore: it empowers the individual and loves the market; it sees the market and the individual as positive energies flowing in the same direction; and it refuses to see the individual as in any way controlled or subsumed by economic forces. Power, therefore, is located simultaneously in two places: the individual self as the locus of willed wealth and the market as the automatic pilot that has displaced its competitors in the field of causality and explanation.

In *The Wealth of Nations*, Adam Smith observes that "as a consequence of the interaction of conflicting interests, 'man is led by an *invisible* hand to promote an end which was no part of his intention.'" For libertarians, the invisible hand of unintended economic good needs the translucent hand of active antiregulation to succeed. Jan Narveson, in a libertarian monograph, stresses that "our rights are fundamentally . . . negative" and this holds true for libertarians' larger view of government.[38] The Cato Institute's Edward Crane likens congressional program initiatives to an addiction. "The argument . . . is that you can't replace something with nothing," Crane observes. "But that sentiment simply reflects the government habit. After all, the American people"—characterized by "responsiveness, compassion, and prudence"—"are not 'nothing.'"[39] Still, the causality refused to government by libertarians is lavishly imputed by them not just to the "people," but to the market. The market has purposes, ethics, and a progressive direction. Like all negative theologies, this form of libertarianism believes in a productive absence that rewards those who trust themselves to it.

In a 1994 essay in the *Cato Journal,* "How Excessive Government Killed Ancient Rome," the example of Rome is offered up by Bruce Bartlett as proof of the universal validity of libertarian antigovernment economic policies. The article illustrates the old adage: "When the only tool you have is a hammer, every problem looks like a nail." Bartlett's section headings include "Free-Market Policies under Augustus"; "Food Subsidies"; "Taxation in the Republic and Early Empire"; "The Rise and Fall of Economic Growth"; "Inflation and Taxation"; "State Socialism"; and "The Fall of Rome." Octavian stands for "Roman economic freedom," Antony and Cleopatra for *both* "Oriental despotism" *and* "State socialism." In this vision of Rome, politics collapses wholly into economic policy. There is no difference between one historical period and another. And even the libertarian individual vanishes into a timeless desire to end taxation. Rome is held over us—still! again!—in a profoundly antihistorical fiscal fable.[40]

The same theme was sounded by Newt Gingrich during his reign as Speaker of the House and leader of the congressional New Right. Urging his listeners to read all about it in Colleen McCullough's historical novels about ancient Rome, Gingrich revived the republic as an unambivalent place where the "nation of law" meets "moral authority."[41] The republic collapsed, he insisted, when it was "corrupted by foreign money, by personal ambition." "Law," for Gingrich, was a personality type, a figure of tough masculine honor that could be sent into single combat against President Clinton. The Roman stoic plays best as a self-wounding figure, offering himself or his favorite son to the ideal of the law in a scene of high pathos. But Gingrich made it his agenda to transform the stoic from a noble loser into a political winner, forgetting that the nobility of Cato exacted suicide.

Because conservative libertarians can blame all historical failures on government economic meddling, it is easy for them to think positively about everything else. Libertarians view state action in response to injustice and need as driven by a false belief that human suffering is increasing. They campaign against an excess of bad news. The libertarian who wants to resist federal initiatives holds that "things are getting better all the time." "Standard of Living Is Rising, 60 Scholars Agree," announces the *Cato Policy Report*. All the contributors concur that "despite the forecasters of doom," they see "no convincing economic reason why these trends toward a better life should not continue indefinitely." [42] Libertarians imagine a new "civil society" that will combine citizenly virtues with private funding. Private funds for the public good may cost the individual money but they do not tax his abstract autonomy. Total voluntarism and total market rationality: self and system will work for the same ends. There will be a civil community, according to this vision, and an ethical one, for the market is by definition virtuous and the death of the state will stimulate the latent virtue of the American people. Government will be transformed into local initiatives suspended meaningfully in the nation's market stream.

Giuliani, the Republican mayor of New York City, apologized in 1998 on behalf of the City of New York for its handling of the 1991 Crown Heights riot in which Yankel Rosenbaum was killed. During his trip to Africa in early April 1998, President Clinton, an empathetic Democrat, offered a near-apology for American participation in the slave trade. As Louis Menand observed in his column for the 1998 Easter issue of the *New Yorker*, their respective apologies put the mayor and the president into the good, if heterogeneous, company of other apologizers motivated by a sense of national or institutional guilt:

> the Internal Revenue Service has apologized to American taxpayers for having a hostile attitude . . . ; the Japanese . . . have apologized for their treatment of British prisoners . . . ; Britain has apologized for being "insensitive" to Nazi victims whose assets it had seized . . . ; the Vatican has apologized . . . for the behavior of Catholics during the Holocaust; a French newspaper has apologized for its position on the Dreyfus Affair; and . . .

Prime Minister Tony Blair has apologized for the Irish potato famine.

Menand speculates that such corporate apologies for long-ago abuses pit niceness against history. Traumas are confronted in order to be forgotten, he suggests, and "the whole effort by large entities like nations and churches to dissociate themselves from the past" seems more like premillennial moral housecleaning than an admission of guilt. [43]

Rather than interpret this epidemic of apology as the result of worldwide amnesia, I view it as caused by the pressure of historical knowledge itself. Apology is not the best outcome of historical awareness, but it is better than none at all. We are confronted with the growing credibility and efficiency of systems through which the sense of historical pain is powerfully communicated. Liberal guilt is generated by the sensation that we all participate in corrupt economies, and that sense of system, most of the time, *is* history today.

Sensibility and liberal guilt now operate on a planetary scale as part of a worldwide exchange of emotions. National and international wrongs, aired through the formidable communicativeness of global media systems, can only fuel the practice of collective apology, stimulating but also attenuating the apologetic impulse. Sympathy is historically minded and not at all amnesiac, but apologies are one-time performances, not sustained programs. The libertarian who feels sullied by the blanket imputation of historical responsibility will resist the theater of sympathy in the name of liberty.

My study of the eighteenth-century interdependence of stoic disinterestedness and weeping men has led me to conclude that libertarian toughness arises in order to prevent government from serving as the medium of "needs talk." Because libertarian masculinity has to eschew the ambivalence of the broader republican tradition, it can only speak in tones of simple antagonism or simple optimism. Libertarians confess to a kind of conservative transcendentalism, a faith that less really is more, that personal versus government power and personal wealth versus public spending are diametrically opposed. The libertarian alliance between selfhood and deregulation accuses Democrats simultaneously of not being *tough* enough and, because of the magical equation that defines the market as rationality itself, of not being *rational* enough. What is specific to libertarians in the 1990s is the equating of sentimentality with government expenditure, and of government expenditure with error. The kind of citizenship recommended by the Cato Institute is not just phobic about government, therefore; it is also phobic about sympathy and, above all, about guilt. There is no sign that the ethos of participatory guilt is going to go away any time soon, however. To the dismay of the libertarians, this means that opportunities for mixed feelings can only multiply.

NOTES

Introduction

Portions of the introduction originally appeared as "A Short History of Liberal Guilt" by Julie Ellison in *Critical Inquiry* 22, no. 2 (winter 1996): 344–71. © 1996 by The University of Chicago. All rights reserved.

1. Robin Toner, "Democrats Offer Emotional Drama in New Hampshire," *New York Times*, Sunday, 16 February 1992, sec. 1, pt. 1, p. 1, col. 3, late edition-final.

2. Kenneth Silverman originates the term "Whig sentimentalism" for the overwrought tone of this line of political writings in *A Cultural History of the American Revolution: Painting, Music, Literature, and the Theatre in the Colonies and the United States from the Treaty of Paris to the Inauguration of George Washington, 1763–1789* (New York: T. Y. Crowell, 1976), 82–87.

3. Andrew Pollack, "Someday Bridges May Have Feelings Too," *New York Times*, 16 February 1992, sec. 4, p. 6, col. 1.

4. W. K. Wimsatt Jr. and M. C. Beardsley, "The Affective Fallacy" *Sewanee Review* 57 (1949).

5. Lloyd Grove, "The Weep Stakes: Pat Schroeder, Keeping Tabs on Tears," *Washington Post*, 23 August 1991, sec. C, 1; Joseph P. Kahn, "When the Tough Get Teary," *Boston Globe*, 2 July 1991, Living sec., 25.

6. *Harper's Magazine* 283 (October 1991): 49–56. Rieff finds in the political effects of universal victimization ("Hitler was a victim") a tendency to erase moral difference and to make blame impossible. He compares the codependency movement to current academic "political correctness":

> Both movements deny the value of any important distinction between the personal and the political; but where the multiculturalists, however much their politics too may be based on feelings, at least try to hold on to certain political categories, the recovery people are interested only in their subjective selves. When *they* say the personal is the political they really mean it.
>
> That the recovery psychotherapists are more radical than the academic multiculturalists becomes most clear when one examines the politics of victimhood, a centerpiece of both movements. In P.C. circles, this idea is inherently self-limiting in the sense that if the concept of oppression is to make any kind of sense, the situation of the various groups of victims—be they blacks, Hispanics, women or gays—must be opposed to that of an oppressor group—these days, straight white males. Proponents of recovery do not think in group terms. They claim that virtually everyone . . . [is] a victim. (50–51)

7. David B. Morris, *The Culture of Pain* (Berkeley: University of California Press, 1991); and Lauren Berlant, *The Queen of America Goes to Washington City: Essays on Sex and Citizenship* (Durham: Duke University Press, 1997), 124–26.

8. Robert Hass, "Families and Prisons," *Michigan Quarterly Review* 30 (fall 1991): 553–72.

9. Adela Pinch, *Strange Fits of Passion: Epistemologies of Emotion, Hume to Austen* (Stanford: Stanford University Press, 1996), 16.

10. Ibid., 167, 10, 166.

11. Judith Butler, *Excitable Speech: A Politics of the Performative* (New York and London: Routledge, 1997), 160.

12. Jacques Derrida, *Politics of Friendship,* trans. George Collins (London: Verso, 1997), viii–x.

13. June Howard, "What Is Sentimentality?" *American Literary History* 11:1 (spring 1999), forthcoming.

14. John Barrell, "Introduction: A Republic of Taste," *The Political Theory of Painting from Reynolds to Hazlitt: "The Body of the Public"* (New Haven: Yale University Press, 1986); *English Literature in History, 1730–80: An Equal, Wide Survey* (London: Hutchinson, 1983), 17–50; and Richard L. Bushman, *The Refinement of America: Persons, Houses, Cities* (New York: Knopf, 1992), 79–89 and chap. 6, "Ambivalence."

15. Jerome McGann, *The Poetics of Sensibility: A Revolution in Literary Style* (Oxford: Oxford University Press, 1996), 7–8, 33.

16. A more expansive chronology in the American setting has been decisively assisted by Liz Barnes, who convincingly abolishes the distinction between sensibility in the "Early Republic" and domesticity in the "antebellum period." Elizabeth Barnes, *States of Sympathy: Seduction and Democracy in the American Novel* (New York: Columbia University Press, 1997).

17. James H. Kavanagh, "Ideology," in *Critical Terms for Literary Study,* ed. Frank Lentricchia and Thomas McLaughlin (Chicago: University of Chicago Press, 1990), 311.

18. Pinch, *Strange Fits of Passion,* esp. chap. 1, "The Philosopher as Man of Feeling: Hume's Book of the Passions."

19. "Vicarious" is a word with a richly ambivalent set of theological, political, and psychological meanings. The term links the notion of the vicar, or surrogate (as in Christ the vicar) to long-distance, virtual, or figurative identifications between self and other. Thus sensibility relies on vicarious participation in the victimization of others.

20. Carroll Smith-Rosenberg, "The Female World of Love and Ritual," *Signs* 1 (1975), reprinted in *Disorderly Conduct: Visions of Gender in Victorian America* (New York: Oxford University Press, 1985); Nancy Cott, *The Bonds of Womanhood: "Woman's Sphere" in New England, 1780–1835* (New Haven: Yale University Press, 1977); Ann Douglas, *The Feminization of American Culture* (New York: Knopf, 1977); Nina Baym, "Melodramas of Beset Manhood: How Theories of American Fiction Exclude Women Authors," *American Quarterly* 33 (1981), reprinted in *The New Feminist Criticism: Essays on Women, Literature, and Theory,* ed. Elaine Showalter (New York: Pantheon, 1985), 63–80; Jane Tompkins, *Sensational Designs: The Cultural Work of American Fiction* (New York: Oxford University Press, 1985); and Cathy N. Davidson, *Revolution and the Word: The Rise of the Novel in America* (New York: Oxford University Press, 1986).

21. Karen Sánchez-Eppler, "Bodily Bonds: The Intersecting Rhetorics of Feminism and Abolition" *Representations* 24 (fall 1988); reprinted in *The Culture of Sentiment:*

Race, Gender, and Sentimentality in Nineteenth-Century America, ed. Shirley Samuels (New York: Oxford University Press, 1992) 92–114.

22. Lauren Berlant, "The Female Complaint" *Social Text* 19–20 (fall 1988): 237–59; and "The Female Woman: Fanny Fern and the Form of Sentiment" in *The Culture of Sentiment,* 265–81.

23. Sedgwick's analysis of homosocial relations among heterosexual men is indispensable, particularly her thoughts on the logic of sentimentality defined in terms of "relations of vicariousness." Her epistemology of the closet, a drama of knowing and not knowing, helps illuminate the place of conspiracy narratives in early modern masculine culture and influenced my epistemological readings of sensibility as a knowledge of systematic relatedness. Eve Sedgwick, *Epistemology of the Closet* (Berkeley: University of California Press, 1990), 152, 186–88.

24. Dana D. Nelson, *The Word in Black and White: Reading "Race" in American Literature 1638–1867* (New York: Oxford University Press, 1992), 67, 77, 86.

25. Julia A. Stern, *The Plight of Feeling: Sympathy and Dissent in the Early American Novel* (Chicago: Chicago University Press, 1997), 17, 40, 151.

26. Laura Wexler, "Tender Violence: Literary Eavesdropping, Domestic Fiction, and Educational Reform," *Yale Journal of Criticism* 5 (fall 1991) reprinted in *The Culture of Sentiment,* 9–38.

27. I am indebted to Wendy Motooka for this passage from Dene Barnett, *The Art of Gesture: The Practices and Principles of Eighteenth Century Acting* (Heidelberg: C. Winter, 1987).

28. Kathleen Wilson, *The Sense of the People: Politics, Culture and Imperialism in England, 1715–1785* (Cambridge: Cambridge University Press, 1995), 157, 162, 203.

29. These characters are both dramatic characters in the usual sense and philosophical characters as defined by Alastair MacIntyre: "Characters are . . . the moral representatives of their culture and they are so because of the way in which moral and metaphysical ideas and theories assume through them an embodied existence in the social world. *Characters* are the masks worn by moral philosophies. . . . Both individuals and roles can, and do, like *characters,* embody moral beliefs, doctrines, and theories, but each does so in its own way. And the way in which *characters* do so can only be sketched by contrast with these." *After Virtue,* 2d ed. (Notre Dame: University of Notre Dame Press, 1984), 28–29.

30. David Marshall's work on sympathy and theatricality also contributes substantially to a better understanding of masculine sensibility in the eighteenth century, although he does not explicitly address the issue of gender. David Marshall, *The Surprising Effects of Sympathy: Marivaux, Diderot, Rousseau, and Mary Shelley* (Chicago: University of Chicago Press, 1988).

31. Adam Smith, *The Theory of Moral Sentiments,* ed. D. D. Raphael and A. L. Macfie (1759; reprint, Indianapolis: Liberty Classics, 1982), 10–13, 306–14. See also MacIntyre's extended account, in *After Virtue,* of how Hume, Smith, and other major figures of the Scottish Enlightenment negotiated questions of sympathy and morality (chaps. 4, 5, 16 passim).

32. In a later era, but one directly related to the liberal 1770s and 1780s, the abolitionist William Knibbs would set forth a scene of white vicarious sentiment in which the "natural joy of prosperity" is overcome by the Christian joy in moral

intervention: "There is nothing more delightful and interesting than to plead the cause of the injured, the degraded and the oppressed. This, under any circumstances, is peculiarly delightful; but it is especially so when the speaker finds himself surrounded by so large a number of his fellow-Christians, who he feels assured never hear of misery but they endeavour to remove it; who never hear of sorrow, but they are anxious to dry the mourner's tears; and who never hear of oppression, but every feeling of their heart rises up in just and holy indignation against the person who inflicts it." "Whiteness at this moment," remarks Catherine Hall, "meant pity and care for lesser peoples, [and] the authority through public campaigns to exercise that concern." The tensions between Smith's and Knibbs's shifting positions reveal the way racial identity, sentimental masculinity, and the social politics of religious difference—including charitable strategies—are simultaneously negotiated. Catherine Hall, *White, Male, and Middle Class: Explorations in Feminism and History* (London: Routledge, 1988), 213. Hall quotes from Knibbs's *Speech at a Public Meeting of the Friends of Christian Mission.*

33. For an overview of the term, see Janet Todd, *Sensibility: An Introduction* (London: Methuen, 1986).

34. Henry Mackenzie, *The Man of Feeling,* ed. Brian Vickers (New York: Oxford University Press, 1987), 59, 61.

35. For a similarly charged handling of the suffering of the racial "other," see the story of "Inkle and Yarico" by Steele in the *Spectator,* discussed at length by Peter Hulme in *Colonial Encounters: Europe and the Native Caribbean, 1492–1797* (New York: Methuen, 1986), 225–63; see also Felicity Nussbaum's "Introduction" to the special issue on "The Politics of Difference" of *Eighteenth-Century Studies* 23 (1990): 375–86.

36. Homi Bhabha, "Postcolonial Authority and Postmodern Guilt," in *Cultural Studies,* ed. Lawrence Grossberg, Cary Nelson, and Paula Treichler (New York: Routledge, 1992), 65.

37. *The Gendering of Melancholia: Feminism, Psychoanalysis, and the Symbolics of Loss in Renaissance Literature* (Ithaca: Cornell University Press, 1992).

38. Gayatri Chakravorty Spivak, *The Post-Colonial Critic: Interviews, Strategies, Dialogues,* ed. Sara Harasym (New York: Routledge, 1990), 115.

39. Joseph Roach, *Cities of the Dead: Circum-Atlantic Performance* (New York: Columbia University Press, 1996).

40. In the epilogue to the anonymous *Romulus and Hersilia* (1682). Paula R. Backscheider, *Spectacular Politics: Theatrical Power and Mass Culture in Early Modern England* (Baltimore: Johns Hopkins University Press, 1993) 106–8.

41. My understanding of late seventeenth-century and early eighteenth-century masculine literary cultures draws on Jessica Munns' work on sexuality and power in the Restoration drama of Otway, *Restoration Politics and Drama: The Plays of Thomas Otway, 1675–1683* (Newark: University of Delaware Press, 1995), 182–94; James Winn's attention to gender and pleasure in Restoration culture, *"When Beauty Fires the Blood": Love and the Arts in the Age of Dryden* (Ann Arbor: University of Michigan Press, 1992); Carolyn Williams's exploration of neoclassicism and gender in *Pope, Homer, and Manliness: Some Aspects of Eighteenth-Century Classical Learning* (London: Routledge, 1993), esp. chap. 2, "Manly Learning"; Philip Ayres' investigations in *Classical Culture and the Idea of Rome in Eighteenth-Century England* (Cambridge: Cambridge University

Press, 1997); Lawrence Klein's account of Shaftesbury's highly political project of Whig legitimation in *Shaftesbury and the Culture of Politeness: Moral Discourse and Cultural Politics in Early Eighteenth-Century England* (Cambridge: Cambridge University Press, 1994); Shawn Maurer's study of how eighteenth-century periodicals instructed middle-class men on social class and marriage in *Proposing Men: Dialectics of Gender and Class in the Eighteenth-Century English Periodical* (Stanford: Stanford University Press, 1998); and G. J. Barker-Benfield's survey, drawing on these sources and many more to conclude that the culture of sensibility is an argument both among and with men, in *The Culture of Sensibility: Sex and Society in Eighteenth-Century Britain* (Chicago: University of Chicago Press, 1992).

42. *The Works of Anna Laetitia Barbauld, with a Memoir by Lucy Aikin Barbauld* (London: Longman, Hurst, Rees, Orme, Brown, and Green, 1825): 226–27.

43. *The Prose of Royall Tyler,* ed. Marius B. Péladeau (The Vermont Historical Society and The Charles E. Tuttle Company, 1972): 143–48.

44. Frederic M. Litto, "Addison's *Cato* in the Colonies," *William and Mary Quarterly,* 3d ser., 23 (July 1966): 448.

45. J. G. A. Pocock, *The Machiavellian Moment: Florentine Political Thought and the Atlantic Republican Tradition* (Princeton: Princeton University Press, 1975), 512. The "Atlantic republican tradition" as described by Pocock was attuned to the affective volatility resulting from unsettling changes in politics, land ownership, mobile property, and sociability in late seventeenth-century England. Without discussing gender, Pocock grapples with the affective complexity of masculine citizenship as he tracks the "apocalyptic" and anxious tone of Whig republicanism down to the American Revolution. He defines republicanism as a critique of the timeless or "imperialist vision of history" according to which "political society was envisaged as the existence among men of the hierarchical order existing in heaven and in nature." Republican discourses, by contrast, "accepted the fact of the republic's mortality" and this is "symbolized by the choice as hero of the unsuccessful rebel Brutus" (53). Strongly identifying with the stoic heroes of English Roman plays, Pocock argues that the republic appeals to "toughly and secularly civic minds" and posits a high degree of continuity between the dilemmas of republican and liberal virtue (80).

46. *Equivocal Beings: Politics, Gender, and Sentimentality in the 1790s* (Chicago: University of Chicago Press, 1995) 199, 14.

Chapter One

1. Lawrence E. Klein, *Shaftesbury and the Culture of Politeness: Moral Discourse and Cultural Politics in Early Eighteenth-Century England* (Cambridge: Cambridge University Press, 1994), 60, 65. See also Robert Voitle, *The Third Earl of Shaftesbury, 1671–1713* (Baton Rouge: Louisiana State University Press, 1984); and K. H. D. Haley, *The First Earl of Shaftesbury* (Oxford: Clarendon Press, 1968).

2. Philip Harth, *Pen for a Party: Dryden's Tory Propaganda in Its Contexts* (Princeton: Princeton University Press, 1993), 19.

3. The relationship between the older and the short-lived younger man was mediated by John Locke. Locke stands in for the missing second generation of Shaftesburys, the "weak" son of the first earl and father of the third. The first earl of Shaftesbury scooped up his grandson and put his education in the hands of Locke.

Locke had presided over the operation that saved the first earl's life and installed the shunt in his abdomen, as subsequent satires depict. The gratitude arising from this mortal intimacy was reinforced by the first earl's enduring admiration for Locke's intellectual and political expertise, and reciprocated by Locke's equally long-standing commitment to the program, if not the style, of the Whig exclusionists. By virtue of his coolness of tone in the *Two Treatises on Government,* Locke has manage to stay separate in our minds from the paranoid mood of the period from 1675 through 1683, when opposition was still factional, even treasonous. But it is precisely Locke's reflective distance that infiltrates the urbane prose of the third earl of Shaftesbury, despite the latter's distaste for his teacher's views. Voitle, *The Third Earl of Shaftesbury,* 119–22, 229–30.

4. Laura Brown, *English Dramatic Form, 1660–1760: An Essay in Generic History* (New Haven: Yale University Press, 1981), 76.

5. Richard Braverman's fine study of such questions is grounded in the assumption that "literary forms mediate . . . dynastic politics" in the period. The influence works two ways, with notions of the family central to both: "literary counterplots . . . redefined the body politic" while writers formulated "political identities in response to the royalist family romance." Richard Braverman, *Plots and Counterplots: Sexual Politics and the Body Politic in English Literature, 1660–1730* (Cambridge: Cambridge University Press, 1993), xii, xiv, xv. I am interested in the somewhat different problem of the historical pressure to understand parliamentary politics as a nonfamilial homosocial institution.

6. Anthony Ashley Cooper, Earl of Shaftesbury, *Characteristics of Men, Manners, Opinions, Times,* ed. John M. Robertson , 2 vols. (Indianapolis: Bobbs-Merrill, 1964), 1 : 74–75. All subsequent references are cited parenthetically by page in the text.

7. Klein, *Shaftesbury and the Culture of Politeness,* 8–9, 15–16.

8. Ibid., 1, 9, 8.

9. Because Klein is interested above all in politeness, he views the politics of the Shaftesbury of 1711 and *Characteristics* as discontinuous with both the politics of the first earl and the third earl's own affiliations of the 1690s. For a discussion of the third earl's engagement with stoicism, see Voitle, *The Third Earl of Shaftesbury,* 135–63.

10. J. R. Jones, *The First Whigs: The Politics of the Exclusion Crisis, 1678–1683* (London: Oxford University Press, 1961), 216–17.

11. Ibid., 17.

12. For an extended survey of the role of Venice as a republic and its relation to the Roman republic, see J. G. A. Pocock, *The Machiavellian Moment: Florentine Political Thought and the Atlantic Republican Tradition* (Princeton: Princeton University Press, 1975), chaps. 7–9.

13. John Loftis, *The Politics of Drama in Augustan England* (Oxford: Clarendon Press, 1969), 16.

14. Harth, *A Pen for a Party,* 45–46.

15. Ibid., 9–11, 16–17, 116–17. See also *Absalom and Achitophel,* comp. Robert W. McHenry Jr., Contexts, no. 3 (Hamden, Conn.: Archon Books, 1986), 255–77.

16. Harth, *A Pen for a Party,* 80–84. It would be useful to know more than we do about the shift from the phenomenon of the king's victimization during the Interreg-

num to the virtuous suffering of the post-Restoration republican. During the seventeenth century, various groups take turns assuming the suffering, ethical position, beginning with the monarchists who mourned Charles I. We have certainly missed some sentimental possibilities within Puritanism. There were no real Whig martyrs until 1683, when the Rye House Plot led to the executions of Russell and Sidney. Sidney's *Discourses*, we should remember, were not published until 1698. Still, the language of sacrificial pathos was firmly in place, augmented by the conventions of the petition movements. The Exclusion Crisis was a period in which opposing camps expressed themselves by competitive outpourings of affection for the king, in the massive campaigns by the Petitioners and the Abhorrers and in the publication by the Crown of the collected "Loyal Addresses."

17. "What has the tyrant made you?" he asks the assembled crowd, and answers, "mechanic laborers, / Drawers of water, taskers, timber-fellers, / Yoked you like bulls, his very jades for luggage / . . . While his lewd sons, though not on work so hard, / Employed your daughters and your wives at home." Nathaniel Lee, *Lucius Junius Brutus*, ed. John Loftis, Regents Restoration Drama Series (Lincoln: Nebraska University Press, 1967), act 2, lines 195–200. All subsequent references are cited by act and line in the text.

18. Stephanie H Jed, *Chaste Thinking: The Rape of Lucretia and the Birth of Humanism* (Bloomington: Indiana University Press, 1989), 49. It is important to note that the significance of Jed's study derives from the central question of her book, which is how a feminist scholar confronts the intellectual and—in the manuscript text—material remains of masculine humanism. See also Braverman, *Plots and Counterplots,* 152.

19. The eroticism of the male breast is not unique to this play, but recurs in Lee's graphic appreciation of the male body, as in the speeches of female characters in *The Rival Queens* (3.1.205, 5.1.35–39).

20. Paul Hammond, "The King's Two Bodies: Representations of Charles II" in *Culture, Politics and Society in Britain, 1600–1800*, ed. Jeremy Black and Jeremy Gregory (Manchester: Manchester University Press, 1991), 38. Hammond argues that political discourses are linked to changes in sexuality and authority in the family. Referring to satirical poems on Charles II, he writes: "If their crudities and fantasies figure a crisis of royal authority, they also reveal—through their very excess, their very instability of tone—a crisis of some kind of masculine sexuality, a crisis in the sway of male power over society at large" (41–42). Writing a decade later, when the analysis of gender in Restoration culture has moved to a much greater degree of specificity, Jessica Munns observes (with reference to *Venice Preserved*): "The definition of manliness is a central issue. . . . Jaffeir's persuasion to revolt and his induction into the conspiracy in Act 2 are couched in terms of entry to a male club dedicated to the eradication of sexual impurities and the empowerment of marginal men":

> Otway was not unique in depicting fathers as cruel. To cite only a few plays of the period, Robert Boyle, Earl of Orrery's *Mustapha* (1665) has the Sultan Solyman putting his son Mustapha to death, John Crowne's *The Ambitious Statesman: or, The Loyal Favourite* (1679) features a father who tortures his son to death. . . . Father-son rivalry is endemic in the literature of the period, yet there is in Otway's work a particular intensity of interest in the morbid psychology of the father as tyrant and

son-hater, with depictions of paternal rage as also sexual rage. Paternal irresponsibility and rage become the hallmark of Otway's dramas, implicating family and state in regressive cycles of mutual destruction . . . the horror of the father who disinherits and murders his sons is matched by agonized movements between resistance and masochistic submission on the part of the son.

Restoration Politics and Drama: The Plays of Thomas Otway, 1675–1683 (Newark: University of Delaware Press, 1995), 32–33.

21. "Belvidera always sees the penis in the phallus, and it is the penis, not some phallic abstraction, that she craves. . . . Belvidera's saving blindness to male codes of honor enables her to see the conspirators as 'hired Slaves, Bravoes, and Common stabbers / Nose-slitters, Ally-lurking Villains!' (3.2.162–63) rather than as a confederacy of heroes." Munns, *Restoration Politics and Drama*, 187–88.

22. Ibid., 188–91.

23. Regarded in this light, the play does not support arguments that, as late seventeenth-century tragedy shifted from heroic action to familial pathos, it became less political. Laura Brown suggests correctly that women take on the role of articulation as a supplement to the weakened, sentimentalized male protagonist and that their function is to maximize the dynamics of pity. Brown draws the opposite conclusion from mine, however. She holds that the onset of pathos marks the end of politics or at least the dissolution of social status in a "classless pathos," whereas I view pathos as strongly political in these contexts. *English Dramatic Form*, 69–70.

24. Brown has commented on the fact that Brutus and his son are "joint protagonists" who, despite the studied contrast between them, take on each other's characteristics. Titus's predicament takes the form of a love-versus-honor dilemma, in which he has to choose between loyalty to the father and loyalty to the woman in his life. But this plot is not really a matter of tension between loyalty to the "family" and loyalty to "the state," or between the claims of the "private" versus the "public" sphere; men love the state as well as their wives, and honor is as much a familial as a political notion. *English Dramatic Form*, 78.

25. Harth, *A Pen for a Party*, 44.

26. John Dryden, *Absalom and Achitophel*, in *John Dryden*, ed. Keith Walker (Oxford: Oxford University Press, 1987), lines 939, 947, 942, 957–60, 961. All further references are cited by line number in the text.

27. James Winn, *When Beauty Fires the Blood: Love and the Arts in the Age of Dryden* (Ann Arbor: University of Michigan Press, 1992), 259.

28. Lauren Berlant, "The Female Complaint," *Social Text* 19–20 (fall 1988): 238, 245.

29. Jones, *The First Whigs*, 209–11.

30. Harth, *A Pen for a Party*, 143.

31. Ibid., 151, 80–86.

32. Jones, *The First Whigs*, 211.

33. Harth, *A Pen for a Party*, 88.

34. Jones, *The First Whigs*, 211.

35. Loftis, *The Politics of Drama in Augustan England*, 20.

36. Thomas Otway, *Venice Preserved*, ed. Malcolm Kelsall, Regents Restoration

Drama Series (Lincoln: Nebraska University Press, 1969), 2.3.146. All subsequent references are cited in the text by act, scene, and line.

37. Rome surfaces as an exemplary idea in the dialogues of Theocles and Philocles, the talking heads of *The Moralists*, with a generational slant. Theocles points out that his friend "might have the same indulgence for Nature or Mankind as for the people of Old Rome, whom . . . I have known you in love with many ways, particularly under the representation of a beautiful youth called the Genius of the People" (2.29). Theocles is instantly convinced that Nature and Mankind are notions of the same order of ontological persuasiveness as the "beautiful youth" signifying "Old Rome."

Chapter Two

An earlier version of chapter 2 originally appeared as Julie Ellison, "Cato's Tears," *English Literary History* 63, no. 3 (fall 1996): 571–601. © 1996 The Johns Hopkins University Press.

1. Kim Hall, *Things of Darkness: Economies of Race and Gender in Early Modern England* (Ithaca: Cornell University Press, 1995).

2. Toni Morrison, *Playing in the Dark: Whiteness and the Literary Imagination* (Cambridge: Harvard University Press, 1992), 13, 6.

3. June Howard, "What Is Sentimentality?" *American Literary History* 11:1 (spring 1999), forthcoming.

4. Ania Loomba, in "Seizing the Book," chap. 6 in *Gender, Race, Renaissance Drama* (Manchester: Manchester University Press, 1989), discusses the ways in which "ambivalence" has been attributed to both subaltern and hegemonic discourses. Bailyn, Fliegelman, and Wood have stressed the highly emotional tone of the opposition Whigs and, later, North American pamphleteers. Bernard Bailyn, *The Ideological Origins of the American Revolution* (Cambridge: Harvard University Press, Belknap Press, 1967), chap. 2; Jay Fliegelman, *Prodigals and Pilgrims: The American Revolution Against Patriarchal Authority* (Cambridge: Cambridge University Press, 1982); and Gordon S. Wood, "Conspiracy and the Paranoid Style: Causality and Deceit in the Eighteenth Century," *William and Mary Quarterly*, 3d series, 39 (July 1982): 401–41. Kenneth Silverman uses the term "Whig Sentimentalism" to describe the overwrought tone of this line of political writings in *A Cultural History of the American Revolution: Painting, Music, Literature, and the Theatre in the Colonies and the United States from the Treaty of Paris to the Inauguration of George Washington, 1763–1789* (New York: T. Y. Crowell, 1976), 82–87.

5. E. M. G. Routh, *Tangier: England's Lost Atlantic Outpost 1661–1684* (London: John Murray, 1912), 11. See also C. R. Pennell, ed., *Piracy and Diplomacy in Seventeenth-Century North Africa: The Journal of Thomas Baker, English Consul in Tripoli, 1677–85* (Rutherford: Fairleigh Dickinson University Press, 1989).

6. John Loftis, *The Politics of Drama in Augustan England* (Oxford: Clarendon Press, 1963), 17. The standard account is J. R. Jones, *The First Whigs: The Politics of the Exclusion Crisis 1678–1683* (London: Oxford University Press, 1961).

7. Jones, *The First Whigs*, 145, 158; K. H. D. Haley, *The First Earl of Shaftesbury* (Oxford: Clarendon Press, 1968), 175, 289, 605, 612, 615; and Routh, *Tangier*, chap. 13, "The English Government and Tangier, 1679–1683."

8. David Harrison Stevens, *Party Politics and English Journalism 1702–1742* (1916; reprint, New York: Russell and Russell, 1967), 17–19, 22–25. On Addison's attendance at a Venetian performance of *Cato Uticense*, which he thought a dreadful play, see Peter Smithers, *The Life of Joseph Addison*, 2d ed. (Oxford: Clarendon Press, 1968), 62–63; on the Italian tour and its relationship to Addison's developing career, see Smithers, chap. 2.

9. Loftis, *The Politics of Drama in Augustan England*, 57–61.

10. The bipartisan approval of the play is evident in the approbation of the *Tory Examiner* and Tory George Sewell's poem, "Observations Upon Cato," in *Addison and Steele: The Critical Heritage*, ed. Edward A. Bloom and Lillian D. Bloom (London: Routledge and Kegan Paul, 1980), 266–71, 281–82. Loftis argues that Addison went out of his way to make the play highly ambiguous in its relation to the party politics of 1713, *The Politics of Drama in Augustan England*, 57–62, a point reinforced by Robert Halsband, "Addison's *Cato* and Lady Mary Wortley Montagu," *PMLA* 65 (December 1950): 1122–29.

11. Michael MacDonald and Terence R. Murphy observe that the admirable qualities of patriotic Roman suicides such as Cato and Lucretia represented a problematic exception in the period from 1500 to 1700, which was marked by more severe punishment of suicide "than ever before or afterwards" (75). In their discussion of "Cato and the Code of Honour," MacDonald and Murphy note that "Georgian intellectuals" were strongly ambivalent: "On the one hand, they admired [the pagan past] more avidly than even their humanist forebears had; on the other, they feared that too great a dependence on classical models promoted values and behaviour that were irreligious" (204–5). *Sleepless Souls: Suicide in Early Modern England* (Oxford: Clarendon Press, 1990). I concur that the management of masculine public honor and reputation stirred up considerable ambivalence in sixteenth- and seventeenth-century England. Nevertheless, ambivalence in secular political and cultural arenas had less to do with strictly religious concerns than with claims to the strategic mixed feelings offered by the stoic-sentimental complex.

12. Joseph Addison, *The Miscellaneous Works of Joseph Addison*, ed A. C. Guthkelch (London: G. Bell and Sons, 1914), vol. 1, act 4, scene 4, lines 139, 135, 141–42. All subsequent references to the play are cited by act, scene, and line in the text.

13. Bercovitch, Fliegelman, and Sundquist have interpreted the history of the American male citizen in terms of familial, and especially paternal, meanings deeply conflated with the idea of the nation itself. *Cato* suggests that this strategy could and did work perfectly well in a British context. British cultural critics, however, have not been attracted to such a hypothesis. See Sacvan Bercovitch *The Puritan Origins of the American Self* (New Haven: Yale University Press, 1975); Fliegelman, *Prodigals and Pilgrims;* and Eric Sundquist, *Home as Found: Authority and Genealogy in Nineteenth-Century American Literature* (Baltimore: Johns Hopkins University Press, 1979).

14. "*Numidia's* grown a scorn among the nations / For breach of publick vows. Our *Punick* faith / Is infamous, and branded to a proverb" (2.5.115–17).

15. I've known young *Juba* rise, before the Sun,
    To beat the thicket where the Tiger slept,
    Or seek the Lion in his dreadful haunts:

    . . . .
    Even in the *Libyan* Dog-days, hunt him down,

> Then charge him close, provoke him to the rage
> Of fangs and claws, and stooping from your Horse
> Rivet the panting savage to the ground. (2.5.11–13, 16–19)

16. Syphax praises North African women in similarly climatic terms (1.4.137–142).

17. For a characterization of contemporary response to Cato's death from "patriotic heartbreak" that includes a comparison to Thomson's *Sophonisba*, see Lincoln B. Faller, *The Popularity of Addison's* Cato *and Lillo's* The London Merchant, *1700–1776* (New York: Garland, 1988), 73, 65–87.

18. Loftis, *The Politics of Drama in Augustan England*, 15–17; and Nathaniel Lee, *Lucius Junius Brutus*, ed. John Loftis, Regents Restoration Drama Series (Lincoln: University of Nebraska Press, 1967), xiii–xviii.

19. Laplanche and Pontalis sum up the psychoanalytic definition of ambivalence: "Specific conflicts in which the positive and negative components of the emotional attitude are simultaneously in evidence and inseparable, and where they constitute a non-dialectical opposition which the subject, saying 'yes' and 'no' at the same time, is incapable of transcending." Jean Laplanche and J. B. Pontalis, *The Language of Psycho-analysis*, trans. Donald Nicholson-Smith (New York: Norton, 1973), 28.

20. Loomba, *Gender, Race, Renaissance Drama*, 94, 144–45.

21. How will my bosom swell with anxious joy,
> When I behold her struggling in my arms,
> With glowing beauty, and disorder'd charms,
> While fear and anger, with alternate grace,
> Pant in her breast, and vary in her face!
> So Pluto, seiz'd of Proserpine, convey'd
> To hell's tremendous gloom th' affrighted maid,
> There grimly smil'd, pleas'd with the beauteous prize,
> Nor envy'd Jove his sun-shine and his skies. (3.7.26–34)

22. John Dennis, "Remarks Upon *Cato, A Tragedy*" (1713) in *The Critical Works of John Dennis*, ed. Edward Niles Hooker (Baltimore: Johns Hopkins Press, 1943), 2:46–47, 54.

23. For an analysis of a similar process at work in a much later (and not precisely analogous) American context, see Walter Benn Michaels, "Race into Culture: A Critical Genealogy of Cultural Identity," *Critical Inquiry* 18 (summer 1992): 655–85. Benn Michaels sums up his argument as follows: "Our sense of culture is characteristically meant to displace race, but part of the argument of this essay has been that culture has turned out to be a way of continuing rather than repudiating racial thought. The appeal to race makes culture an object of affect and that gives notions like losing our culture, preserving it, stealing someone else's culture, restoring people's culture to them, and so on, their pathos" (684–85).

24. James Sambrook, *James Thomson (1700–1748): A Life* (Oxford: Clarendon Press, 1991), 128–30.

25. Thomson's *Sophonisba* was firmly conventionalized through six earlier French plays on the subject (including that by Corneille) and English versions by Marston, Nabbes, and Lee. Sambrook, *James Thomson*, 81–82. On the attraction of Frederick Prince of Wales to both *Sophonisba* and *Cato*, see Faller, *The Popularity of Addison's Cato*, 29–33.

26. James Thomson, *Sophonisba*, in *The Plays of James Thomson*, ed. Percy G.

Adams (New York: Garland Publishing, 1979), 4.3.25. All subsequent references are cited by act, scene, and line in the text.

27. Patricia Parker notes that *The "Aeneid" of Thomas Phaer and Thomas Twyne* (1573) describes Dido as the queen of "Moores, that have of dooble toong the name" and describes Carthaginians both as "Moors" and as "white Moors in Affrike." Parker observes, "The overriding distinction throughout remains 'Trojan/Roman' as opposed to 'Moor' and 'Affrike.' Sidonian-Carthaginian Dido is clearly identified with the 'Affrika' . . . Aeneas is commanded to 'forsake' . . . and Carthage is part of 'Barbarie' as described at the opening of 'Iohn Leo his First Booke.'" "Fantasies of 'Race' and 'Gender': Africa, *Othello,* and Bringing to Light," in *Women, "Race," and Writing in the Early Modern Period,* ed. Margo Hendricks and Patricia Parker (London: Routledge, 1994), 318–19 n. 38. On Carthage, Queen Elizabeth, and Dido, see also Stephen Orgel, "Shakespeare and the Cannibals" in *Cannibals, Witches, and Divorce: Estranging the Renaissance,* ed. Marjorie Garber (Baltimore: Johns Hopkins University Press, 1987).

28. Eve Kosofsky Sedgwick, *Epistemology of the Closet* (Berkeley: University of California Press, 1990), 145.

29. John Trenchard, *Cato's Letters,* 4 vols. (London, 1723–24). See also Marie P. McMahon, *The Radical Whigs, John Trenchard and Thomas Gordon: Libertarian Loyalists to the New House of Hanover* (Lanham: University Press of America, 1989); J. G. A. Pocock, *The Machiavellian Moment: Florentine Political Thought and the Atlantic Republican Tradition* (Princeton: Princeton University Press, 1975), 426–27, chap. 13, 467–77, 528–531; and Charles Bechdolt Realey, *The London Journal and Its Authors, 1720–1723* (Lawrence: University of Kansas Department of Journalism Press, 1935).

30. Benjamin Franklin, for example, drew on both works, quoting from Addison's Cato's final soliloquy (5.1.15–18) for the motto of his *Virtue Book* and adopting from *Cato's Letters* the signifying name of Cato to serve as one of the speakers in his *Busy-Body* essays, or moral dialogues, of 1729. Frederic M. Litto, "Addison's *Cato* in the Colonies," *William and Mary Quarterly,* 3d series, 23 (July 1966): 444–46, 440–42. Bernard Bailyn long ago argued that the truculent voices of Whig opposition ideologues, marginal in British politics, became dominant in colonial debates leading up to independence. One may question the causal force of the rhetorical centrality of *Cato's Letters* and other oppositional works between the Stamp Act Crisis and the outbreak of war. Nonetheless, the ubiquitousness of this and similar texts—established in newspaper and pamphlet debates through allusion, echo, and authorial pseudonyms—is undeniable. Bernard Bailyn, "Sources of Political Culture," chap. 1 in *The Origins of American Politics* (New York: Vintage, 1970); and *The Ideological Origins of the American Revolution,* 35–54.

31. Litto, "Addison's *Cato* in the Colonies," 431–49. See also Fliegelman, *Prodigals and Pilgrims,* 151–54.

32. Litto, "Addison's *Cato* in the Colonies," 441–42. See also Caroline Robbins, *The Eighteenth-Century Commonwealthman: Studies in the Transmission, Development, and Circumstances of English Liberal Thought from the Restoration. of Charles II until the War with the Thirteen Colonies* (Cambridge: Harvard University Press, 1959); and Gordon S. Wood, *The Creation of the American Republic, 1776–1787* (New York: Norton, 1969), chap. 1.

33. I am grateful to David Anthony for bringing this piece of information back for me from the American Antiquarian Society.

34. Adam Smith, *The Theory of Moral Sentiments* (Indianapolis: Liberty Bell Press, 1982), part 1, section 3, chapter 1, 14, 49. All subsequent references are cited by part, section, chapter, and page in the text.

35. Clarence Major, ed., *Juba to Jive: A Dictionary of African-American Slang* (New York: Penguin, 1994), 263; and Saidiya V. Hartman, *Scenes of Subjection: Terror, Slavery, and Self-Making in Nineteenth-Century America* (New York: Oxford University Press, 1997).

36. Maria Edgeworth, *Belinda,* Everyman Edition (London: J. M. Dent, 1993), 327–28. All subsequent references are cited by page in the text.

Chapter Three

1. Margaret R. Somers, "Citizenship and the Place of the Public Sphere: Law, Community, and Political Culture in the Transition to Democracy," *American Sociological Review* 58, no. 5 (October 1993), 589–687.

2. Lauren Berlant, *The Anatomy of National Fantasy: Hawthorne, Utpoia, and Everyday Life* (Chicago: University of Chicago Press, 1991), 5.

3. M. H. Abrams, "Structure and Style in the Greater Romantic Lyric," in *Romanticism and Consciousness: Essays in Criticism,* ed. Harold Bloom (New York: Norton, 1970), 201–29. On the "loco-descriptive" poem, see p. 208.

4. Kathleen Wilson, "The Good, the Bad, and the Impotent: Imperialism and the Politics of Identity in Georgian England," in *The Consumption of Culture, 1600–1800: Image, Object, Text,* ed. Ann Bermingham and John Brewer (London and New York: Routledge, 1995), 242.

5. "[E]mpire was linked . . . to opposition and libertarian ideologies, to strategies of extra-parliamentary organization and resistance, and to the form and content of popular political consciousness." In the 1730s and early 1740s the "imperial project . . . was represented as the ultimate patriotic one: it diffused wealth among the entire population, protected domestic freedoms (including freedom of trade and navigation . . .) from the threats of both foreign powers and rapacious ministries, coaxed 'public-spiritedness' from British subjects, and extended Britons' birthrights to the colonies . . . [P]opular imperialism became attached to anti-aristocratic critiques of the state and polity" (Wilson, "The Good, the Bad, and the Impotent," 248). On cosmopolitanism, see Timothy Brennan, *At Home in the World: Cosmopolitanism Now* (Cambridge: Harvard University Press, 1997). "As it actually unfolds today in left cultural theory, the discourse on cosmopolitanism . . . is deeply humane, learned, and frankly—even belligerently—anti-imperial. . . . [T]he ethics of cosmopolitanism are as desirable as they are embattled" (15). For Brennan, cosmopolitanism today includes "the death of the nation-state, transculturation (rather than . . . one-sided assimilation), cultural hybridity (rather than a . . . contrast between the foreign and the indigenous), and postmodernity (as the view that consumption is politically exciting, viable, and wholly one's own)", and it favors "a single, internally rich and disparate plurality" (2). See also David Hancock, *Citizens of the World: London Merchants and the Integration of the British Atlantic Community, 1735–1785* (Cambridge: Cambridge University Press, 1995).

6. John Barrell, *Poetry, Language, and Politics* (Manchester: Manchester University Press, 1988). Barrell argues that, in the eighteenth-century poetry of landscape, "a new kind of perceiving subject is produced: one which, by its ability to divide, organ-

ise and reflect upon its experiences, differentiates itself from those experiences, and survives and transcends them." Thomson's landscapes are "the appropriate products of a class which, because it could afford to travel, to move from place to place, had developed a means of constructing its relations with places in a way that represented, exactly, the degree of its abstraction, emancipation, from particular localities and their power to determine our 'knowledge' and our 'being'" (133–34). See also Barrell, *The Political Theory of Painting from Reynolds to Hazlitt: "The Body of the Public"* (New Haven: Yale University Press, 1986), 63–66.

7. James Thomson, *Winter. A Poem* (London, 1726), lines 274–76.

8. Thomson, "Winter," *The Poetical Works of James Thomson* (London: William Pickering, 1830), lines 572–74, 499.

9. Thomson, "Winter," *Poetical Works,* lines 507–8.

10. Barrell, *The Political Theory of Painting from Reynolds to Hazlitt,* 6.

11. Thomson, "Summer," *Poetical Works,* lines 951–58.

12. On Dennis's political stance, see *The Critical Works of John Dennis,* 2 vols. ed. Edward Niles Hooker (Baltimore: Johns Hopkins Press, 1943), 2:xlvi. Dennis dedicated his *Essay on the Navy* (1702) to Thomas Herbert, eighth earl of Pembroke, his patron for two decades, and at various times first lord of the admiralty and lord high admiral (2:xxi–xxii). Subsequent references to *The Critical Works* are abbreviated as *CW* and are cited in the text by volume and page.

13. Richard White, *The Middle Ground: Indians, Empires, and Republics in the Great Lakes Region, 1650–1815* (Cambridge: Cambridge University Press, 1991), 117, 120–21, 150–51.

14. Joseph Roach, *Cities of the Dead: Circum-Atlantic Performance* (New York: Columbia University Press, 1996), chap. 4. Dennis's *Liberty Asserted* debuted six years prior to the famous visit of the "Mohawk Kings" to London in 1710, when the Iroquois alliance petitioned the queen for military intervention against the Hurons and the French. As Roach shows, literary and performative reactions to the 1710 visit were manifold. They included Addison's two *Spectator* issues of Friday, April 27, 1711 (no. 50), and Friday, May 4, 1711 (no. 56), and a performance of Davenant's musical *Macbeth,* revived "For the Entertainment of the Four INDIAN KINGS lately arriv'd."

15. White, *The Middle Ground,* 15–19, 66–75, 30–31, 35. For example, one finds references to the adoption of captive Indians belonging to different leagues by one another and of Europeans by Indians; intertribal marriage and marriages between Indians and Europeans, especially the French; the considerable authority of women, particularly among the matrilineal Hurons; and the recurring anxiety about Indian conspiracies felt by Europeans in North America.

16. "I have introduced the Characters of two Frenchmen, Frontenac and Miramont, who are both of them Men of Honour; but the difference between them is this, that Miramont, who declares against Arbitrary Pow'r, is altogether without Blemish, and the Faults and Defects in Frontenac's Character, are plainly deriv'd from his Zeal for their present Government" (*CW* 1:323).

17. John Dennis, *Liberty Asserted* (London, 1704), act 1, scene 2, lines 104–5. Subsequent references are cited by act, scene, and line in the text.

18. See Harold Forster, *Edward Young: The Poet of the Night Thoughts, 1683–1765* (Arlburgh: Erskine Press, 1986),163–64.

19. Ibid., 32–33.

20. Ibid., 71.
21. If Men shall ask who brought thee to thy End,
    Tell them, The Moor, and they will not despise thee.
    If cold white Mortals censure this great Deed,
    Warn them, they judge not of superior Beings
    Souls made of Fire, and Children of the Sun,
    With whom Revenge is Virtue.

Edward Young, *The Revenge* (London, 1721), act 5, lines 445–50. Subsequent references are cited in the text by act, scene (where appropriate), and line.

22. Edward Young, *Night Thoughts,* ed. Stephen Cornford (Cambridge: Cambridge University Press, 1989), section 5, lines 518–20. Subsequent references are cited in the text by section and line.

23. Forster, *Edward Young,* 30, 59.

24. Francis Parkman, *The Conspiracy of Pontiac,* vol. 1 (Lincoln and London: University of Nebraska Press, 1994), 131–32. Subsequent references are cited in the text by page. Parkman's note credits this story to a Scottish midshipman, later a professor of natural philosophy at Edinborough. Kathleen Wilson notes: "The recovery of British patriotism and manliness through the imperial cause was epitomized . . . by the death of General James Wolfe at the Battle of Quebec. . . . In a significant anticipation of Benjamin West's famous painting . . . a tableau of this historic moment . . . ended a performance at the Manchester Theatre in 1763 . . . : 'the General expiring in the Arms of Minerva, while she crowns him with a Laurel; the Figure of Hope with a broken Anchor, weeping over him, an Emblem of past Recovery. Britannia, the Genius of England, seated in Commerce, with an Indian Prince kneeling at her Feet, resigning up America: And Fame, triumphing over Death, with this Motto: He can never be lost, Who Saves His Country'" ("The Good, the Bad, and the Impotent," 251). Gray's poem has often been connected to the death of his intimate friend, Richard West. West died in 1742 immediately following the breakdown of Gray's relationship with Horace Walpole, so it is not surprising that the themes of death and friendship are joined in the *Elegy.* Roger Lonsdale, ed., *Thomas Gray and William Collins: Poetical Works* (Oxford: Oxford University Press, 1977), xii–xiii, 33–34. References to Gray's poems are from this edition and are cited parenthetically in the text by line.

25. White, *The Middle Ground,* 270, 297, 313. For a detailed history, see Howard H. Peckham, *Pontiac and the Indian Uprising* (1947; reprint, with a foreword by John C. Dann, Detroit: Wayne State University Press, 1994).

26. Elizabeth Rogers divorce petition, State of New Hampshire, 11 February 1778 (William L. Clements Library, University of Michigan), 1.

27. John C. Dann, ed., "North West Passage Revisited, a Collection of New Documents on Robert Rogers' Northwest Passage Expedition," *American Magazine and Historical Chronicle* 2:1 (Ann Arbor: University Microfilms, William L. Clements Library, University of Michigan).

28. John R. Cuneo, *Robert Rogers of the Rangers* (New York: Oxford University Press, 1959), 174–77.

29. Dann, "North West Passage Revisited," 24.

30. Elizabeth Rogers divorce petition, 1.

31. Cuneo, *Robert Rogers of the Rangers,* 180–82.

32. Ibid., 182.

33. Peckham, *Pontiac and the Indian Uprising,* 317.

34. Ibid., 309–311.

35. *Ponteach: or the Savages of America* (London, 1766), act 2, scene 3, lines 19–20. Subsequent references are cited parenthetically in the text by act, scene, and line number.

Chapter Four

An earlier version of chapter 4 originally appeared as "The Politics of Fancy in the Age of Sensibility" by Julie Ellison in *Re-visioning Romanticism: British Women Writers 1776–1837,* eds. Carol Shiner Wilson and Joel Haefner (Philadelphia: University of Pennsylvania Press, 1994).

1. Judith Sargent Murray, "On the Equality of the Sexes," in *Selected Writings of Judith Sargent Murray,* ed. Sharon M. Harris (New York: Oxford University Press, 1995), 4–5. Written in 1779, the essay was first published in *Massachusetts Magazine* 2 (March 1790): 133.

2. See Lora Romero, "Vanishing Americans: Gender, Empire, and New Historicism" *American Literature* 63 (September 1991).

3. Roger Lonsdale, ed. *Eighteenth-Century Women Poets: An Oxford Anthology* (Oxford and New York: Oxford University Press, 1989), 364. Lonsdale notes the different versions of the source of the music: "Mrs Thrale recorded that it was William Seward who had come across the original music. . . . Mrs Hunter herself in 1802 . . . stated that she heard a gentleman who had lived among the Cherokees 'sing a wild air, which he assured me it was customary for those people to chaunt with a barbarous jargon, implying contempt for their enemies in the moments of torture and death'" (532–33 n).

4. William Wordsworth, *The Poems,* ed. John O. Hayden (New Haven, Conn.: Yale University Press, 1981), 1:871, 275–76, 945.

5. Charlotte Smith, "Elegiac Sonnets and Other Poems," in *The Poems of Charlotte Smith,* ed. Stuart Curran (New York: Oxford University Press, 1993), 50.

6. Ibid., "Sonnet LXI," 54, lines 1, 3–4, 9–12.

7. James Engell, *The Creative Imagination: Enlightenment to Romanticism* (Cambridge: Harvard University Press, 1981), 172–96.

8. Here I paraphrase my characterization of fancy in "'Nice Arts' and 'Potent Enginery': The Gendered Economy of Wordsworth's Fancy," *Centennial Review* 33 (fall 1989): 442, 446–47.

9. Ibid.; Alan Liu, "The Politics of the Picturesque," chap. 3 of *Wordsworth: The Sense of History* (Stanford: Stanford University Press, 1989); and Nanora Sweet, "History, Imperialism, and the Aesthetics of the Beautiful: Hemans and the Post-Napoleonic Moment," in *At the Limits of Romanticism: Essays in Cultural, Feminist, and Materialist Criticism,* ed. Mary A. Favret and Nicola J. Watson (Bloomington: Indiana University Press, 1994), 170–84.

10. *The Plays and Poems of Mercy Otis Warren,* ed. Benjamin Franklin V (Delmar, N.Y.: Scholars' Facsimiles and Reprints, 1980), 100. The passage cited is taken from "To a Young Gentleman in Europe" (1784), Warren's prefatory letter to *The Ladies of Castile,* which appeared in *Poems, Dramatic and Miscellaneous* (1790).

11. Murray, "On the Equality of the Sexes," 4–11.

12. Ross Chambers explores the politics of the melancholy or "suicidal" text in terms that illuminate the status of otherness in the literature of sensibility. His approach has the signal advantage of linking melancholia to the most difficult evaluative question posed by the work of white middle-class women writers of the late eighteenth century: What is the proportion of resistance to appropriation, of resistance in one area (say, race or American independence) to conventionality in another (such as gender or class)? Ross Chambers, "The Suicide Tactic: Writing in the Language of the Other," chap. 3 in *Room for Maneuver: Reading (the) Oppositional (in) Narrative* (Chicago: University of Chicago Press, 1991). Crucial to Donna Landry's reading of Wheatley is Homi Bhabha's view of the resistant potential of hybridity, a discourse that "doubles, doubly displaces, and disrupts the self-proclaimed 'authoritative' representations of the imperialist power"—a language, in other words, that displays the tension between minoritized and majoritized languages proposed by Chambers: "the effect of colonial power is . . . the *production* of hybridisation . . . [which] reveals the ambivalence at the source of traditional discourses on authority and enables a form of subversion, founded on that uncertainty, that turns the discursive conditions of dominance into the grounds of intervention" (quoted in Donna Landry, *The Muses of Resistance: Laboring-Class Women's Poetry in Britain, 1739–1796* [Cambridge: Cambridge University Press, 1990], 218).

13. Anna Letitia Barbauld, *Poems* (London, 1773), 1–12; Judith Sargent Murray, *The Gleaner* (Schenectady, N.Y.: Union College Press, 1992); and Mercy Otis Warren, *Poems, Dramatic and Miscellaneous* (Boston: I. Thomas and E. T. Andrews, 1790), 13–96.

14. Anna Letitia Barbauld, "A Summer Evening's Meditation," *The Works of Anna Letitia Barbauld, with a Memoir by Lucy Aiken* (London: Longman, 1825), p. 126, lines 73–78. Subsequent references are cited by line in the text.

15. R. Radhakrishnan, "Nationalism, Gender, and the Narrative of Identity" in *Nationalisms and Sexualities*, ed. Andrew Parker et al. (New York: Routledge, 1992), 81–84.

16. John Barrell, "An Unerring Gaze: The Prospect of Society in the Poetry of James Thomson and John Dyer," chap. 1 of *English Literature in History, 1730–80: An Equal, Wide Survey* (New York: St. Martin's Press, 1983).

17. John Aiken and A. Aiken, *Miscellaneous Pieces in Prose* (London, 1773), 190–214.

18. For a detailed discussion of antislavery poetry by women, focusing on contributions to the 1787 parliamentary campaign for abolition, see Moira Ferguson, *Subject to Others: British Women Writers and Colonial Slavery, 1670–1834* (New York: Routledge, 1992).

19. Ferguson points out that the character of the corrupted mistress of a slave-owning family would have been familiar from Sarah Scott's novel, *Sir George Ellison* (1766), set in Jamaica (Moira Ferguson, "British Women Writers and an Emerging Abolitionist Discourse," *The Eighteenth Century: Theory and Interpretation* 33 [spring 1992]: 17).

20. Marlon Ross, *The Contours of Masculine Desire: Romanticism and the Rise of Women's Poetry* (New York: Oxford University Press, 1989), 221–24.

21. Barbauld, *The Works*, 232–50.

22. The attack on "Eighteen Hundred and Eleven" in the *Anti-Jacobin* of 12 August 1812 counters the favorable notice of the *Monthly Review*. Quoting the *Monthly's*

approving claim that "poets are prophets as well as satirists," the *Anti-Jacobin* expresses its "sovereign contempt for the prophetic powers of Mrs. Barbauld," especially because those powers depict "the ruins of England with so much more spirit than . . . her beauties."

23. *Quarterly Review* 7 (June 1812): 311.

24. On "Eighteen Hundred and Eleven," Marlon Ross comments, "In a sure, strong voice, Barbauld predicts England's fate as irreversible. How ironic that this tour de force should be executed by a woman who believes that women should not become authors and should refrain from entering the masculine world of politics and knowledge." *The Contours of Masculine Desire*, 226.

25. While Barbauld's fantasy of London in ruins is ridiculed, a few pages earlier Roscoe is urged to abandon the mode of rational argument and to speak sentimentally on behalf of slaves: "Whence is it, that an amiable and benevolent man, expressly writing on political affairs, can count over . . . from bead to bead, the miserable round of mewling complaints about peace, taxes, and corruption, without stealing, from the monotony of ave's to Reform, a single thought for the suffering and struggles of the most interesting people in Europe; without stopping to shed 'one human tear,' either of indignation over the record of their cruel wrongs, or of sympathy, hope, and solicitude, over the yet unfinished history of their glorious efforts for deliverance?" *Quarterly Review* 7 (June 1812): 281. The pamphlets under review included *A Letter to Henry Brougham . . . on the Subject of Reform in the Representation of the People in Parliament* and *An Answer to a letter from Mr. John Merritt on the Subject of Parliamentary Reform.*

26. In David Brion Davis's "Calendar of Events," the prominence of the abolition issue in New England at this time is clear: In 1771, "A bill passed by the Massachusetts assembly to end slave importation fails to win the governor's assent." In 1773, "Massachusetts blacks petition the legislature for relief from oppression; Leicester and other Massachusetts towns instruct their representatives to work for laws against both slavery and the slave trade. . . . Samuel Hopkins and Ezra Stiles send a circular letter to New England churches, urging them to oppose the slave trade." *The Problem of Slavery in the Age of Revolution, 1770–1823* (Ithaca: Cornell University Press, 1975). See also Roger Bruns, *Am I Not A Man and a Brother: The Anti-Slavery Crusade of Revolutionary America, 1688–1788* (New York: Chelsea House, 1977); and Duncan J. MacLeod, *Slavery, Race and the American Revolution* (London: Cambridge University Press, 1974).

27. Phillis Wheatley, *The Collected Works of Phillis Wheatley*, ed. John Shields, The Schomburg Library of Nineteenth-Century Black Women Writers (New York: Oxford University Press, 1988). All subsequent references are cited by poem and line in the text.

28. Landry finds "a buried idiom of subversion . . . an awareness of revolutionary and abolitionist consciousness that Wheatley can only intimate but not openly embrace" (*The Muses of Resistance*, 219). John Shields concurs with Landry's reading in his observations on the gist of Wheatley's revisions from broadside to book, which show that on the subject of slavery she is being careful "not to ruffle the feathers of her overwhelmingly white, and at first, often British audience." *The Collected Works of Phillis Wheatley*, 195–96.

29. "Slavery, a Poem," from *Works of Hannah More* (London: T. Cadell, 1788), p. 28, lines 110–19.

30. Ferguson, "British Women Writers," 7–11.

31. See Mikhtar Ali Isani, "The British Reception of Wheatley's Poems on Various Subjects," *Journal of Negro History* 66 (summer 1981): 144–49; James A. Rawley, "The World of Phillis Wheatley," *New England Quarterly* 50 (December 1977): 666–77; and William H. Robinson, "Phillis Wheatley in London," *CLA Journal* 21 (1977): 187–201.

32. The earlier draft is lustier, with its link between Dartmouth's "paternal Sway" regarded exultantly by a New England "big with Hopes" (lines 4–5).

Chapter Five

An earlier version of chapter 5 originally appeared as "Race and Sensibility in the Early Republic: Ann Eliza Bleecker and Sarah Wentworth Morton" by Julie Ellison in *American Literature: A Journal of Literary History, Criticism, and Bibliography* 65, no. 3 (Fall 1993): 445–74. © 1993 by Duke University Press.

1. Werner Sollers, *Beyond Ethnicity: Consent and Descent in American Culture* (New York: Oxford University Press, 1986), 104, 128–29.

2. Renato Rosaldo, *Culture and Truth: The Remaking of Social Analysis* (Boston: Beacon Press, 1989), 70.

3. Dana N. Nelson, *The Word in Black and White: Reading "Race" in American Literature 1638–1867* (New York: Oxford University Press, 1992), 67, 145.

4. Bleecker and Morton are representative of a general preoccupation with race among women writers. For a detailed discussion of antislavery poetry by women, see Moira Ferguson, *Subject to Others: British Women Writers and Colonial Slavery, 1760–1834* (New York and London: Routledge, 1992). On race relations during the American Revolution, see David Brion Davis, *The Problem of Slavery in the Age of Revolution 1770–1823* (Ithaca: Cornell University Press, 1975); Gary B. Nash, *Race, Class and Politics: Essays on American Colonial and Revolutionary Society* (Urbana: University of Illinois Press, 1986), especially ch. 11, "Forging Freedom: The Emancipation Experience in the Northern Seaports, 1775–1820"; Roger Bruns, *Am I Not a Man and a Brother: The Anti-Slavery Crusade of Revolutionary American, 1688–1788* (New York: Chelsea House, 1977); and Duncan J. MacLeod, *Slavery, Race and the American Revolution* (Cambridge: Cambridge University Press, 1974). See also Sidney Kaplan and Emma Nogrady Kaplan, *The Black Presence in the Era of the American Revolution*, rev. ed. (Amherst: University of Massachusetts Press, 1989).

5. See Barbara Graymont, *The Iroquois in the American Revolution* (Syracuse: Syracuse University Press, 1972); Isabel Thompson Kelsay, *Joseph Brant 1743–1807: Man of Two Worlds* (Syracuse: Syracuse University Press, 1984); Thomas S. Abler, ed., *Chainbreaker: The Revolutionary War: Memoirs of Governor Blacksnake as told to Benjamin Williams* (Lincoln: University of Nebraska Press, 1989); and Gary B. Nash, *Race, Class and Politics: Essays on American Colonial and Revolutionary Society*. See also Thomas J. Davis, *A Rumor of Revolt: The "Great Negro Plot" in Colonial New York* (New York: Free Press, 1985) chs. 1–3; and Stefan Beilinski, "Episodes in the Coming of Age of an Early American Community: Albany, N.Y., 1780–1793," in *World of the Founders: New York Communities in the Federal Period*, ed. Stephen L. Schechter and Wendell Tripp (Albany: New York State Commission on the Bicentennial of the United States Constitution, 1990), 117–19.

6. *Ouabi, or the Virtues of Nature, an Indian Tale in Four Cantos* (Boston: I. Thomas

and E. T. Andrews, 1790). All subsequent references to *Ouabi* are cited parenthetically by page number in the text. Sarah Wentworth Morton's poems of maternal mourning appear in *My Mind and Its Thoughts:* "Stanzas / To my late lovely and beloved daughter Charlotte, at the age of fifteen," 67–68; "Memento, / For my Infant, who lived but eighteen hours," 255–56; "Lamentations / of an unfortunate mother, over the tomb of her only son (1)," 260–61; "Stanzas, / occasioned by the question of a friend, 'What has preserved you?'" 263; "Lines / enclosing the beautiful ringlets of my son," 264; "Apostrophe / to the memory of my beloved daughter Charlotte, / Fragment," 264–65; "Lines, / to those who have said, 'You are tranquil,'" 265–66.

7. Also operative in Morton's cultural politics is her distaste for new styles of commercial wealth, dramatized in her indignant opposition to the conversion of her family's ancestral home into a bank by her husband, Perez Morton. See "Lines to the Mansion of My Ancestors, on Seeing it Occupied as a Banking Establishment," *My Mind and Its Thoughts,* 30–31.

8. *The Posthumous Works of Ann Eliza Bleecker in Prose and Verse. To which is added, A Collection of Essays, Prose and Poetical, by Margaretta V. Faugeres* (New York, 1793), 146. All subsequent references are cited parenthetically by page number in the text. Published by Faugeres in 1793, Bleecker's *Posthumous Works* includes poems; correspondence; *The History of Maria Kittle;* and "The Story of Henry and Anne," the tale of a poor couple's emigration to America from quasi-feudal Europe. The citation is from a letter that accompanies a manuscript of *The History of Maria Kittle.* "I take the freedom to trouble you with a little history," Bleecker explains, "written some time ago for Susan [Susan Ten Eyck, Bleecker's half-sister], which being altogether a fact, may give you some idea of savage cruelty, and at the same time will justify our fears in your opinion" (146). It would be necessary to delve into local records to ascertain definitely if the black men and women Bleecker refers to as "old Merkee" and "a young mulatto girl" were slaves, but the prevalence of slave-holding in upstate New York late into the century and Bleecker's locutions suggest that this is the case. In one letter she refers to Merkee and the white servant together as simply "two servants," which may suggest that Merkee is not a slave (179). But see Nash, *Race, Class, and Politics,* on the names of slaves and freed African Americans in northern cities. "Merkee" resembles what Nash identifies as slave names, rather than the names of free blacks (294–98).

9. John Barrell, *English Literature in History, 1730–80: An Equal, Wide Survey* (New York: St. Martin's Press, 1983), especially ch. 1, "An Unerring Gaze: The Prospect of Society in the Poetry of James Thomson and John Dyer."

10. Lina Mainiero, ed., *American Women Writers,* s.v. "Ann Eliza Bleecker" by L. W. Koengeter (New York: Frederick Ungar, 1979), 1:77.

11. Richard Slotkin, *Regeneration Through Violence: The Mythology of the American Frontier 1600–1860* (Middletown, Conn.: Wesleyan University Press, 1973). Slotkin's reading of eighteenth-century captivity narratives in terms of "a representative of the kind of heroism that natural, uncultivated, American man is capable of'" (189) is distinctly unhelpful with regard to captivity narratives by and about women. The late eighteenth-century boom in captivity narratives was not caused simply by the settlers' desire to stage an "empowering" assimilation of Native American regions. Nor is it

solely the result of the wish to define "the American character by proclaiming the rejection of British culture" as Captain Greg Sieminski proposes in "The Puritan Captivity Narrative and the Politics of the American Revolution" (*American Quarterly* 42, no. 1 [March 1990], 36). Mitchell Breitweiser, in *American Puritanism and the Defense of Mourning: Religion, Grief, and Ethnology in Mary White Rowlandson's Captivity Narrative* (Madison: University of Wisconsin Press, 1990), deals with an earlier text organized by female mourning and racial difference. Breitweiser's emphasis on the relationship between Puritan religious ideology and the shock of "the real" in Rowlandson's narrative has some parallels to Bleecker's response to trauma. See also Annette Kolodny, *The Land Before Her: Fantasy and Experience of the American Frontiers, 1630–1860* (Chapel Hill: University of North Carolina Press, 1984), 27–28; and Rafia Zafar, *We Wear the Mask: African-Americans Write American Literature* (New York: Columbia University Press, 1997). The republication of Rowlandson's 1682 *Narrative* in Boston six times between 1770 and 1773 suggests, as Sieminski proposes, that feminine captivity could represent the colonies' overall enslavement to the British tyrant, as well as Boston's particular status as the victim of a British "massacre," a term for Indian attacks. But the conflation of tyrants and savages as enemies of North American domestic sanctuaries reinforces the republic's civility as well as its capacity for resistance. Sieminski, "The Puritan Captivity Narrative," 37–39.

12. Shirley Samuels calls attention to a later embodiment of the image of Native American violence against white women in her discussion of Horace Greenough's sculpture titled *Rescue Group* (1853): "A mother and child cower beneath the raised tomahawk of a fierce Indian. Behind him a gigantic frontiersman grasps the Indian's tomahawk-wielding hand." No gigantic frontiersmen appear in Bleecker's fearful fantasy—just the triad of mother, child, and Indian. Bleecker's works give us a glimpse of how a frontier woman writer handles the representational conventions that paired "violence against women and violence against Indians," "the female body and the native race." *Romantics of the Republic: Women, the Family, and Violence in the Literature of the Early American Novel* (New York: Oxford University Press, 1996): 107–12.

13. Donna Landry provides a useful context in her analysis of the relationships between class, gender, and genre in eighteenth-century pastoral and georgic poetry, "Pastoral and Georgic Transformations," *The Muses of Resistance: Laboring-Class Women's Poetry in Britain, 1739–1796* (Cambridge and New York: Cambridge University Press, 1990), 22–29.

14. Lauren Berlant, "The Female Complaint," *Social Text* 19–20 (fall 1988), 237–59.

15. Dryden's version reads as follows:
> Alas! I lost *Creusa:* hard to tell
> If by her fatal Destiny she fell,
> Or weary sate, or wander'd with affright;
> But she was lost for ever to my sight.
>
> . . . .
>
> What mad expressions did my Tongue refuse?
> Whom did I not of Gods or Men accuse?
> This was the fatal Blow, that pain'd me more
> Than all I felt from ruin'd Troy before.

Stung with my Loss, and raving with Despair,
Abandoning my now forgotten Care,
Of Counsel, Comfort, and of Hope bereft,
My Sire, my Son, my Country Gods, I left. (lines 1002–1005, 1010–1017)
Edward Niles Hooker et al., eds., *The Works of John Dryden,* 20 vols. (Berkeley: University of California Press, 1956–89) 5 (1987): 379–414.

16. Cathy N. Davidson, *Revolution and the Word: The Rise of the Novel in America* (New York: Oxford University Press, 1986), 289 n. 32. See also 85, 90, 96, 101–102.

17. Morton, *My Mind and Its Thoughts,* 7–9.

18. Davidson, *Revolution and the Word,* 106.

19. "There is now a living instance of a like propensity. A gentleman of fortune, born in America, and educated in all the refinements and luxuries of Great Britain, has lately attached himself to a female savage . . . and in consequence of his inclination, has relinquished his own country and connections, incorporated himself into the society, and adopted the manners of the virtuous, though uncultivated Indian." Morton, "Introduction," *Ouabi, Or the Virtues of Nature, An Indian Tale in Four Cantos* (1790), vi.

20. "Sanctioned by such authorities I flatter myself, allowing for the justifiable embellishments of poetry, that I shall not be considered an enthusiast in my descriptions. The liberal reader will, I trust, make many allowances for the various imperfections of the work, from a consideration of my sex and education; the one by education incident to weakness, the other from duty devoted to domestic avocations. And I am induced to hope, that the attempting a subject wholly American will in some respect entitle me to the partial eye of the patriot; that, as a young author, I shall be received with tenderness, and, as an involuntary one, be criticized with candor" (Ibid., viii). Morton is an "involuntary" author because she publishes "in compliance with the solicitations of . . . friends" (v).

21. On the discourse of the "Vanishing American," see Lora Romeros, "Vanishing Americans: Gender, Empire, and the New Historicism," *American Literature* 63, no. 3 (September 1991): 385–404; Philip Deloria, *Playing Indian* (New Haven: Yale University Press, 1998); Brian W. Dippie, *The Vanishing American: White Attitudes and U.S. Indian Policy* (Middletown, Conn.: Wesleyan University Press, 1982); and Slotkin, *Regeneration Through Violence,* 357–69.

22. The same preference for a spirit of resistance over one of resignation comes through in Morton, "The African Chief," *My Mind and Its Thoughts,* 201–2.

23. David S. Shields provides a wonderful account of the masculine campus at American colleges. *Civil Tongues and Polite Letters in British America* (Chapel Hill, N.C.: Institute for Early American History and Culture, 1997), chap. 7, "The College, the Press and the Public."

24. In the 1771 text, Indian genocide forms part of the standard "Black Legend" that was used to make the English look good by comparison to the Inquisitorial Spanish. The Spanish-English comparison, explicit or implied, organizes the treatment of conquest from Dryden's *The Indian Emperour* to Hemans's "The Forest Sanctuary," and it is important to place North American examples like Freneau's in this tradition.

25. Philip Freneau, *The Poems of Philip Freneau,* 2 vols. ed. Fred Lewis Pattee (New York: Russell and Russell, 1963), 1.35–37. Subsequent references are cited by page number in the text.

26. In the culture of the Atlantic theater late in the eighteenth century, the prospect becomes particularly well adapted to the nonrealistic treatment of political crisis. One thinks here not only of the poems I have already enumerated, in which fancy drives prospective invention, but also of Freneau's "The Pictures of Columbus" (1774/1788). The first section, titled "Columbus making Maps," represents the explorer not only as a framed picture but as a prospective artist himself. Freneau's contemporary, Joel Barlow, wrote two Columbus poems permeated by fancy, as well: *The Vision of Columbus* (1787) and *The Columbiad* (1825). The frontispiece of *The Columbiad* reads, "Hesper appearing to Columbus in prison." Barlow had followed Freneau onto the collegiate stage in 1778, delivering his first published verse, "The Prospect of Peace," at the "public examinations" at Yale. See also Dwight's "America: Or, A Poem on the Settlement of the British Colonies."

27. As soon as the Revolution ended, political discourse in the United States took place in an atmosphere of resentment and aggressive suspicion. Freneau became notorious for promoting this tone in his newspapers, poems, and magazine contributions; the phrase, "That rascal, Freneau" was George Washington's. This proclivity for the language of rage carries the indignation at Britain over to the Indians in this poem.

28. Much later, Longfellow's surreal narrative poem, *Evangeline, A Tale of Acadie* (1847), certainly one of the most interesting treatments of a displaced nation figured as a melancholy woman, can be read in these terms.

29. William C. Dowling, *Poetry and Ideology in Revolutionary Connecticut* (Athens: University of Georgia Press, 1990), 92.

Chapter Six

Portions of chapter 6 originally appeared as Julie Ellison, "Cato's Tears," *English Literary History* 63, no. 3 (fall 1996): 571–601. © 1996 by The Johns Hopkins University Press.

1. See, for example, the proposal for regional cultural centers offered by William R. Ferris, chair of the National Endowment for the Humanities (http://www.neh.fed.us/html/corner/corn9805.html); the American Folklife Festival produced by the Smithsonian Center for Folklife Programs and Cultural Studies, "a research-based presentation of contemporary living cultural traditions . . . that embody the creative vitality of community-based traditions" (http://www.si.edu/folklife/center.htm#festival); the site-based memory projects described in Dolores Hayden in *The Power of Place: Urban Landscapes as Public History* (Cambridge: MIT Press, 1995); the Arts of Citizenship Program at the University of Michigan; and the West Philadelphia Project at the University of Pennsylvania.

2. Patricia Yaeger, *The Geography of Identity* (Ann Arbor: University of Michigan Press, 1996), 18. Paul Gilroy, one of many cultural critics to promote models of systematic interrelatedness, posits "the black Atlantic world" as a "rim culture," "a webbed network," a world of "complicity and syncretic interdependency," and of "stereophonic bilingual, or bifocal cultural forms," a structure shaped by "intercultural positionality." *The Black Atlantic: Modernity and Double Consciousness* (Cambridge: Harvard University Press, 1993), 29, 31, 3, 6.

3. Paul Baepler, "The Barbary Captivity Narrative in Early America," *Early American Literature* 30 (1995): 95, 116 n. 3. Baepler observes that using such narratives

to criticize North African slaveholding only became common in the nineteenth century, even though as early as 1700 Samuel Sewell "suggests that the colonists are complicit in Barbary captivity by holding Africans as slaves in America." As Baepler has demonstrated, the Barbary captivity narratives "give us a rare glimpse of how the British and early Americans imagined Africans and both justified and questioned institutionalized slavery" (113). See also Lotfi Ben Rejeb, "America's Captive Freeman in North Africa: The Comparative Method in Abolitionist Persuasion," *Slavery and Abolition* 9, no. 1 (1988): 57–71. Christopher Looby's wonderful reading of voice in Washington Irving's *Salmagundi* (1807–8) focuses on the letters written by the Tripolitan prisoner, Mustapha Rub-A-Dub Keli Khan. But, while Looby shows that American "LOGOCRACY" is a form of "discursive legitimation," he nowhere mentions that the United States was still facing an awkward situation in North Africa. *Voicing America: Language, Literary Form, and the Origins of the United States* (Chicago: University of Chicago Press, 1996): 79–81.

4. Jared Gardner offers illuminating analyses of the intersection of race and citizenship (but not gender) in both *The Algerine Captive* and *Edgar Huntly* (*Master Plots: Race and the Founding of an American Literature, 1787–1845* [Baltimore: Johns Hopkins University Press, 1998], 53). He views these works as "importantly national," however, whereas I consider them evidence of the way in which even the discourse of nationalism and the particular constructions of race on which nationalism relies partake of a well-established transnational culture of sensitive, racially marked masculinity.

5. Gordon S. Wood, "Conspiracy and the Paranoid Style: Causality and Deceit in the Eighteenth Century," *William and Mary Quarterly* 39 (1982): 401, 410, 421–25.

6. Eve Kosofsky Sedgwick, *Epistemology of the Closet* (Berkeley: University of California Press, 1990): 186, n. 10.

7. *Edgar Huntly* appeared in later American editions of Brown's works starting in 1827; it also appeared in London in an 1803 Minerva Press edition, with a second London edition in 1821, reprinted in 1831.

8. Sidney J. Krause, "Historical Essay," *Edgar Huntly*, vol. 4 of *Bicentennial Edition of the Novels and Related Works of Charles Brockden Brown*, ed. Sydney J. Krause and S. W. Reid. (Kent, Ohio: Kent State University Press, 1984), 303.

9. *Edgar Huntly* also belongs to the genre of exile or tracking narratives such as Charlotte Smith's "The Emigrants" (1793), nineteenth-century works like Burney's *The Wanderer* (1802–12, 1814), Hemans's "The Forest Sanctuary" (1825), and Longfellow's *Evangeline* (1847). British as well as American characters display the mobile fancy characteristic of early republican literature. The "loco-descriptive" patterns described by M. H. Abrams as an attribute of eighteenth-century poetry are a nearly universal transgeneric idiom that constitutes place through mobility. "Structure and Style in the Greater Romantic Lyric," in *From Sensibility to Romanticism*, ed. Frederick W. Hilles and Harold Bloom (London: Oxford University Press, 1965), 535.

10. On deterritorialization and reterritorialization, see Yaeger, *The Geography of Identity*, 10–12, 16–17.

11. Charles Brockden Brown, *Edgar Huntly or, Memoirs of a Sleep-Walker*, ed. Norman S. Grabo (New York: Penguin, 1988), 280–81. Subsequent references are cited in the text by page number.

12. Carroll Smith-Rosenberg, "Subject Female: Authorizing American Identity," *American Literary History* 5, no. 3 (1993): 481–511. See also Paul Downes, "Sleep-

Walking Out of the Revolution: Brown's *Edgar Huntly*," *Eighteenth-Century Studies* 29, no. 4 (1996): 413–31. Downes reads the novel as organized by the tension between "the appeal of . . . an order . . . secured by the suppression of radical speculation . . . and a moral commitment to full revelation" of the content of Waldegrave's radicalism (416).

13. Yaeger, *The Geography of Identity*, 23, 25, 15.

14. Clithero himself recalls the immediate "cordial intimacy" that he had felt for Sarsefield in Ireland and the friendship that sprang up as Sarsefield recounted his Far Eastern and Mediterranean adventures, including—not incidentally—"time . . . spent immured in caverns and carousing with robbers" (58). The young Huntly was Sarsefield's "favorite scholar and . . . companion of all his pedestrian excursions" (92–93).

15. I draw here on Lora Romero's subtle discussion of the way in which "prodigy" illuminates the affiliations of the micro- and the macropolitical. "Vanishing Americans: Gender, Empire, and New Historicism," in *The Culture of Sentiment: Race, Gender, and Sentimentality in Nineteenth-Century America*, ed. Shirley Samuels (New York: Oxford University Press, 1992), 117.

16. Michel de Certeau, *The Practice of Everyday Life*, quoted by Yaeger, *The Geography of Identity*, 21.

17. The figure of the Moor and of the sub-Saharan African pervaded the literature and spectacles of early modern England. Kim F. Hall, whom I applaud for her decision to "hold onto the idea of a language of race in the early modern period" (6), gives the best account of the relationship between the social presence of Africans in Renaissance England, the representational practices that marketed the display of racial difference as cosmopolitanism to English elites, and the trading economy along the Barbary coast that produced profits large enough that a "sense of wealth and novelty infuses English literature and is tied to representations of race" (17) (*Things of Darkness: Economies of Race and Gender in Early Modern England* [Ithaca: Cornell University Press, 1995]). Hall traces the emergence of racial categories from mercantile and colonial experience. How the theatricality of African difference in English culture subtends the complicated power of African characters like Othello, Juba, and Sophonisba is one of the challenging questions posed by Hall's excellent study. See also Peter Fryer, *Staying Power: The History of Black People in Britain* (London: Pluto Press, 1984), chaps. 1–4; and Margo Hendricks and Patricia Parker, *Women, "Race," and Writing in the Early Modern Period* (London: Routledge, 1994).

18. Baepler, "The Barbary Captivity Narrative," 107. Baepler notes, first, that the Barbary captivity narrative predated that of the North American Indian, and second, that both the North African and Indian captivity narratives relied on the "figure of the suffering captive as God's chosen penitent" (95–98). Samuel C. Chew provides an overview of the infrastructure of fund-raising, prisoner exchange, and humanitarian activities linking Tudor England to North African states, often through Catholic orders and other intermediaries, in *The Crescent and the Rose: Islam and England during the Renaissance* (New York: Oxford University Press, 1937). Rafia Zafar, in *We Wear the Mask: African Americans Write American Literature, 1760–1870* (New York: Columbia University Press, 1997), focuses on the difference between texts by white captives and those written by blacks, including Briton Hammon and John Marrant. She is exactly right to point out how genres were combined, as accounts "of religious

redemption came to be spiced up with tales of Indian uprising, psychological and physical torture, adoption into a strange ethnic or racial world . . . and exotic travels." Zafar's discussions of the way in which Indian captivity and African slavery were narrated provide important contexts for the copresence in *Edgar Huntly* of an interpolated tale of Indian captivity and the memory of Waldegrave, who "was a teacher of the Negro free-school when he died" (136), as well as for the connection between white and black slavery in *The Algerine Captive* (42, 52–53, 43, 55, 67–68).

19. For studies of North Africans in the United States, see Allan D. Austin, *African Muslims in Antebellum America: A Sourcebook* (New York: Garland, 1984); and Ronald A. T. Judy, *(Dis)Forming the American Canon: African-Arabic Slave Narratives and the Vernacular* (Minneapolis: University of Minnesota Press, 1993). B. R. Burg points us toward the erotics of Mediterranean piracy and Barbary captivity. *Sodomy and the Pirate Tradition: English Sea Rovers in the Seventeenth-Century Caribbean* (New York: New York University Press, 1983). See also Stephen Clissold, *The Barbary Slaves* (London: Paul Elek, 1977), 42–43; and Baepler, "The Barbary Captivity Narrative," 111.

20. *Port folio* (Philadelphia, 1804): 234–35. For an interesting reading of classical allusion in Charles Brockden Brown's *Wieland* that takes seriously "the fantasmatic relation that political leaders of the revolutionary era enjoined to the heroes of classical antiquity," see Looby, *Voicing America*, 158–65.

21. Cicero's oration holds forth indignantly against the praetor, and his rage seems to carry over into another article on the same page, a diatribe against the "foreign outcasts" and "Jacobins" that have been "vomited on our shores." *Port folio* (Philadelphia, 1804): 235.

22. William Ray, *Horrors of Slavery or, the American Tars in Tripoli* (Troy, N.Y.: Printed by Oliver Lyon, 1808), 29–32.

23. *The American in Algiers, or the Patriot of Seventy-Six in Captivity. A Poem, in Two Cantos*, vol. 1 (New York: J. Buel, 1797), 5, 9–10 (Ann Arbor: University Microfilms, William L. Clement Library, University of Michigan). Subsequent references are cited by page number in the text.

24. Royall Tyler's great-uncle apparently died in captivity in North Africa. Baepler, "The Barbary Captivity Narrative," 115.

25. Royall Tyler, *The Algerine Captive; or, the Life and Adventures of Doctor Updike Underhill: Six Years a Prisoner Among the Algerines*, 2 vols. (Walpole, New Hampshire: Printed by David Carlisle, 1797): 1:143–45 (Ann Arbor: University Microfilms, William L. Clements Library, University of Michigan).

26. Behind many of these literary veterans of the 1780s stands Smollett's Lieutenant Obadiah Lismahago, who elicits a wave of "compassion" and "pity warmed with indignation." Lismahago's mutilation by and captivity among American Indians parodies the genre right down to the death song and spawns romantic feelings in Tabitha that are likened to those of Desdemona, "who loved the Moore *for the dangers he had past.*" Tobias George Smollett, *The Expedition of Humphrey Clinker* (New York: Holt, Rinehart and Winston, 1950) 218–28. Tyler's play, *The Contrast* (1787), features the unpretentious avatar of Revolutionary virtue, Colonel Manly. Manly's sensibility is a sign of obsolescence. He is devoted to "antiquated, anti-gallant notions" that are obsolete in the new urban consumer culture of postrevolutionary New York: "His conversation is like a rich, old-fashioned brocade—it will stand alone; every sentence is a sentiment." He wears his old regimental coat, takes pride in his "poverty of . . .

appearance," and remains committed to the needy veterans who served under him. "I came hither to solicit the honourable Congress," he announces, in order "that a number of my brave old soldiers may be put upon the pension-list, who were, at first, not judged to be so materially wounded as to need the public assistance." Gilbert Imlay's novel was published in London 1793 by Joseph Johnson as *The Emigrants, &c. or The History of an Expatriated Family*. In Colonel Arl—ton, Imlay develops the ideal of the gentlemanly "officer veteran" who survives his romantic melancholia to become a hard-working civic activist and the founder of a utopian community for veterans on the Ohio River. See Julie Ellison, "There and Back: Transatlantic Novels and Anglo-American Careers," in *The Past as Prologue: Essays to Celebrate the Twenty-Fifth Anniversary of ASECS,* ed. Carla Hay and Syndy M. Conger (New York: Published for the American Society for Eighteenth-Century Studies by AMS Press, 1995).

Conclusion

Portions of the conclusion originally appeared as "A Short History of Liberal Guilt" by Julie Ellison in *Critical Inquiry* 2, no. 2 (winter 1996): 344–71. © 1996 by The University of Chicago. All rights reserved.

1. The notion of racial guilt had emerged earlier. The "guilt thesis" in southern historiography, which refers to the purported ambivalence of slave owners during the Civil War, was articulated in the fifties, in the early stages of the Civil Rights movement. The defeat of the Confederacy, suggested historians Bell Wiley and C. Vann Woodward, can be partially attributed to a distinctive southern guilt. Gaines M. Foster, "Guilt Over Slavery: A Historiographical Analysis," *Journal of Southern History* 56, no. 4 (1990): 670–71, 674–75.

2. Michael Omi and Howard Winant, *Racial Formation in the United States from the 1960s to the 1990s* (New York: Routledge, 1994):147–59.

3. Ibid., 147–48. See also David R. Roediger, "The Racial Crisis of American Liberalism," in *Towards the Abolition of Whiteness* (London: Verso, 1994): 121–26. A debate over the shifting ground of liberalism on race issues appeared in *Reconstruction* in articles by Peter Erickson, Stephen Steinberg, and others. *Reconstruction* 2, no. 1 (1992).

4. Lauren Berlant, "'68, or Something" *Critical Inquiry* 21, no. 1 (autumn 1994): 125–28, 137.

5. Eve Kosofsky Sedgwick, *The Epistemology of the Closet* (Berkeley: University of California Press, 1990), 145–46.

6. Susan Jeffords, *Hard Bodies: Hollywood Masculinity in the Reagan Era* (New Brunswick: Rutgers University Press, 1994): 109, 116–18, 176–77.

7. Under these conditions, it is not surprising that the dynamics of sympathy and the prestige of performance have arrived on the intellectual scene together. Performance can be critical shorthand for public cultures in which political knowledge depends on audiences. Saidiya V. Hartman's analysis of race mediated by performance applies with special pertinence to the case of liberal guilt, which involves the social display of cross-racial sympathy in one or both directions. *Performing Blackness: Staging Subjection and Resistance in Antebellum Culture* (New York: Oxford University Press, 1995). I am grateful to Professor Hartman for allowing me to read and cite her manuscript in advance of publication.

8. I strongly agree with Daniel Born that "guilt is engendered by seeing system-

atic connections." "Private Gardens, Public Swamps: *Howards End* and the Revaluation of Liberal Guilt," *Novel* 25 (winter 1992): 158.

9. Shelby Steele, "White Guilt," *American Scholar* 59 (autumn 1990): 497.

10. Omi and Winant, *Racial Formation in the United States,* 117, 134.

11. Shelby Steele, "Affirmative Action Must Go," *New York Times,* 1 March 1995, final edition, sec. A, p. 19.

12. Judith N. Shklar, *Ordinary Vices* (Cambridge: Belknap Press of Harvard University Press, 1984), 237, 3, 248, 226–27.

13. Ibid., 17, 23, 21.

14. Nancy Fraser, *Unruly Practices: Power, Discourse, and Gender in Contemporary Social Theory* (Minneapolis: University of Minnesota Press, 1989): 103; and Richard Rorty, *Contingency, Irony, and Solidarity* (Cambridge: Cambridge University Press, 1989): xv, 198.

15. Fraser, *Unruly Practices,* 162, 164–65, 169–70.

16. "Left-liberal spectrum" is Peter Erickson's term. "Multiculturalism and the Problem of Liberalism," *Reconstruction* 2, no. 1 (1992): 97.

17. Bernard Williams, *Shame and Necessity* (Berkeley: University of California Press, 1993), 94.

18. Liberal guilt is not far from the existential shame developed by Sartre in *Being and Nothingness,* where the specifically ocular crisis of shame marks the subject's alienated entry into the social world under the gaze of another human being. Sartre shows how unequally painful social encounters can occur in the parallel universe of similarly embarrassed philosophical subject-object relations. Jean-Paul Sartre, *Being and Nothingness* (New York: Washington Square Press, 1956), 360–61, 384.

19. Elizabeth Barnes brings to light Thatcher Thayer's *Vicarious Element in Nature and Its Relation to Christ* (1888) and uses it to explore the idealization and disembodiment of sympathy in very helpful ways. *States of Sympathy: Seduction and Democracy in the American Novel* (New York: Columbia University Press, 1997), 115–20.

20. Patricia J. Williams, *The Alchemy of Race and Rights* (Cambridge: Harvard University Press, 1991), 17, 21–22.

21. Ibid., 27.

22. Charles Lamb, *Elia, 1823* facsimile edition (Oxford: Woodstock, 1991), 274. I am indebted to Chip Tucker for directing me to this passage.

23. Lauren Berlant, "The Female Complaint" *Social Text* 19–20 (1988): 245, 253.

24. Berenice Fisher, "Guilt and Shame in the Women's Movement: The Radical Ideal of Action and Its Meaning for Feminist Intellectuals," *Feminist Studies* 10, no. 2 (1984): 185–212.

25. The process by which eighteenth- and nineteenth-century viewers sympathized with suffering—"the bourgeois weeping over the spectacle of poverty . . . the man swooning over the spectacle of female virtue under siege"—in turn generated embarrassment or skepticism about the viewer's position, Sedgwick argues: "For a spectator to misrepresent the quality or locus of his or her implicit participation in a scene . . . would be to enact . . . the worst meaning of the epithet [sentimental]. . . . The prurient; the morbid; the wishful; the snobbish; the knowing; the arch: these denote subcategories of the sentimental, to the extent that each involves a covert reason for . . . identification through a spectatorial route." *The Epistemology of the Closet,* 151.

26. Gayatri Chakravorty Spivak, *The Post-Colonial Critic: Interviews, Strategies, Dialogues* (New York: Routledge, 1990), 121–22.

27. "The strategic objective of being 'outside' is not to be outside theory but to be its exorbitant object," Homi Bhabha remarks in a similar vein, "to overcome the pedagogical predictability of the sententious professor." "Postcolonial Authority and Postmodern Guilt," in *Cultural Studies,* ed. Lawrence Grossberg et al. (New York: Routledge, 1991), 57.

28. Spivak, *The Post-Colonial Critic,* 9, 57, 62; *In Other Worlds: Essays in Cultural Politics* (New York and London: Methuen, 1987): 136.

29. The turn to agency is important in this context. Lawrence Grossberg deplores the politics of the eighties as "political positions [that] exist as entirely affective investments, separated from any ability to act." If the right wing "depoliticizes politics, it . . . repoliticizes everyday life" by setting into motion "affective epidemics" of "moral panic" that occupy pernicious "structures of identification and belonging." Grossberg tries to imagine forms of "agency" that permit a return to action by the left and recommends social feeling as the basis for positive change. He calls for an end to identity politics in favor of a pragmatic call for coalition, constituting a "we" that emerges from a widespread sense of "affective subjectivity" and a willingness on the left to speak with "authority." Grossberg thus defends himself sentimentally against an oversentimentalized society. He fights one strategy of inappropriate feeling with counterfeelings that are vicarious in a different way. His work exemplifies the current dialogue between leftist critique and transvaluations of feeling. *We Gotta Get Out of This Place: Popular Conservatism and Postmodern Culture* (New York: Routledge,1992), 279–81, 284, 377, 379–80.

30. "A Man on Horseback" *Atlantic Monthly* 277 (January 1996): 50–52. Despite academic interest in the collected essays of Trenchard and Gordon, the first new edition of all 144 of *Cato's Letters* in almost 250 years has been published, not by a university press, but by the Liberty Fund—a conservative educational foundation in Indianapolis that sponsors the Liberty Press. The two-volume hardcover edition of *Cato's Letters* costs only about thirty dollars. Unfortunately it makes available, not the 1723–24 first edition, but an edition of 1877.

31. "What Happened to Civility: The Example of George Washington." *Reader's Digest* 147 (August 1995): 41–42.

32. "Why Not Bring Back the Czars? Restoring the Romanovs to Reign, Not Rule" *Time* 138 (November 1991): 102.

33. Robert Nozick, "Why Do Intellectuals Oppose Capitalism?" *Cato Policy Report* 20, no. 1 (Jan.–Feb. 1998). See also Gerald P. O'Driscoll Jr., "The Meaning of Hayek," *Cato Policy Report* 17, no. 6 (Nov.–Dec. 1995): 9. "The Talk of the Town" in *The New Yorker* announced that Charles Murray, author of *The Bell Curve,* had "outed himself as a Libertarian, and, in a new book, *What It Means to Be A Libertarian,* lays out a vision of government which is to mainstream conservatism what the bikini is to thermal underwear." *The New Yorker,* 18 Nov. 1998: 39.

34. Kathleen Wilson, *The Sense of the People: Politics, Culture, and Imperialism in England 1715–1785* (Cambridge: Cambridge University Press, 1995): 118–119.

35. John Trenchard and Thomas Gordon, *Cato's Letters,* in *The English Libertarian Heritage, from the Writings of John Trenchard and Thomas Gordon in the Independent Whig and Cato's Letters,* ed. David Jacobson (Indianapolis: Bobbs Merrill, 1966), 2:95–96.

36. Dwight R. Lee and Richard B. McKenzie, *Failure and Progress: The Bright Side of the Dismal Science* (Washington: Cato Institute, 1993).

37. Tom G. Palmer, "Myths of Individualism" *Cato Policy Report* 18, no. 5 (Sept.–Oct. 1996). www.cato.org/pubs/policy_reporter/cpr-18n5-1.html.

38. Jan Narveson, *The Libertarian Idea* (Philadelphia: Temple University Press, 1988): 269.

39. Edward H. Crane, "The Government Habit," *Cato Policy Report* 17, no. 6 (Nov.–Dec. 1995). http://www.cato.org/pubs/policy_report/pr-nd-ec.html.

40. Bruce Bartlett, "How Excessive Government Killed Ancient Rome" *Cato Journal* 14, no. 2 (fall 1994).

41. Frank Bruni, "Gingrich Sees Echo of Ancient Rome in America Today," *New York Times,* 3 May 1998, 30. The Roman novels of Colleen McCullough are costume dramas that trade on the aesthetics of quantity. They are advertised as being massive or "epic" in scope, full of the "color" of history. McCullough's thoroughly researched Romans are appetitive entrepreneurs of power and pleasure. Her books do not mourn the loss of the republic, but celebrate imperial sensations. See, for example, *The First Man in Rome* (New York: Avon, 1990).

42. "Standard of Living Is Rising, 60 Scholars Agree," *Cato Policy Report* (Nov.–Dec. 1995): 13.

43. Louis Menand, "Comment," *The New Yorker* (13 April 1998) 5–6.

INDEX